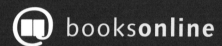 **books**online

Read this book online today:

With SAP PRESS BooksOnline we offer you online access to knowledge from the leading SAP experts. Whether you use it as a beneficial supplement or as an alternative to the printed book, with SAP PRESS BooksOnline you can:

- Access your book anywhere, at any time. All you need is an Internet connection.
- Perform full text searches on your book and on the entire SAP PRESS library.
- Build your own personalized SAP library.

The SAP PRESS customer advantage:

Register this book today at *www.sap-press.com* and obtain exclusive free trial access to its online version. If you like it (and we think you will), you can choose to purchase permanent, unrestricted access to the online edition at a very special price!

Here's how to get started:

1. Visit *www.sap-press.com*.
2. Click on the link for SAP PRESS BooksOnline and login (or create an account).
3. Enter your free trial license key, shown below in the corner of the page.
4. Try out your online book with full, unrestricted access for a limited time!

Your personal free trial **license key**
for this online book is:

100 Things You Should Know About
Financial Accounting with SAP®

 **PRESS**

SAP PRESS is a joint initiative of SAP and Galileo Press. The know-how offered by SAP specialists combined with the expertise of the Galileo Press publishing house offers the reader expert books in the field. SAP PRESS features first-hand information and expert advice, and provides useful skills for professional decision-making.

SAP PRESS offers a variety of books on technical and business related topics for the SAP user. For further information, please visit our website: *www.sap-press.com*.

Veeriah Narayanan
Customizing Financial Accounting in SAP
2012, app. 780 pp.
978-1-59229-377-3

Naeem Arif and Sheikh Tauseef
SAP ERP Financials: Configuration and Design
2011, app. 650 pp.
978-1-59229-393-3

Manish Patel
Discover SAP ERP Financials
2008, 544 pp.
978-1-59229-184-7

John Jordon
100 Things You Should Know About Controlling with SAP
2011, 289 pp.
978-1-59229-341-4

Paul Ovigele

100 Things You Should Know About
Financial Accounting with SAP®

Galileo Press

Bonn • Boston

Galileo Press is named after the Italian physicist, mathematician and philosopher Galileo Galilei (1564–1642). He is known as one of the founders of modern science and an advocate of our contemporary, heliocentric worldview. His words *Eppur si muove* (And yet it moves) have become legendary. The Galileo Press logo depicts Jupiter orbited by the four Galilean moons, which were discovered by Galileo in 1610.

Editor Laura Korslund
Technical Reviewer Vincenzo Sopracolle
Copyeditor Ruth Saavedra
Cover Design Graham Geary
Photo Credit iStockphoto.com/STEVECOLEcss
Layout Design Graham Geary
Production Graham Geary
Typesetting Publishers' Design and Production Services, Inc.
Printed and bound in Canada

ISBN 978-1-59229-364-3

© 2011 by Galileo Press Inc., Boston (MA)
1st Edition 2011

Library of Congress Cataloging-in-Publication Data
Ovigele, Paul.
100 things you should know about financial accounting with SAP /
Paul Ovigele. — 1st ed.
p. cm.
Includes index.
ISBN-13: 978-1-59229-364-3
ISBN-10: 1-59229-364-6
1. SAP ERP. 2. Accounting—Computer programs. 3. Accounting—Data processing. I. Title.
II. Title: One hundred things you should know about financial accounting with SAP.
HF5679.O86 2011
657.0285'53—dc23
2011014960

Contents at a Glance

Dear Reader,

Have you ever spent frustrating and painful hours trying to figure out how to customize a display in the Financial Accounting component in SAP ERP Financials? If so, the newest book from the best-selling *100 Things* series will be sure to ease your troubles, as it unlocks the secrets of an SAP expert for you to use. This book provides key users and even consultants with 100 tips and workarounds you can use to increase productivity, save time, and improve the ease-of-use for your SAP system. The tips have been carefully selected to provide a collection of the best, most useful, and rarest information. With these tips, your experience with SAP will be friendlier and easier, and you may think "I had no idea you could do that this way!" or "I wish I had known how to do that a long time ago!"

Thanks to the expertise of Paul Ovigele, this book will put you in the best possible position to truly maximize your time and make your job easier. Throughout the course of writing the manuscript, Paul impressed me with his in-depth knowledge, dedication to providing readers with the best possible information, and patience with the editorial process. You are now the recipient of this knowledge and dedication, and I'm confident that you'll benefit greatly from both.

We appreciate your business, and welcome your feedback. Your comments and suggestions are the most useful tools to help us improve our books for you, the reader. We encourage you to visit our website at *www.sap-press.com* and share your feedback about this work.

Thank you for purchasing a book from SAP PRESS!

Laura Korslund
Editor, SAP PRESS

Galileo Press
Boston, MA

laura.korslund@galileo-press.com
www.sap-press.com

Contents

Acknowledgments

I'd like to acknowledge my wife Whitney and my children Sebastian and Sloane for accommodating my busy schedule while I was writing this book.

I'd also like to acknowledge Laura Korslund for her work in editing the manuscript.

Introduction

This book is one of the first of a new series based on 100 ideas for various SAP software components. It is designed to make reading and understanding SAP ERP more interesting and accessible for your day-to-day work. You can flip through this book and search for ideas on each page to see if any of the 100 topics catches your attention. If so, you can read through the concept or tip in a matter of minutes and decide whether you'd like to research the topic further.

The Financial Accounting component in SAP ERP (also known as the FI component) delivers complete, integrated financial management software to ensure compliance and predictability of business performance. It is an essential building block of your enterprise business strategy — providing a solid foundation to expand your business, realize greater efficiencies across key processes, and ensure compliant and accurate accounting and financial reporting. It consists of the submodules General Ledger Accounting, Accounts Receivable, Accounts Payable, Bank Accounting, Fixed Assets, and Travel Management.

Each tip in this book aims to replicate a scenario where a skilled SAP expert is by your side, demonstrating how to best and most efficiently accomplish a task. It assumes a basic knowledge of functionality in the FI component (or the ability and access to find this information) on the part of the user. The information provided in this book is not readily available on the Internet. Rather, it represents lessons that I have learned from my more than 13 years of experience in the different FI components with clients, both large and small, across a number of industries in several countries, as well as valuable "nuggets" provided to me by other experienced FI consultants, for which I am grateful.

This book is broken down into 10 parts, each representing a processing function, rather than division by FI submodule, because there are several ideas that can apply to multiple submodules. This book does not claim to be an exhaustive account of all you need to know to use the FI component of SAP ERP. Rather, I have tried to include problem-solving tips and tricks for areas that are less than well covered in the available literature. As its end goal, this book aims to become an indispensable companion for those trying to navigate the FI component in an efficient, user-friendly way. Let's quickly discuss the different parts of this book.

Part 1, *Master Data*, provides useful tips on how to easily maintain and control master data objects, such as with the hierarchical maintenance of general ledger accounts and sensitive fields in the customer and vendor master to monitor and approve any changes.

Part 2, *Transaction Processing*, provides tips on quicker ways to perform Financial Accounting transactions, such as matching incoming payments to invoices by the number of days overdue and reversing a reversal document without having to repost all of the items.

Parts 3 and 4, *Display* and *Data Analysis*, give you ideas on how to access data from the system in specific formats, lists, and output types by making certain settings in the system. For example, you are shown how to maintain default settings for how reports are downloaded to Microsoft Excel; you also learn how to create a sort key to arrange your item display lists according to specific fields.

Parts 5, 6, and 7, *Account Assignment*, *Environment*, and *Integration*, focus more on the system configuration settings that determine how you are able to post to accounts automatically, where user entry defaults are maintained, and how data from other components flows seamlessly into the Financial Accounting component. For example, you will learn the setting needed to display the financial and logistics documents in a purchasing invoice posting, how to set up alternative reconciliation accounts for customers and vendors, and how to handle delivery costs on purchase orders.

Part 8, *Reporting*, describes different ways of customizing and accessing reports in the system to meet specific needs, such as how to add extra fields to certain standard customer, vendor, and fixed asset reports and how to create and use drilldown reports.

And finally, Parts 9 and 10, *Data Update* and *Technical*, provide tips on how and where to use various programs and transactions that are more technical in nature (which may sometimes require the assistance of an ABAP or Basis expert) to update, modify, or delete certain data from the database or to access certain screen functionality. For example, you will learn how to delete finance master data from the system and to configure screen variants for Financial Accounting and Logistics Invoice Verification transactions.

For more information on Financial Accounting with SAP, visit *www.sap-press.com*, where you can find further reading material in this area.

Part 1

Master Data

Things You'll Learn in this Section

The importance of master data in the finance components cannot be over-emphasized. Most accounting transactions are based on some type of master data or other. Master data in SAP systems involves creating data records to be stored on a long-term basis for several business processes. Examples of this data include customers, vendors, fixed assets, and general ledger accounts.

The more fields that are entered in the master data, the less data entry needs to be entered on the transactional level. This is why many SAP implementation projects dedicate a huge amount of time to cleansing and validating master data before it is loaded into the SAP system. Incorrect entries and settings in master data records lead to incorrect transactions being posted, and this situation could be exponential if several transactions based on the same master data are processed in parallel. Correcting these kinds of errors at the backend is much more costly than spending the time to ensure that the data correct before it is used.

In most cases, the master data that the finance department relies on comes from other components. Normally, the finance department is not responsible for maintaining the master data. However, the department should understand how master data is created to identify the root cause of an issue by looking at the field values and settings.

This section focuses largely on the master data that the finance team is responsible for, such as the General Ledger, customer, vendor, and fixed asset master and the profit center master (which was brought into the Financial Accounting component with mySAP ERP 2004). The themes we address in this part involve making master data easier to maintain, more flexible, and more secure. We also provide ideas on how to easily maintain general ledger accounts, create cost elements automatically, control changes to customer and vendor fields, derive segments, and define currency types.

Tip 1

Easily Maintaining General Ledger Accounts

You can maintain multiple general ledger accounts by using the hierarchical display setting.

Creating and maintaining a general ledger account is usually done by first accessing Transaction FS00. This method is fine if you are creating or maintaining a single account and you have all of the relevant data you need to find the account, such as the account number range, company code data, and descriptions. However, if you want to have quick access to multiple accounts during maintenance in order to easily scan through similar accounts that you want to copy from, then your best option is to use the HIERARCHY DISPLAY functionality.

✓ And Here's How...

You can access the HIERARCHY DISPLAY setting by going to Transaction FS00 (General Ledger Account Master Data) and selecting the menu option SETTINGS • HIERARCHY DISPLAY.

You will see a dialog box asking whether you want to display the accounts in a navigation tree or not. Choose to display the accounts in a navigation tree, and restart the transaction. You can exit the current transaction, restart it, or type "Transaction /nFS00" in the command field to access the screen, as shown in Figure 1.

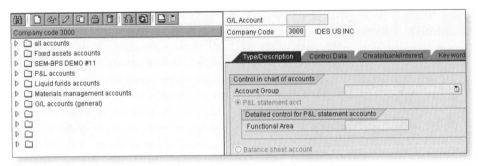

⌃ *Figure 1 Hierarchical Display of General Ledger Account Master*

The folders that are displayed in the left part of the screen represent the account groups that the general ledger accounts belong to. You use the account groups to control the number range intervals of the accounts per chart of account. The account groups also control the field statuses (suppressed, optional, required, or displayed) of the fields that are available in the account master record. You can click on the triangle icons beside the account group folders to view the general ledger accounts that exist in those groups.

The right part of the screen is the traditional Master Data Maintenance screen for a general ledger account. By double-clicking on an account on the left part of the screen, you can maintain or display the details of the account on the right part of the screen. You can use the icons shown at the top of the screen to quickly access the functionality for maintaining the accounts. If you want to create a new account in a particular number range, you can easily check the hierarchy to see what the next available number is. You can then select the account that you want to copy from, click on the COPY icon, and enter the account number you want to create.

By using the FIND icon (), you can search for an account's number or description in a company code. This is useful when you are creating an account that may already exist as a different number. By putting all or part of the description in the search field, you will find out if there is a similar account in the same or a different account range. The BLOCK and MARK FOR DELETION icons are available here, as they are with the normal maintenance view. However, it is easier to scan through several accounts with the hierarchical view and check or maintain the block and deletion settings.

Last, you can easily change the view from one company code to another by clicking on the CHANGE COMPANY CODE icon ().

Tip 2

Creating Cost Elements Automatically

You can automatically create a cost element when a new profit and loss account is saved.

Once you have created a general ledger profit and loss account, you need to create a cost element. If your company creates accounts manually, you may run the risk of forgetting to create the cost element. Therefore, it is easier to set up the process where the system creates the primary cost elements automatically.

✓ And Here's How...

To create cost elements automatically, you first need to set up the range of cost element numbers to be created, along with their corresponding cost element categories. Access Transaction OKB2 or follow the Implementation Guide (IMG) menu path:

> CONTROLLING • COST ELEMENT ACCOUNTING • MASTER DATA • COST ELEMENTS • AUTOMATIC CREATION OF PRIMARY AND SECONDARY COST ELEMENTS • MAKE DEFAULT SETTINGS

Enter the relevant chart of accounts and press Enter, which brings you to the screen where you can assign the cost elements, as displayed in Figure 1.

You can enter either ranges of cost elements or individual cost elements in each row. The cost element category determines for which business transaction the cost element can be used, and whether it is a primary or secondary cost element.

Automatic Generation of Cost Elements: Default Setting			
Acct from	Account to	CElem cat.	Short Descript.
440030	440030	12	Sales deduction
450100	450199	11	Revenues
610000	612999	1	Primary costs/cost-reducing revenues
630000	639999	1	Primary costs/cost-reducing revenues
650000	669999	1	Primary costs/cost-reducing revenues

⌃ *Figure 1 Automatic Generation of Cost Elements*

You need to enable the system to create the cost element once the new general ledger account is created. To do this, follow the configuration menu path:

FINANCIAL ACCOUNTING (NEW) • GENERAL LEDGER ACCOUNTING (NEW) • MASTER DATA • G/L ACCOUNTS • PREPARATIONS • EDIT CHART OF ACCOUNTS LIST

Double-click on the relevant chart of accounts and change the CONTROLLING INTEGRATION setting displayed into AUTOMATIC CREATION OF COST ELEMENTS, as shown in Figure 2.

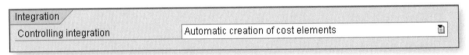

Integration	
Controlling integration	Automatic creation of cost elements

⌃ *Figure 2 Controlling Integration Setting in Chart of Accounts*

The next time a general ledger account that is within the relevant number range is created and saved, the corresponding cost element master record will be set up as well. This will carry over the description that was entered in the general ledger account and the cost element category that was set up in Transaction OKB2.

If you already created your general ledger accounts and retroactively want to create the cost elements automatically based on these accounts, you need to run a batch session to update the profit and loss accounts that you specified in Transaction OKB2 as cost elements. To do this, go to Transaction OKB3 to create the batch input session and enter the relevant data.

You run the batch session using Transaction SM35. Depending on the number of cost elements being created, you can run the session in either the foreground or the background.

Tip **3**

Paying Vendors with Multiple Bank Accounts

By assigning partner bank types to each vendor bank account, you can easily pay vendors who have multiple banks.

If you are making payments using an automatic bank transfer payment method (such as by wire or ACH), the system will normally expect you to select just one bank account that is specified in the vendor's master record. However, in some cases your vendor (or customer) may have several bank accounts and may request that you make a payment to a specific one, depending on the invoice that is being paid. Alternatively, they may require that you make payments to multiple banks, depending on when the payment is made.

And Here's How...

To meet this payment requirement, you need to set up partner bank types in the vendor master record so you can select the bank to which you want to make the payment. Partner bank types are alphanumeric keys of up to four characters, but can be made up of any combination of letters and numbers the business wants to use. You can enter the partner bank type by following these steps:

1. Go to Transaction FK01 to create the vendor master record or FK02 to change the record.
2. Go to the Payment Transactions screen in the GENERAL DATA tab.
3. Enter the various bank accounts of the vendor, as shown in Figure 1.
4. Enter unique keys for each bank in the PARTNER BANK TYPE column, which is denoted BNKT.

Ctry	Bank Key	Bank Account	Acct holder	C	IBAN	IBANValue		BnkT
US	031100380	5675800989	JOE BLOGGS		⇨			PB1
US	031100380	3216544798	JOE BLOGGS		⇨			PB2

⌃ *Figure 1 Multiple Banks in Vendor Master*

There are a couple of ways to specify which partner bank type can be used on an invoice.

Option 1

The first is when you are creating the invoice using either Transaction FB60 for direct invoices or MIRO for purchasing invoices. When you have entered the details as usual, go to the PAYMENT tab. In the PART. BANK field, you can specify which of the partner bank types entered in the vendor master record you want to use.

Option 2

If you forgot to enter the partner bank type when creating the invoice or did not have the relevant information at the time of posting, you can also specify the bank type by going to Transaction FB02 to change the invoice. When you have entered the invoice number and year to display the lines, double-click on the vendor line and click on the ADDITIONAL DATA tab. This takes you to the screen shown in Figure 2. Then use the drop-down menu on the PART. BANK TYPE field to select the option that relates to the bank you want to use.

⌃ *Figure 2 Additional Data Screen*

This second option may be necessary when you are creating invoices through automated settlement processes such as consignment (using Transaction MRKO) or evaluated receipt settlement (using Transaction MRRL). With these processes, the partner bank type field is not available when the invoice is created, so you have to retroactively populate the field on the invoice document.

Tip 4

Maintaining IBAN in the Master Records

You can populate the IBAN for a vendor or customer by generating it from the bank account number or by direct input.

The International Bank Account Number (IBAN) is required as the primary account identifier in Europe. Payments not bearing an IBAN may be delayed or rejected. However, some European vendors still only provide their bank branch and account number, and not their IBAN.

In this tip, we will show you the easiest way to generate and maintain the IBAN in your master records.

✔ And Here's How...

You can automatically populate the IBAN in the vendor master by going to Transaction FK01 and entering the country, bank key (and in some countries, such as Italy, the bank control key), and account number in the PAYMENT TRANSACTION screen of the GENERAL DATA section.

You generate the IBAN by clicking on the IBAN arrow. You first get a message saying "Check and confirm the proposed IBAN." When you confirm this message, the system proposes the IBAN from the account details that you entered, as shown in Figure 1.

⌃ *Figure 1 Automatic Generation of IBAN*

If the system proposes a number that is different from the one the vendor has provided, you can simply edit the values proposed by the system. You will see a message saying "The IBAN entered does not match the bank details." This can be overwritten. Once the IBAN has been populated, there is a green mark underneath the IBAN arrow.

At times, the reverse is the case, where the vendor provides the IBAN but not his bank details. You therefore need to generate the country, bank key, bank control key, and bank account number from the IBAN.

To do this, click on the IBAN arrow without entering any other bank details. Enter the IBAN and click on the GENERATE BANK DETAILS button. You will get the IBAN CONVERTER pop-up box with the bank country, key, and account details. Once you have confirmed the details, the relevant bank fields are populated accordingly.

Another scenario may arise where you know the IBAN, but you do not want to enter (or generate) the bank details, as the vendor has not provided them. In this case, you need to allow users to enter the bank details without the account number. To do this, follow the IMG menu path:

> FINANCIAL ACCOUNTING (NEW) • ACCOUNTS RECEIVABLE AND ACCOUNTS PAYABLE • ACTIVATE IBAN WITHOUT BANK ACCOUNT NUMBER

This takes you to the screen shown in Figure 2.

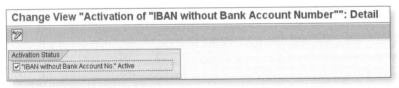

≫ *Figure 2 Activate IBAN without Bank Account Number*

When you select the "IBAN WITHOUT ACCOUNT NO." ACTIVE box, you can enter the IBAN without the system requiring the bank account details. When you enter the IBAN in this case, the IBAN converter box will have the ACCT NUMBER UNKNOWN checkbox selected automatically. If, however, you want the account number to be generated, simply unselect this box and click on the GENERATE BANK DETAILS button as already described.

Tip 5

Defining Sensitive Fields

You can define fields in the customer and vendor master as "sensitive" to control any changes made to them.

Certain fields in the vendor and customer master, such as bank account details, addresses, and tax identification numbers need to be monitored to ensure that any changes made to them have been approved for accuracy and legitimacy. If these fields are freely modifiable without the necessary approval, these actions could lead to issues of fraud or payment errors.

✅ And Here's How...

Fields in the customer and vendor master can be set as *sensitive* so that any changes made to them will in turn block them for payment until an authorized person approves and releases them.

To define fields as sensitive, follow this configuration menu path:

> FINANCIAL ACCOUNTING • ACCOUNTS RECEIVABLE AND ACCOUNTS PAYABLE • CUSTOMER ACCOUNTS • MASTER DATA • PREPARATIONS FOR CREATING CUSTOMER MASTER DATA • DEFINE SENSITIVE FIELDS FOR DUAL CONTROL (CUSTOMERS)

Click on NEW ENTRIES, then drop down on the field name and double-click on any fields you want to make sensitive. As an example, we have marked the BANK KEY and BANK ACCOUNT fields as sensitive in Figure 1.

Field name	Field Label
KNBK-BANKL	Bank Key
KNBK-BANKN	Bank Account

« Figure 1 *Define Sensitive Fields*

When you try to change one of the fields that have been made sensitive, the system displays the message "Change to general data must be confirmed". You are still allowed to save your changes. However, if anyone subsequently tries to display or change the customer/vendor master data before confirmation of the sensitive field changes, the system will give a message saying that the change has not been confirmed. The customer/vendor account will be blocked for payment until the change is confirmed by an authorized person (such as a supervisor).

It is not obvious that the vendor/customer is blocked for payment from simply looking at the invoice documents. During the payment run, the system puts the invoices for the relevant customer/vendor in an exception list and indicates that there are unconfirmed changes to the master record. You can go to Transaction S_ALR_87012090 to view changes that have been made to sensitive fields for vendors or Transaction S_ALR_87012183 for customers. To confirm the change (for vendors, for example) either use Transaction FK08 or follow the menu path:

> Accounting • Financial Accounting • Accounts Receivable • Master Record • Confirmation of Change • Single

To confirm multiple vendor changes, follow the same menu path but choose the option List, or go to Transaction FK09 to be taken to the screen shown in Figure 2.

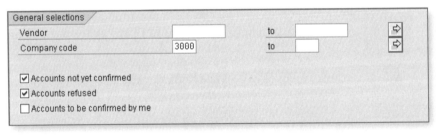

⇡   *Figure 2 Confirm Multiple Vendor Changes*

The person responsible for confirming the changes should have the relevant authorization for this transaction. For obvious reasons, in most cases this authorization profile should not be given to the person who makes the changes. The authorized person can display which fields have been changed and then choose to confirm or refuse the changes.

Tip 6

Direct Posting to Asset Reconciliation Accounts

You can make direct postings to asset reconciliation accounts by changing the RECONCILIATION CONTROL indicator.

Reconciliation accounts ensure that data from a subledger account flows seamlessly to SAP General Ledger. It is normally not possible to make direct postings to a reconciliation account to preserve the integrity of the data passed from the subledgers. However, you may sometimes find this process of making direct postings necessary in Fixed Asset Accounting, because during migration SAP General Ledger and the asset subledger are updated separately.

✔ And Here's How...

Even though it is not possible to change the reconciliation setting on an asset account in the general ledger master after postings have been made, you can bypass this roadblock with a couple of different methods. First, you can use Transaction ABF1, which looks like the standard "complex" posting transaction, except that it allows you to directly enter the asset reconciliation account alongside the asset posting key (70, 75, and so on). Second, you can use Transaction OAMK or follow the configuration menu path:

> FINANCIAL ACCOUNTING (NEW) • ASSET ACCOUNTING • PREPARATION FOR PRODUCTION STARTUP • PRODUCTION STARTUP • SET OR RESET RECONCILIATION ACCOUNTS

This will take you to the screen shown in Figure 1.

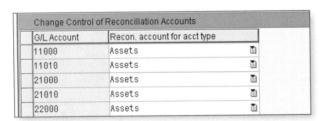

The settings are made by company code. Select the company code you want to change and click on the CHANGE CONTROL OF RECONCILIATION ACCOUNTS folder. This brings you to the screen shown in Figure 2, which allows you to choose the accounts you want to set as reconciliation accounts or allows you to remove this setting.

« *Figure 2 Change Control of Reconciliation Accounts*

The only accounts that appear in the list are the balance sheet accounts that have been configured in Transaction AO90.

To make a mass change setting, you can use the buttons at the bottom of the Change Control of Reconciliation Accounts screen, which is illustrated in Figure 3.

⊼ *Figure 3 Mass Reset Buttons*

The SET RECONCILIATION IND. FOR ALL ACCOUNTS button puts the reconciliation indicator on all of the accounts in the company code, whereas the DELETE RECONCILIATION IND. FOR ALL ACCOUNTS button takes the indicator off. You can also use this transaction to change an account from having an ASSET indicator to another reconciliation indicator, such as CUSTOMER or VENDOR.

Tip 7

Assigning Cost Centers on Assets

You can assign cost centers to assets for different time intervals and to assets in different company codes.

The cost center assignment is made in the TIME DEPENDENT tab of the asset master data and can be set for a specific validity period. The validity period functionality is important because an asset can belong to one cost center for a specific time period and then belong to another cost center in a different time period. However, you may not want cost centers to be managed as time-dependent if the assets will always belong to the same cost center.

✓ And Here's How...

To disable the time-dependency of cost centers in the asset master record, you can go to the IMG menu path:

> FINANCIAL ACCOUNTING (NEW) • ASSET ACCOUNTING • MASTER DATA • SPECIFY TIME-INDEPENDENT MANAGEMENT OF ORGANIZATIONAL UNITS

When you select the TIME-INDEPENDENT ORGANIZATIONAL UNITS box, as shown in Figure 1, the system disables the time-dependency functionality for a cost center in an asset master record.

CoCd	Company Name	Time-independent organiz. units
3000	IDES US INC	☑

⌃ *Figure 1 Specify Time-Independent Organizational Units*

This means that when you enter or change the cost center assignment for an asset, it is valid for all time intervals. If you change the cost center with this setting active, the system will create an automatic transfer document from the old to the new cost center. One requirement of the standard system, however, is that the cost center that is assigned to an asset should belong to the same company code as the asset. If this is not the case, the system issues an error message.

There may be cases where your business holds an asset in another department that belongs to a different company code. Here you need to override this standard system restriction. To do this, use Transaction AO90 or follow the IMG menu path:

> FINANCIAL ACCOUNTING (NEW) • ASSET ACCOUNTING • MASTER DATA • SPECIFY COST CENTER CHECK ACROSS COMPANY CODES

The settings are made by company code. Select the corresponding box, as shown in Figure 2, and the system will allow you to enter a cost center with a different company code from the asset.

	CoCd	Company Name	Across co.codes
	3000	IDES US INC	☑

⌃ *Figure 2 Specify Cost Center Check across Company Codes*

The standard system check normally checks that the cost center is in the same company code as the asset. However, with this setting, the system only checks that the cost center is in the same controlling area to which the company code of the fixed asset is assigned.

If you produce balance sheet reports by profit center, this setting will be significant because of the assignment of the cost center to the profit center. The transactions for the asset are shown on a profit center in a different company code from the asset account. Note that for the profit center to be derived from the cost center on the asset, the field status group of the general ledger account that is assigned for the asset's acquisition and production costs (APCs) should have the profit center set to OPTIONAL.

Tip 8

Netting Off Customer and Vendor Items

For customers who are also vendors, you can offset the payables against their receivables.

In some cases, you may have business partners that are both vendors and customers. They may require combined clearing of their open items during the payment run and dunning programs. You need to change a few settings in the master data in order for this process to work correctly, which we will discuss in this tip.

✅ And Here's How...

In the vendor master (Transaction FK02) go to the CONTROL tab of the GENERAL DATA section. Enter the customer number of the vendor in the CUSTOMER field, as shown in Figure 1.

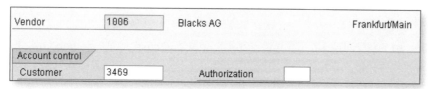

≫ *Figure 1 Customer Field in Vendor Master*

After making this entry, go to the PAYMENT TRANSACTIONS ACCOUNTING tab of the COMPANY CODE DATA section and select the CLRG WITH CUST. (Clearing with Customer) box that is displayed in Figure 2.

≪ Figure 2 *Clearing with Customer Checkbox*

This checkbox is only activated after you enter the customer in the vendor master. If you do not select this box, you will not be able to clear customer and vendor items together; however, you will be able to view their line items together in the customer or vendor line item display transactions.

If you also need to separately process the vendor items from a customer clearing transaction, go to the customer master (Transaction FD02), and then click on the PAYMENT TRANSACTIONS ACCOUNTING tab of the COMPANY CODE DATA section. Select the CLEARING WITH VENDOR box, which is displayed in Figure 3.

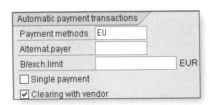

≪ Figure 3 *Clearing with Vendor Checkbox*

When you perform a payment run in Transaction F110, the system nets off the items of both the customer and vendor and proposes to pay only the difference. If you are performing any of the manual clearing functions for customers and vendors, the system shows the open items of the combined accounts. Before you consider activating this clearing functionality, ensure that it is legal to offset receivables with payables in the country in which the company code is located.

If you want to display the open items of the vendor and customer together, you can do this by going to the vendor line item display in Transaction FBL1N and selecting the CUSTOMER ITEMS box, as displayed in Figure 4.

≪ Figure 4 *Activate Customer Items in Vendor Item Display*

Tip 9

Deriving Segments

You can create full balance sheets below the company code level by activating and deriving the segment field.

The segment is an object that was introduced with SAP General Ledger. It is a division of the company that can be used to create external financial statement reports. For the segment to be assigned to financial documents, you first need to know how to derive it.

Because segments are relatively new, we find that they still generate a lot of questions from SAP customers. In this tip, we will show you how to create and derive segments so that they can be used for financial statement reporting.

✓ And Here's How...

First, you need to assign both the profit center scenario (FIN_PCA) and segment scenario (FIN_SEGM) to your ledgers; this is because the most common way of deriving a segment is through a profit center. You can do this via the IMG menu path:

> FINANCIAL ACCOUNTING (NEW) • FINANCIAL ACCOUNTING BASIC SETTINGS (NEW) • LEDGERS • LEDGER • ASSIGN SCENARIOS AND CUSTOMER FIELDS TO LEDGERS

Select the relevant ledger(s), click on the SCENARIOS folder, and add the PROFIT CENTER UPDATE and SEGMENTATION scenarios to the ledger, as shown in Figure 1.

Scenario for General Ledger	Long Text
FIN_PCA	Profit Center Update
FIN_SEGM	Segmentation
FIN_UKV	Cost of Sales Accounting

« Figure 1 *Assign Scenarios to the General Ledger*

You need to define the segment field as a document splitting characteristic. To do this, go to the IMG menu path:

> FINANCIAL ACCOUNTING (NEW) • GENERAL LEDGER ACCOUNTING (NEW) • BUSINESS TRANSACTIONS • DOCUMENT SPLITTING • DEFINE DOCUMENT SPLITTING CHARACTERISTICS FOR GENERAL LEDGER ACCOUNTING

Select the SEGMENT field and select the ZERO-BALANCE checkbox. To ensure that every financial document contains a segment, we recommend that you also select the MANDATORY checkbox, as shown in Figure 2, so that an error message is issued for documents that do not contain a segment.

Document Splitting Characteristic for General Ledgers					
Field		Zero balance	Partner field		Mandatory Field
Profit Center		☐	PPRCTR		☐
Segment		☑	PSEGMENT		☑

⌃ *Figure 2 Document Splitting Characteristics*

You define the segment as a configuration setting (as opposed to a master data setting), similar to the profit center. To define the segment, go to the following IMG menu path:

> ENTERPRISE STRUCTURE • DEFINITION • DEFINE SEGMENT

If you want to be able to modify the segment field in the profit center master after transactions have been posted, go to Transaction SM30, go to view V_FAGL_SEGM_PRCT, and select the CHANGE SEG. IN PRCTR checkbox.

Some companies do not use profit centers, so they would not be able to derive a segment using the process described above. If this is the case, you can use the Business Add-In (BAdI) FAGL_DERIVE_SEGMENT. Here, you can insert your own program logic for how the segment should be derived. You can also derive a segment by using FI substitutions. To do this, access Transaction OBBH and define a prerequisite and a substitution rule.

Finally, you can manually enter a segment when posting an accounting document. To do so, you need to enable the segment field status for the relevant general ledger accounts in Transaction OBC4 and for the relevant posting keys in Transaction OB41.

For more information on segment derivation, refer to Online Services System (OSS) Note 686531.

Tip **10**

Defining Currency Types

You can define up to three currencies for a company code by using currency types

If you are a multinational company (or one that belongs to an international group), then you will probably need to maintain more than one currency for your company code to satisfy group reporting requirements, to peg it with a more stable currency, or for management reporting purposes.

One way to do this would be to manually translate all transactions in your company code to all the different currencies that you need to report in. However, this could be a painstaking process and may lead to errors. The more efficient way for you to accomplish this would be to take advantage of the parallel currency functionality, which automatically translates every financial transaction into the different currencies set up for that company code.

A company code can have up to three local currencies, also known as parallel currencies, by using one of the following currency types:

▶ **Company code currency**
The currency of the country in which the company code is located

▶ **Group currency**
The currency that is specified in the client table T000

▶ **Hard currency**
Benchmark currency that is normally used in countries with high inflation

▶ **Index-based currency**
A fictitious currency normally used in countries with high inflation

▶ **Global company currency**
A currency that is used for affiliated companies

And Here's How...

You can set currency types for the leading ledger of a company code in the following IMG menu path:

> FINANCIAL ACCOUNTING (NEW) • FINANCIAL ACCOUNTING BASIC SETTINGS (NEW) • LEDGERS • LEDGER • DEFINE CURRENCIES OF LEADING LEDGER

Double-clicking on the relevant company code takes you to the screen shown in Figure 1, which shows each currency type linked to a valuation, valuation exchange rate type, source currency, and translation date.

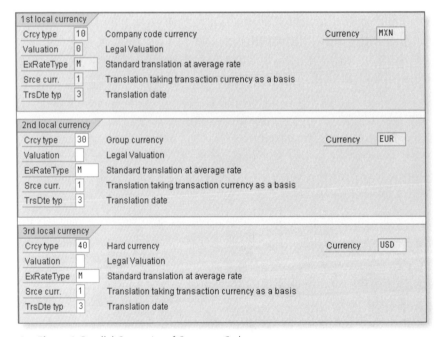

≈ *Figure 1 Parallel Currencies of Company Code*

The CURRENCY TYPE defines the currency's function in your SAP system. This could be the currency of the country, the currency of the company's parent entity, or another related currency. It is also used in conjunction with the valuation method if you use parallel valuation. The VALUATION view is used with parallel valuation functionality to view business transactions by dimensions such as legal, group, or profit center valuation. If you do not use parallel valuation functionality, then all currency types will be set to LEGAL.

The EXCHANGE rate type controls which type of rate—buying, selling, or average— is used to translate the currencies. This is normally set to M for average rate. The SOURCE CURRENCY determines which currency to use for translation and should normally be set to 1 for transaction currency. The TRANSLATION DATE TYPE deter- mines which date in the document will be compared with the valid-from date in the exchange rate table to decide which exchange rate will be used in the document.

In addition to these currencies, there is also the document, or transaction currency, which is any currency in which the document was posted.

Tip 11

Creating Trading Partners

You can use a trading partner to identify transactions with affiliated companies for consolidation purposes.

You want to distinguish transactions made with affiliated companies from those made with other business partners. This way you can report on sales and purchases that are made within the corporate group separately from those that are made externally. You can then perform any eliminations that need to be made when performing a consolidation function.

If you do not use trading partners, then you would need to set up a separate general ledger account to represent transactions relating to each affiliated company. Depending on the size of the group your company belongs to, this could lead to a significant increase in the number of general ledger accounts in your system.

✓ And Here's How...

You can create a trading partner (or company) by going to the IMG menu path:

> ENTERPRISE STRUCTURE • DEFINITION • FINANCIAL ACCOUNTING • DEFINE COMPANY

You will see the screen displayed in Figure 1, where you can enter the appropriate company information.

Company	3000
Company name	IDES US INC
Name of company 2	

Detailed information

Street	1230 Lincoln Avenue
PO Box	
Postal code	10019
City	New York
Country	US
Language Key	EN
Currency	USD

Figure 1 *Define Company (Trading Partner)*

If your company is responsible for group eliminations, you need to set up the affiliates as company codes and assign them to trading partners. To do this, go to the IMG menu path:

ENTERPRISE STRUCTURE • ASSIGNMENT • ASSIGN COMPANY CODE TO COMPANY

You then enter the trading partner number that represents the company code, as shown in Figure 2.

CoCd	City	Company
3000	New York	3000

Figure 2 *Assign Company to Company Code*

When you have set up the trading partners, you can assign them to the affiliate companies' vendor and customer master records. To do this, go to the CONTROL tab of the GENERAL DATA section in either the customer (FD02) or vendor (FK02) master data and add the relevant trading partner number, as shown in Figure 3.

Account control

Customer		Authorization	
Trading Partner	3000	Corporate Group	

Figure 3 *Trading Partner Field in Vendor Master*

With this setting, when a posting is made to this vendor or customer, the trading partner field is populated for both the receivables/payables entry and the offsetting account entry. This facilitates the elimination of the receivables and payables as well as the revenue and cost between affiliated companies. You can also assign a trading partner to a general ledger account to achieve the same objective as above.

To do this, insert the trading partner in the TYPE/DESCRIPTION tab of the general ledger master using Transaction FS00. If you want to directly input the trading partner in the document, enable the trading partner field in the document type. To do this, go to the document type configuration Transaction OBA7, and in the CONTROL DATA section, select the checkboxes INTER-COMPANY POSTINGS and ENTER TRADING PARTNER, as shown in Figure 4.

« *Figure 4* Activate Intercompany Posting in Document Type

By checking only the ENTER TRADING PARTNER checkbox, you can enter only one trading partner at the header level, which will apply to all the line items of a document. By checking both the ENTER TRADING PARTNER and INTER-COMPANY POSTINGS checkboxes, you can enter multiple trading partners at the line item level of a document.

Part 2

Transaction Processing

Things You'll Learn in this Section

Financial transactions are processed in the normal course of business. The frequency and nature of the transactions that are processed depends on the specific business scenario and the policy of the organization. Transaction processing is normally done more frequently than master data processing, and therefore, the methods of performing these transactions are usually more unique to the users, as they have most likely formed a habit of doing things in a certain way. In this manner, users often find different workarounds to compensate for any system gaps or processing errors when they process transactions. SAP, however, provides various features to reduce the time and effort users need to process data and create journal entries by using certain functionalities (which are not always known to the user) within the transactions.

You use transaction processing to carry out system activities that form part of a process. The completion of one activity is necessary for the next activity in a process chain to be executed. In an enterprise resource planning (ERP) system such as SAP ERP, it is important that the processing of transactions is as smooth, timely, and accurate as possible so that the related processes can be carried out expediently. However, sometimes you might find that the transactions you perform frequently are prone to entry errors and may cause a bottleneck in the process. There are also situations where you carry out a time-intensive activity repeatedly due to force of habit and perform manual workarounds where necessary.

In this part of the book, we will show you some alternative processes to avoid the laborious and sometimes error-prone methods you've been using. You will learn unique ways to clear customer open items, specify specific types of documents to be included in a payment run, match a vendor invoice to multiple purchase orders in a single screen, and post advance payments.

Tip 12

Clearing Customer Invoices

Customer open items can be selected with greater or lesser detail for payment by using extra clearing options.

When you receive payments from customers, selecting and matching the items to be cleared can be difficult when the items to be paid have not been referenced. This may be the case because you have to wade through a pile of invoices to find which one is being paid. If you are using an automated process such as the Electronic Bank Statement, there is normally an interpretation algorithm that is used to determine the items to be paid. However, with the manual processes you would need to formulate your own logic to decide how to apply the payment.

In this tip, we will show you several ways to reduce the manual effort of searching through the open items to be cleared.

✓ And Here's How...

The most common way of processing customer payments manually is by using Transaction F-28 or via the following menu path:

> FINANCIAL ACCOUNTING • ACCOUNTS RECEIVABLE • DOCUMENT ENTRY • INCOMING PAYMENTS.

In cases where the customer payment does not specify which invoices need to be cleared, you can apply the payment to the items according to their days overdue by selecting the DISTRIBUTE BY AGE checkbox in the OPEN ITEM SELECTION section of the initial screen, as displayed in Figure 1.

« **Figure 1** *Distribute by Age Checkbox in*
Open Item Selection

When you subsequently click on the PROCESS OPEN ITEMS button, the system proposes the items to be cleared in the order of the number of days they are outstanding. You can see from the DAYS IN ARREARS column that the items that have been selected are those that have been overdue the longest. If the next item to be selected is more than the balance that is left on the payment, then the system enters the remaining amount in the DIFFERENCE POSTINGS box (shown in Figure 2), thus suggesting that this balance be posted back to the customer's account.

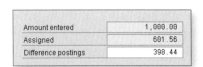

« **Figure 2** *Difference Postings*

Another possible scenario is that the customer is paying one or several invoices that they have not specified with the payment, but you believe it would be too time-consuming to locate the invoices that add up to the payment amount. To expedite the process of finding the location of these items, select the AUTOMATIC SEARCH checkbox in the initial screen of Transaction F-28. When you click on the PROCESS OPEN ITEMS button, the system selects all of the items that add up to the amount entered in the initial screen.

If the tallied items come close to the amount entered (within a 10% variance, which is the standard), the system shows the pop-up box displayed in Figure 3, which gives you the proposed amount to be cleared and asks whether you accept it.

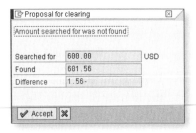

« **Figure 3** *Proposed Amount and Difference*

If you select ACCEPT, the system leaves the balance as NOT ASSIGNED, and you can clear the balance against other items or leave it on the customer's account.

Tip 13

Reversing a Reversal Document

If you cannot reverse a document because it has cleared items, you can use the "Post with Reference" with reversal functionality.

Sometimes you may need to reverse a document that already has cleared items. This may happen when one of the general ledger account lines on an invoice has been cleared, or when the document that you are trying to reverse is a reversal document. Normally you cannot reverse a document that contains a reversal indicator, but in this tip we will present a workaround to this problem.

And Here's How...

You can reference a document with cleared items by using Transaction FBR2, which takes you to the screen shown in Figure 1. Enter the DOCUMENT NUMBER and COMPANY CODE that you want to reference, and then select the GENERATE REVERSE POSTING box.

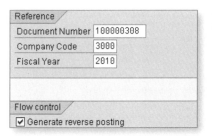

« Figure 1 *Post with Reference with Reversal Generation*

When you press the [Enter] button, the system will take you to the header and first line of the document. If you keep pressing [Enter], you will be taken to subsequent lines in the document. When you reach the last line of the document, the system will show the overview screen displayed in Figure 2, which shows all of the lines and their respective posting keys and amounts.

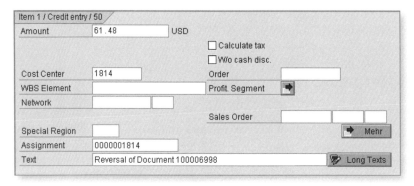

Document Date	02/05/2010	Type	SA	Company Code	3000
Posting Date	02/05/2010	Period	2	Currency	USD
Document Number	INTERNAL	Fiscal Year	2010	Translatn Date	02/05/2010
Reference				Cross-CC no.	
Doc.Header Text				Trading part.BA	

Items in document currency

```
     PK  BusA Acct                            USD    Amount      Tax amnt
 001 50  7000 0000476900 Other general expen         61.48-
 002 40  7000 0000113100 Citibank Account            61.48
```

⌃ *Figure 2* Document Overview

You can change the text on the header or any of the lines by double-clicking on the line. For example, by double-clicking on line 001, you can enter the item text, as shown in the TEXT field in Figure 3, to indicate that this is a reversal document.

Item 1 / Credit entry / 50

Amount	61.48	USD	
		☐ Calculate tax	
		☐ W/o cash disc.	
Cost Center	1814	Order	
WBS Element		Profit. Segment	➡
Network			
		Sales Order	
Special Region			➡ Mehr
Assignment	0000001814		
Text	Reversal of Document 100006998		📝 Long Texts

⌃ *Figure 3* Reversal Document Item Text

You can click on the DOCUMENT OVERVIEW button (🔲) to go back to the Post Document Display Overview screen and post the document.

A few other ways of accessing the Post with Reference transaction are as follows:

▸ In an Enjoy Transaction (for example Transaction FB50 for the general ledger, FB60 for vendors, or FB70 for customers), select the menu option GOTO • POST WITH REFERENCE.

▸ In a Complex Posting transaction (for example Transaction F-01 for the general ledger, F-43 for vendors, or F-22 for customers), select the menu option DOCUMENT • POST WITH REFERENCE.

Defining Ledger Groups

You can use ledger groups to facilitate simultaneous updating of accounting documents in several ledgers.

If you need to produce financial statements according to different accounting standards such as US GAAP and IFRS, you must create adjustment entries that reflect the different accounting treatments that are defined by these standards. You can do this either by creating extra general ledger accounts to record these adjustments or by using parallel ledgers, which gives you a manageable number of general ledger accounts. You can create parallel ledgers to represent the different accounting standards, along with the leading ledger that is the principle ledger for financial statement consolidation.

You can produce these financial statements by defining ledger groups. Ledger groups are a combination of individual ledgers that can be used as a means of updating all ledgers in the group through a single general ledger transaction. This process is used in cases where parallel ledgers are set up for parallel accounting processes and when similar updates need to be made to certain ledgers, but not to others.

✓ And Here's How...

To define a ledger group, you first need to define a ledger by following the IMG menu path:

> FINANCIAL ACCOUNTING (NEW) • LEDGERS • LEDGER • DEFINE LEDGERS FOR GENERAL LEDGER ACCOUNTING

The screen in Figure 1 is displayed.

Define Ledgers in General Ledger Accounting			
Ld	Ledger Name	Totals Table	Leading
XX	Test New Ledger	FAGLFLEXT	☐

⌃ *Figure 1 Define Ledgers in General Ledger Accounting*

Here, you define a two-character key for your ledger in the Lᴅ field, give it a name, and assign it to the general ledger totals table FAGLFLEXT. You then define whether the ledger is the leading ledger by selecting the Lᴇᴀᴅɪɴɢ checkbox. Once you define the ledger as the leading ledger, a ledger group with the same name is automatically created. You can add other ledgers to this ledger group by following the IMG menu path:

Fɪɴᴀɴᴄɪᴀʟ Aᴄᴄᴏᴜɴᴛɪɴɢ (Nᴇᴡ) • Lᴇᴅɢᴇʀs • Lᴇᴅɢᴇʀ • Dᴇꜰɪɴᴇ Lᴇᴅɢᴇʀ Gʀᴏᴜᴘ

The ledger that this ledger group is derived from is automatically flagged as the representative ledger of that ledger group. The representative ledger controls the posting periods that are allowed when postings are made to that ledger group. You can assign the posting period variant to the representative ledger (if the representative ledger is not the leading ledger) via the IMG menu path:

Fɪɴᴀɴᴄɪᴀʟ Aᴄᴄᴏᴜɴᴛɪɴɢ (Nᴇᴡ) • Lᴇᴅɢᴇʀs • Lᴇᴅɢᴇʀ • Dᴇꜰɪɴᴇ ᴀɴᴅ Aᴄᴛɪᴠᴀᴛᴇ Nᴏɴ-Lᴇᴀᴅɪɴɢ Lᴇᴅɢᴇʀs

This takes you to the screen shown in Figure 2.

Settings for Non-Leading Ledgers in General Ledger									
CoCd	Company Name	C1	Crcy 1	C2	Crcy 2	C3	Crcy 3	FV	Var.
3000	IDES US INC	10	USD					K4	3000

⌃ *Figure 2 Settings for Non-Leading Ledgers*

You can then control the posting periods for that variant using Transaction OB52. When you post a document to an open posting period in the representative ledger, the document is posted to all other ledgers in the ledger group, even if their posting periods are closed. You therefore need to make sure that you synchronize the posting periods of all ledgers within a group.

The accounting transactions you can use to post directly to a ledger group are Transactions FB01L, FB50L, and ABF1L. If a ledger group is not specifically assigned in an accounting transaction, then all ledgers in the system are updated with the posting.

Recording Advance Payments

You can use special general ledger transactions to record advance payments and clear them when the payment is made.

You might find yourself in a unique situation where a vendor asks you to pay a certain amount up front before delivery is made. You can use the down payment functionality of your system to accomplish this. This involves creating a down payment request (which is a noted item), then either creating a down payment or running the payment program.

✅ And Here's How...

To access the settings for a down payment request, go to Transaction OBYR or access the settings via the IMG menu path:

> FINANCIAL ACCOUNTING (NEW) • ACCOUNTS RECEIVABLE AND ACCOUNTS PAYABLE • BUSINESS TRANSACTIONS • DOWN PAYMENTS MADE • DEFINE ALTERNATIVE ACCOUNTS FOR DOWN PAYMENTS

Double-click on the SPECIAL GENERAL LEDGER indicator F and click on PROPERTIES to access the screen shown in Figure 1.

Notice that the NOTED ITEMS checkbox and the radio button for DOWN PAYMENT/ DOWN PAYMENT REQUEST are selected. This checkbox can only be selected for SPECIAL GENERAL LEDGER indicator F. As part of the standard system setting, you cannot select this checkbox for any other down payment indicator.

Properties		Special G/L transaction types	
Noted items	☑	◉ Down payment/Down payment request	
Rel.to credit limit	☐	○ Bill of exchange/Bill request	
Commitments warning	☐	○ Others	
Target sp.G/L ind.	AIMB		

Posting Key			
Debit		Credit	
29		39	Down payment request

≫ *Figure 1 Special General Ledger Indicator Properties*

In the TARGET SP. G/L IND. field, enter the down payment indicators that can be created from this down payment request (you can find the list of special general ledger indicators and their meanings in the initial screen of Transaction OBYR). Click on the ACCOUNTS button, and you will come to the screen displayed in Figure 2. This screen shows the reconciliation accounts (which are linked to the vendor) that the down payment request can be used for, as well as the special general ledger accounts that will be used when the down payment request is posted.

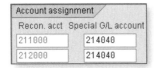

Account assignment	
Recon. acct	Special G/L account
211000	214040
212000	214040

≪ *Figure 2 Special General Ledger Account Assignment to Reconciliation Accounts*

To post a down payment request, go to Transaction F-47 or access the screen via the following menu path:

> ACCOUNTING • FINANCIAL ACCOUNTING • ACCOUNTS PAYABLE • DOCUMENT ENTRY • DOWN PAYMENT • REQUEST

You enter the document header details as normal, along with the vendor account and the relevant SPECIAL GENERAL LEDGER indicator (TRG.SP.G/L IND. field), as shown in Figure 3. This special general ledger indicator is not the down payment request indicator, but is one of the target special general ledger indicators configured in the properties of indicator F.

Vendor	
Account	1111
Trg.sp.G/L ind.	A

≪ *Figure 3 Special General Ledger Indicator for Down Payment Request*

Click on the NEW ITEM button to enter the amount, due date, and other relevant information, and then post the document. When viewing the vendor line items in Transaction FBL1N, you need to select the NOTED ITEMS checkbox to view the down payment request, which is displayed in Figure 4.

« *Figure 4 Enable Noted Items in Line Item Display*

Although noted items can be viewed in vendor (and customer) line item display reports, they do not update transaction figures, so they do form part of the balance of the vendor, customer, or general ledger accounts.

Payment Run Free Selection

You can include or exclude certain documents from a payment run, based on specific criteria.

You may want to restrict the list of selected open items in the payment proposal to be more specific with the items that you want to include or exclude in the payment run. This will help to streamline the list of items that is shown in the payment proposal and make it easier to review. For example, you may want the payment proposal to include specific document numbers for a vendor or customer, items with only a credit balance, or only items that contain a certain field value (for example, a specific group key) in the vendor and customer master.

✅ And Here's How...

To modify your list of open items, go to the FREE SELECTION tab of the payment program in Transaction F110. Select the dropdown option on the FIELD NAME field to see the pop-up box shown in Figure 1. You can choose between the DOCUMENT, VENDOR MASTER RECORD, and CUSTOMER MASTER RECORD.

« Figure 1 *Free Selection Options*

Each of these options gives you the list of table fields that are available for that selection. You can use most fields from the following tables to define your free selection conditions: BKPF and BSEG for documents, LFA1 and LFB1 for vendors, and KNA1 and KNB1 for customers.

Select the field you want to use, and enter the values to include from that field. For multiple values, you can separate the values using a comma (with no spaces between the comma and the values). For example, to enter profit centers 1000, 2000, and 3000, enter the values as "1000,2000,3000". For ranges, enter the values in parentheses and separate them with a comma. For example, a document number range from 100001 to 100008 is entered as "(100001,100008)". If you are entering date fields as your selection criteria, you should enter them in the format YYYYMMDD; for example, November 4, 2010, becomes "20101104". Examples of these values are displayed in Figure 2.

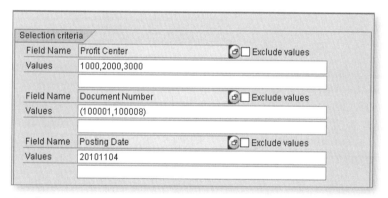

⚱ *Figure 2* *Free Selection Field Values*

You can also exclude the values that you have entered from the payment proposal by selecting the EXCLUDE VALUES checkbox. You can choose up to three selection criteria fields (such as document number, posting date, and amount), and each of these can have three fields from different tables, from the same table, or a mix of both.

Note that the system does not validate that the value you entered exists in the field table. It only validates that the field length and character specifications are correct. You will only find out if you entered incorrect values when you execute the payment proposal and do not get the data you requested. Depending on the number of items in the payment proposal, this may be difficult to identify, so it is important that you ensure that the values you enter in the filter criteria are accurate.

Using Enjoy Transactions versus Complex Postings

You need to know when to use Enjoy Transactions versus "complex posting" transactions to process accounting documents.

The standard accounting posting Transaction F-02 allows you to work with specific processes, such as the manual entry of tax items for general ledger documents, as well as transfers from one vendor or customer to another. However, this is a time-consuming exercise, as you need to enter a lot of data in the fields and to navigate to as many screens as there are line items. It is possible to become lost when entering the account to be posted to on one screen and the amount that relates to that account on the next screen. Furthermore, if you have another account line to post to, this account is entered on the same screen as the amount of the previous account line, and it's amount is entered on the next screen.

It is therefore confusing to align the accounts with their related amounts. To simplify the process, you can use the Enjoy Transaction, where you enter all of the accounts and amounts in a single screen.

✓ And Here's How...

The Enjoy Transaction is a single screen where you can enter, hold, simulate, park, and post a document, as well as retrieve templates using minimal entries and keystrokes. It is used for accounting documents such as general ledger postings, incoming invoices and credit memos, and outgoing invoices and credit memos. You can access the Enjoy Transaction for general ledger postings by going to Transaction FB50 or via the following menu path:

ACCOUNTING • FINANCIAL ACCOUNTING • GENERAL LEDGER • POSTING • ENTER GENERAL LEDGER ACCOUNT DOCUMENT

You will see the buttons shown in Figure 1, which will help you simplify the data entry process.

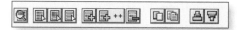

« Figure 1 *Enjoy Transaction Quick Access Buttons*

For example, the COPY LINES button (⬚) copies the line you select to the line immediately below it. If you have multiple lines that have similar values in almost all of the fields, you can use this function to replicate the line and then change only the relevant fields. If you want to store the account and amount entries as a template, use the menu option:

EDIT • ACCOUNT ASSIGNMENT TEMPLATE • SAVE ACCOUNT ASSIGNMENT TEMPLATE

Give the template any name. You can access the account assignment template by clicking on the TREE OPTIONS button (⬚ Tree on) and selecting the template you saved. In Figure 2, you can see that using the TREE OPTIONS button also gives you access to held documents and screen variants.

« Figure 2 *Tree Options View*

The Enjoy Transaction screen has some restrictions, one being that if you are in a vendor or customer transaction (i.e. FB60 or FB70), you cannot control to what type of offsetting account you post. You only have the option of posting to a general ledger account because you cannot change the posting keys as you would with the complex transaction. Therefore, you may need to switch to a complex transaction screen from an Enjoy posting screen. To do this, after you have entered the vendor details, follow the menu path ENVIRONMENT • COMPLEX POSTING to find the screen shown in Figure 3.

⌃ *Figure 3 Complex Posting Screen*

You will see the document overview with the single vendor line. To enter another vendor's account, you can enter the relevant posting key and account at the bottom of the screen as you would when you are using a complex posting transaction.

It is important to note that if you try to switch back to the Enjoy Transaction, you will lose all your data! Therefore, make certain you have made all of the necessary entries in the Enjoy Transaction format before you switch to complex posting. You can make any subsequent changes to the lines by double-clicking on the line in the complex posting format.

Deriving Profit Centers from Customer or Vendor Transfers

You can take advantage of passive splitting to derive the profit center on postings between vendors or customers.

If your company needs to have a balance sheet by profit center (or another dimension such as segment or business area), then you need to ensure that some or all balance sheet account transactions contain a profit center. However, when processing a transfer posting from one vendor or customer to the other, the system will not know what document splitting characteristic (for example, profit center) the posting should have. The reason for this is as the general ledger reconciliation accounts that are linked to customers and vendors are balance sheet accounts, the active splitting rules (which look for the account assignment of the offsetting account) do not work.

So, to ensure that every accounting posting contains a profit center, you have to set the system up appropriately.

✓ And Here's How...

First, you need to define the profit center field as a document splitting characteristic and make it a required entry. You can do this by following the IMG menu path:

> FINANCIAL ACCOUNTING (NEW) • GENERAL LEDGER ACCOUNTING (NEW) • BUSINESS TRANSACTIONS • DOCUMENT SPLITTING • DEFINE DOCUMENT SPLITTING CHARACTERISTICS FOR GENERAL LEDGER ACCOUNTING

The screen in Figure 1 is displayed.

Document Splitting Characteristic for General Ledgers					
Field		Zero balance	Partner field		Mandatory Field
Business Area	🗎	☑	PARGB	🗎	☐
Profit Center	🗎	☑	PPRCTR	🗎	☑
Segment	🗎	☑	PSEGMENT	🗎	☐

⌃ *Figure 1 Document Splitting Characteristics*

For the defined profit center characteristic, select the MANDATORY FIELD checkbox. By choosing this box, an error message will be issued any time a document does not have a profit center. One scenario where this is likely to happen is with the example described on the previous page, where you are making a posting from one balance sheet account with no default profit center assignment to another balance sheet account.

You might normally post from one customer to another by using the SAP complex posting Transaction F-22 or by switching from an Enjoy Transaction (as described in Tip 17). However, the system will not have a profit center assignment on any of the lines in the document, because the profit center field cannot be directly entered on a customer line. Therefore, you will probably receive the error message we just described if you have set the profit center field as a mandatory document splitting characteristic.

The correct way to post this document is to take advantage of the document splitting functionality. There are two main types of document splitting:

▶ **Active splitting**
At least one of the lines on the document contains a profit center. In this case, the balance sheet line is split into as many lines as there are profit centers on the document, in the same ratio that the profit center amounts are split.

▶ **Passive splitting**
The profit center is inherited from a line on the original document that is being post-processed. Passive splitting therefore normally applies to "post with clearing" documents, because this is the only way you can post a document by selecting and matching another document that has already been posted.

We will use an example to demonstrate how the profit center can be derived from a posting. An invoice to customer 600 has been posted and is shown in the document display (use Transaction FB03) screen in Figure 2.

Itm	PK	Account	Description	Amount	Curr.	Profit Center	Segment
1	01	600	IDES US - (Inter-Company Accou	1,000.00	EUR		
2	50	800200	Revenues	1,000.00-	EUR	NGL_1020	MANF

≫ **Figure 2** Document Display (Entry View)

The default document display shows the entry view, which is how the transaction was originally posted. You can see that the profit center (and segment) is only assigned to the revenue line.

To see how the system displays this document after document splitting, click on the GENERAL LEDGER VIEW button to see the display as shown in Figure 3.

Itm	PK	L.item	Account	Description	Amount	Curr.	Profit Center	Segment
1	01	000001	145000	Accounts Receivable	1,000.00	EUR	NGL_1020	MANF
2	50	000002	800200	Revenues	1,000.00-	EUR	NGL_1020	MANF

≫ **Figure 3** Document Display (General Ledger View)

Note that in the GENERAL LEDGER view, the system does not show the customer number. Instead, it shows the reconciliation account that is linked to the customer. For customer 600, the reconciliation account is 145000.

However, if later on you find that the invoice should have gone to customer 1000 instead of customer 600, you can rectify this mistake by following these steps: Go to Transaction FB05 and enter the header and line details for customer 1000, and then click on the CHOOSE OPEN ITEMS button, which will take you to the screen shown in Figure 4.

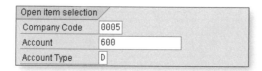

« **Figure 4** Choose Open Items Screen

Enter customer 600 and click the PROCESS OPEN ITEMS button to see the screen shown in Figure 5.

« **Figure 5**
Process Open
Items Screen

Select the amount to be transferred to customer 1000 and post the document.

When you display the document using Transaction FB03, you will see that the profit center that was derived from the revenue line on the original document has been inherited in the correct customer's document. When you view it using the entry view, you will see the transfer from customer 600 to customer 1000 as shown in Figure 6.

Itm	PK	Account	Description	Amount	Curr.	Profit Center	Segment
1	01	1000	Becker Berlin	1,000.00	EUR		
2	15	600	IDES US - (Inter-Company	1,000.00-	EUR		

⌃ *Figure 6 Transfer from Customer 600 to Customer 1000*

Clicking on GENERAL LEDGER VIEW takes you to the screen shown in Figure 7.

Itm	PK	L.item	Account	Description	Amount	Curr.	Profit Center	Segment
1	01	000001	140000	Trade Receivables -	1,000.00	EUR	NGL_1020	MANF
2	15	000002	145000	Accounts Receivable	1,000.00-	EUR	NGL_1020	MANF

⌃ *Figure 7 General Ledger View of Transfer Document*

You will see that the profit center (and segment) that was on the original invoice has now been inherited by customer 1000 (which is shown as reconciliation account 140000).

Tip 19

Posting Fast Invoice Entry for MIRO

You can match vendor invoices against multiple purchase orders using a single screen transaction.

Transaction MIRO is widely used by most account payable departments that use SAP software. These departments could be posting as few as one or as many as a thousand invoices per day. This transaction, however, only allows the input of one purchase order per invoice on a single screen.

If you need to enter several invoices that contain several purchase order lines, consider using Transaction MIRA to accomplish this process quickly.

✓ And Here's How...

You can access the Fast Invoice Entry screen by going to Transaction MIRA or via the menu path:

> LOGISTICS • MATERIALS MANAGEMENT • LOGISTICS INVOICE VERIFICATION • DOCU-MENT ENTRY • ENTER INVOICE FOR INVOICE VERIFICATION IN THE BACKGROUND

The top part of the screen looks exactly like the MIRO transaction. The bottom part of the screen is shown in Figure 1.

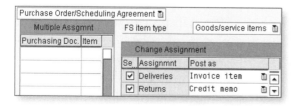

« *Figure 1 Fast Invoice Entry Screen*

In the MULTIPLE ASSIGNMENT part of the screen you can enter as many purchase orders as exist on the vendor invoice.

One thing to note about this transaction is that you cannot change any of the line item details that have been defaulted from the purchase order, such as the amount, quantity, or account assignments. If you want to make a change here, then you should revert back to standard invoice verification Transaction MIRO.

Use Transaction MIRA when you expect the invoice details to be largely similar to those on the purchasing document and therefore do not need any significant changes. When you have completed the document, click on the SCHEDULE BACK-GROUND VERIFICATION button, which looks like the normal POST button. This stores the invoice verification in the background until you run the settlement program RMBABG00 by going to Transaction SE38. This takes you to the screen displayed in Figure 2.

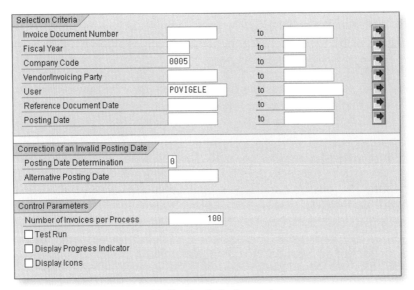

⌃ *Figure 2 Logistics Invoice Verification in Background*

This program can either be processed directly or set up as a background job using Transaction SM36. You can use parameters such AS INVOICE DOCUMENT NUMBER, COMPANY CODE, USER, etc., to filter the documents that will be posted, or leave the values open so that all documents that have been saved in the MIRA transaction are processed. The program checks and validates the invoices and posts them if there are no errors. It also produces a log that tells you which documents cannot be posted.

Tip 20

Manually Clearing Multiple Accounts

You can combine several accounts in the manual clearing transaction to allow matching of items from different accounts.

You might find yourself in a situation where you want to clear more than one account using the clearing transaction. Additionally, there are specific circumstances where you may want to clear items that do not have a common field that you can match (unlike with the automatic clearing functionality, where each line needs to have a matching field that the system can use as a criteria for performing the clearing).

To be able to work with clearing items from multiple accounts, we will tell you how to accomplish this task by using a manual clearing transaction.

✓ And Here's How...

To manually clear multiple accounts, go to Transaction F-03 (note that this process also applies to the other clearing transactions such as F-44 for vendors, F-32 for customers, and so on), enter the initial general ledger account that you want to clear, and press [Enter] to display the open items for clearing. As displayed in Figure 1, you can select the open items that you want to clear.

Account	Document Number	Document Date	Posting	Bus	Day	USD Gross
113101	1500000041	03/09/2005	50	3000	0	120,430.35-
113101	1500000042	03/09/2005	50	3000	0	9,603.00-

⌃ *Figure 1 Process Open Items Screen*

If you want to add the open items of multiple accounts to the same clearing screen, you need to do the following: Click on the DOCUMENT OVERVIEW button and then click on CHOOSE OPEN ITEMS to show the screen displayed in Figure 2. This screen already contains the company code and account that you are clearing.

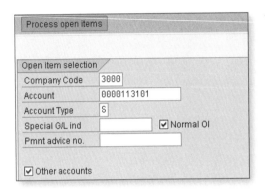

« Figure 2 Choose Open Items Screen

Select the OTHER ACCOUNTS checkbox and click on the PROCESS OPEN ITEMS button to see the screen shown in Figure 3, where you can add additional accounts. First, enter the relevant account type for the accounts, and then enter the accounts and company codes. Either select the STANDARD OIs checkbox if there are no special general ledger transactions to be considered, or enter the relevant special general ledger indicators.

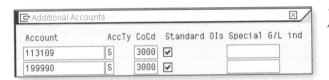

« Figure 3 Additional Accounts Screen

Press the ⌈Enter⌉ key, and you will see that the open items from the additional accounts (shown in Figure 4) have been added to the list.

Account	Document Number	Document Date	Posting	Business A	Days	USD Gross
113101	1500000041	03/09/2005	50	3000	0	120,430.35-
113101	1500000042	03/09/2005	50	3000	0	9,603.00-
113109	1400000000	07/28/2000	40	3500	0	2,496.00
199990	100003949	01/01/2009	50	5000	0	154,000.00-
199990	100003950	01/01/2009	50	5000	0	89,550.00-
113109	100000294	07/05/2002	50	6000	0	130,583,333.31-

⌃ **Figure 4** Additional Accounts in Clearing Screen

Tip **21**

Posting to Special Periods

You can use special periods for adjustment postings that do not affect the monthly balances in the affected year.

When performing your periodic processes, you want to be able to post audit or tax adjustments to periods that do not affect the balances in your normal periods, but do affect the balance for the whole year. In standard SAP, there are usually 12 normal posting periods and 4 special periods, the idea being that each special period can be used to make adjustments to each quarter of the fiscal year.

In this tip, we will show you how to maintain and make postings to special periods, which you can use for any adjustments that you do not want to form part of the balance of your normal periods.

✓ And Here's How...

Set up special periods by going to Transaction OB29 or following the IMG menu path:

> FINANCIAL ACCOUNTING (NEW) • FINANCIAL ACCOUNTING GLOBAL SETTINGS (NEW) • LEDGERS • FISCAL YEAR AND POSTING PERIODS • MAINTAIN FISCAL YEAR VARIANT (MAINTAIN SHORTENED FISCAL YEAR)

The screen in Figure 1 is then displayed.

	FV	Description	Number of posting periods	No.of special periods
Fiscal year variants				
	K4	Calendar year, 4 spec. periods	12	4
	PS	July - June, 4 special periods	12	4
	Q1	Quarters	4	

⌃ *Figure 1 Fiscal Year Variant with Special Periods*

Enter the special periods that correspond to the relevant fiscal year variant in the No. of Special Periods column. The system allows you to enter more than four special periods, but you cannot enter more than 16 total periods.

To enable posting to the special periods, you need to ensure that these periods are open. To do this, use the standard period maintenance table (Transaction OB52). It is normal to open the special periods of the previous year in the second posting interval in this table. This way, you can keep the normal periods of the previous fiscal year closed and maintain the normal periods of the current fiscal year in the first posting interval. This is displayed in the screen shown in Figure 2.

Var.	A	From acct	To account	From per.1	Year	To period	Year	From per.2	Year	To period	Year	AuGr
3000	+			1	2010	12	2010	13	2009	16	2009	
3000	A		ZZZZZZZZZZ	1	2010	12	2010	13	2009	16	2009	
3000	D		ZZZZZZZZZZ	1	2010	12	2010	13	2009	16	2009	
3000	K		ZZZZZZZZZZ	1	2010	12	2010	13	2009	16	2009	

⌃ **Figure 2** *Period Maintenance Table*

To post to the special periods when entering a general ledger document (for instance in Transaction FB50), first ensure that the posting date you entered falls in the last period of the fiscal year. For example, if you are using a January to December calendar-based fiscal year variant, your posting date should be between December 1 and 31. You should also enable the posting period to be entered in the screen to specify to which of the special periods is to be posted. If you do not enter any posting period, the system will automatically use period 12, which is based on the posting date you entered. To allow the posting period to be entered in an Enjoy Transaction, click on the Editing Options button and select both the Display Periods and the Posting in Special Periods Possible checkboxes, as shown in Figure 3.

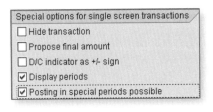

« **Figure 3** *Enable Posting to Special Periods*

If you do not select the Display periods checkbox, you will not be able to enter the special periods.

Part 3
Display

Things You'll Learn in this Section

There are several reasons why either a consultant or end user would need to display data in a company's SAP system, such as responding to an account query for a customer or vendor, viewing the outstanding items in a bank account, or finding out how much depreciation has been recorded on a fixed asset. There are a number of ways, ranging from simple to complex, to extract data from your SAP system. You can display the data directly on the screen, print it out, or download it to an external application.

Displaying data is one of the most common tasks that is carried out by SAP system end-users. The beauty of the system is that you, as an end user, can configure your own display screens often without requiring the help of a consultant or programmer. You also have several functions that are usually found in spreadsheet programs, such as sorting columns in a list, filtering data for specific values, totaling and subtotaling amount columns, and hiding and moving column positions. These tools provide you with a lot of flexibility with regard to how you can view lists and reports. You can save any of the settings that have been made as a variant for yourself alone, or (with the proper authorization) for anyone who uses that report. If you are not satisfied with SAP's functionality for arranging and customizing the screen, you can always download the report to Microsoft Excel (in HTML, XML, or XXL format) or Microsoft Word.

Another aspect of SAP's display functionality is that you should be able to enter the minimum amount of data in a field to get the data output you want. For example, if you are working within a certain company code and you go to another screen that requires a company code, the system will automatically populate the company code field with the one you were working on in the previous screen. Additionally, the field memory stores the last few values that you entered so that you can simply press the [Backspace] key or [Spacebar] to retrieve a value you entered in the past.

This part of the book will provide tips on how to sort, search, and maintain certain display settings in order to make the data in the system easier to analyze and interpret. For example, we will show you how to use worklists for quick display and processing of data. Also, you will learn how to add special fields and mass change fields to line item display reports.

Displaying Parallel Currencies

You can display the alternative currencies of a company code and post to them directly in several ways.

As we discussed in Part 1, every company code can have up to two parallel currencies, which are translated at historical exchange rates and set in the currency tables. When you display a document for a company code, you can also display the amounts that were updated in these currencies. Without this functionality, you would have to manually translate the company code currency into the parallel currencies.

And Here's How...

Access the Display Document transaction (FB03), double-click on one of the lines in the document, and click on the ADDITIONAL DATA button, which takes you to the screen shown in Figure 1. You will see the parallel currency amounts (which are made in the configuration screen of Transaction OB22).

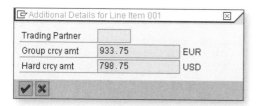

« Figure 1 *Parallel Currencies in a Document*

You can also view the parallel currencies when displaying the balance of a general ledger account in Transaction FAGLB03. When you have displayed the balances per period, click on the CHANGE DISPLAY CURRENCY button to see the screen shown in Figure 2. You can choose in which parallel currency you want to display the balances.

《 Figure 2 *Parallel Currencies in Balance Display*

Crcy Type Descriptn	Crcy	Currency Description
Company code currenc	MXN	Mexican Peso
Group currency	EUR	Euro (EMU currency a
Hard currency	USD	American Dollar

When you display the line items of the account (do this by double-clicking on one of the amounts in the Balance Display screen), you can view the parallel currency amounts by pulling in the relevant columns using the CHANGE LAYOUT button. This will take you to the screen displayed in Figure 3.

DocumentNo	Typ	Doc. Date	PK	Amount in local cur.	LCurr	Amount in loc.curr.2	LCur2	Amt in loc.curr. 3	LCur3
5000000000	WE	06/15/2000	96	260.00-	MXN	32.37-	EUR	27.69-	USD
5000000001	WE	06/15/2000	96	3,800.00-	MXN	473.10-	EUR	404.70-	USD
5000000002	WE	06/15/2000	96	3,900.00-	MXN	485.55-	EUR	415.35-	USD
5000000003	WE	06/15/2000	96	2,400.00-	MXN	298.80-	EUR	255.60-	USD
5100000000	RE	06/15/2000	86	260.00	MXN	32.37	EUR	27.69	USD
*				10,100.00-	MXN				

≪ Figure 3 *Parallel Currencies in Line Item Display*

Note that the AMOUNT IN LOCAL CURRENCY field relates to the company code currency. The AMOUNT IN LOCAL CURRENCY 2 field relates to the first parallel currency set up in Transaction OB22 (in this case the group currency). The field AMOUNT IN LOCAL CURRENCY 3 relates to the second parallel currency set up in Transaction OB22 (in this case, the hard currency).

Sometimes you may need to make an adjustment to the parallel currency amounts without changing the company code currency amount. To post a document only to the parallel currencies (and thereby post a zero amount in the first company code currency), go to the following menu path:

> ACCOUNTING • FINANCIAL ACCOUNTING • GENERAL LEDGER • POSTING • VALUATE FOREIGN CURRENCY

Enter the document header and line item data as you would with a normal accounting document. However, do not enter any value in any of the amounts fields (that is, neither the AMOUNT nor the AMOUNT IN LC fields) if you only want to post to the parallel currencies. Instead, click on the ADDITIONAL DATA button, which will display the parallel currency amount fields ready for input.

Downloading to Excel

You can maintain Excel download settings for line item reports.

Most financial line item display reports can be downloaded directly to Microsoft Excel. You can easily choose which spreadsheet format to download the data to, but you need to know how to create, modify, and delete the default download settings. In this tip, we will show you how to modify these settings so that you have the ability to change the download format as required.

✅ And Here's How...

The usual way of activating a direct Excel download from the financial line item display reports is to follow the menu option LIST • EXPORT • SPREADSHEET from the display screen.

The first time you do this, you will see a pop-up box as displayed in Figure 1.

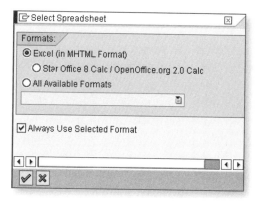

« Figure 1 *Spreadsheet Download Formats*

This box gives you various formats to choose from. If you select the ALWAYS USE SELECTED FORMAT checkbox, the system will save whichever option you last chose as a default. This is a good option if you always use the same format, as it saves you from selecting the option over and over again. However, once you have saved the setting, you are essentially stuck with it (keep reading for solutions to this problem). This setting will apply to all reports that are downloaded directly to Excel, so you will not have the flexibility of choosing different download options for different reports.

Remove Default Setting

If you want to remove the default setting for Excel downloads, go to Transaction SE38 (or SA38, depending on your authorization level) and enter program SALV_BS_ADMIN_MAINTAIN. This program may only be maintainable by your Basis team or a few select power users. The screen in Figure 2 is displayed.

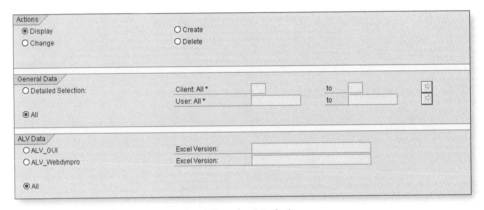

⌃ *Figure 2 Screen for Maintaining Excel Download Defaults*

When you execute the program, you will see that the screen is divided into three sections. The first section, ACTION, is where you select what you want to do in the program—DISPLAY, CREATE, CHANGE, or DELETE. If, for example, you had saved a default download format and now want to delete it, select the DELETE option. Then, in the GENERAL DATA section, select the DETAILED SELECTION option and enter the relevant client number and user name. You do not need to make any change in the third section, ALV DATA, for this purpose. When you click on the EXECUTE button, you will see a line with your user name and the Excel download option that you have saved. Highlight this line and click on the DELETE button, and a pop-up message box will appear, specifying how many lines are selected for deletion and if you want to delete them. Select Y (for Yes) to delete the line(s).

Make or Change Default Setting

If you want to make or change a default format using this program, you can select the CREATE or CHANGE option in the ACTIONS section. Then enter the relevant client and user(s) in the GENERAL DATA section, select the ALV_GUI option in the ALV section, and enter the Excel format that you want to set as or change to be the current default.

Sorting the Payment Run Output List

You can use sort variants to define how the payment program correspondence is sorted.

The payment program creates payment media such as checks and bills of exchange, as well as payment advice notes, depending on the payment methods used. You may want to sort the items by certain criteria such as by vendor name, postal code, or accounting clerk to help manage the processing of these outputs. If you do not specify how the system is to sort this material, the system will sort the items according to the SAP vendor numbers, which is not normally in a logical sequence that can be used to easily search for or group the payment media.

And Here's How...

You can find the screen to configure item sorting by accessing the IMG menu path:

> FINANCIAL ACCOUNTING (NEW) • ACCOUNTS RECEIVABLE AND ACCOUNTS PAYABLE • BUSINESS TRANSACTIONS • AUTOMATIC OUTGOING PAYMENTS • PAYMENT MEDIA • SORT VARIANTS

To define the variants for the correspondence output (for example, to control the sort order in which the checks are printed), click on the PAYMENT MEDIA: DEFINE SORT VARIANTS step. Then click on the CREATE button, which takes you to the screen shown in Figure 1. Here you can give the SORT VARIANT a two-character key and a description.

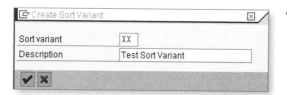

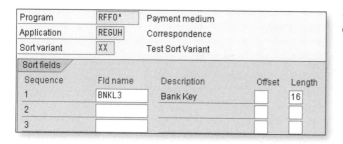

« Figure 1 Create Sort Variant

Pressing the ⌈Enter⌋ button takes you to the screen shown in Figure 2, where you can define the sequence of fields by which you want the media to be sorted.

« Figure 2 Sort Variant Configuration Screen

The dropdown options in the FLD NAME field show you which fields are available. If you need the field characters to start from a certain position, you can put the position number in the OFFSET field. For example, let's say your sort variant was by bank key, and a vendor's bank key number was 890135622. When you choose an offset number of 4, the sort variant will be based on the value 135622, because the number 1 is the fourth character in the field value.

If you do not put anything in the OFFSET field, then the system will use the whole field value. If you want only a specific number of characters from the field value to be used for the sort character, you can enter the number in the LENGTH field.

You can now insert the sort variant into the relevant payment methods to be used in the payment run. You can accomplish this by accessing Transaction FBZP and clicking on the PMNT METHODS IN COMPANY CODE button. You then double-click on the relevant company code and payment method, and click on the FORM DATA button to open up the fields in that section. Next, go to the subsection labeled SORTING OF THE (shown in Figure 3) and enter the sort variants you created for correspondence and line items in the corresponding fields.

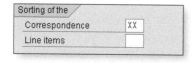

« Figure 3 Assign Sort Variant to Payment Method

Using the Document Display Editing Options

You can display a document using the document or reference number, as well as by the DATA ENTRY or GENERAL LEDGER view.

In the initial screen of the standard document display transaction, you can see the SAP document number, the company code, and the fiscal year. However, when vendors query specific invoices, it is normal for them to give their own invoice number as opposed to the SAP document number. In this case, you may want to adapt the document screen so that you can easily look up a document based on the vendor's invoice number. Let's look at this display configuration process in the solution.

✅ And Here's How...

You can display accounting document numbers by using Transaction FB03 (Document Display) or via the menu path:

> FINANCIAL ACCOUNTING • GENERAL LEDGER (OR ACCOUNTS RECEIVABLE OR ACCOUNTS PAYABLE) • DOCUMENT • DISPLAY

To enable entry of this field in the Document Display screen, click on the EDITING OPTIONS button. In the DISPLAY DOCUMENTS USING section shown in Figure 1, select the REFERENCE NO. box and click on the SAVE button.

« *Figure 1 Reference Number Checkbox*

The system shows you a message stating: "The options were entered in the user master record." This means this reference number field setting is stored in the user's profile and will always be used as default until it is changed and resaved. The original screen is displayed with the reference number field, as shown in Figure 2.

⌃ *Figure 2 Reference Number Field in the Document Display Screen*

You can only enter either the document number or the reference number, not both. There are two views that you can use to display documents.

▶ The standard view is called the DATA ENTRY view, which shows your standard double entry postings according to the items that have been posted.

▶ With SAP General Ledger, there is now also the GENERAL LEDGER view, which contains the line items split according to the document splitting characteristics and zero-balancing items.

To default the GENERAL LEDGER view when displaying an accounting document, click on the EDITING OPTIONS button, and select the GENERAL LEDGER VIEW checkbox in the DISPLAY DOCUMENTS USING section, as shown in Figure 3.

《 *Figure 3 General Ledger View Checkbox*

Tip **26**

Resetting Cleared Items en Masse

You can reset multiple cleared items by using a simple Legacy System Migration Workbench (LSMW) recording.

When you reset a cleared item, you generally must remove any clearing data from the line item of a document, thereby changing its status from cleared to open. This is a standard practice using Transaction FBRA. A drawback of this transaction, however, is that you can only reset one cleared document at a time.

Let's look at how you can reset hundreds of incorrect clearing documents quickly and easily using LSMW.

✔ And Here's How...

By using the LSMW tool, you can easily create an upload sheet with the clearing document numbers, company code, and fiscal year that you can load into the system to reset the cleared items. If you are new to this somewhat complex process, we suggest that you look up information on how LSMWs are created in SAP's online help system at *http://help.sap.com*. We will only address the key areas that need to be set up to deal with mass resetting of cleared items in this tip.

Go to Transaction LSMW and create your project, subproject, and object. Then select Goto • Recordings and give the recording any name (in this example, we use the name ZFBRA, as shown in Figure 1).

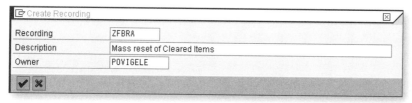

⌃ *Figure 1* *Create LSMW Recording*

When you save the recording, three recorded fields will be available: DOCUMENT NUMBER OF THE CLEARING DOCUMENT (AUGBL), COMPANY CODE (BUKRS), and FISCAL YEAR (GJAHR). To save the file structure, you need to perform the following five steps (note that at each step you select the radio button connected to the step and EXECUTE (⊕)):

1. **Maintain object attributes.**
   Select the BATCH INPUT RECORDING radio button, enter the recording name, and click SAVE.

2. **Maintain source structures.**
   Click on the buttons CHANGE (✎) and CREATE (▯), and give the source stricture a name (for example, ZZFBRA) and description.

3. **Maintain source fields.**
   Click on CHANGE, then click once on the source field name and then on the TABLE MAINTENANCE button (▦). Enter the values shown in Table 1 and click the SAVE button twice.

Field Name	Type	Length	Field Description
AUGBL	C	10	Clearing document
BUKRS	C	4	Company code
GJAHR	C	4	Fiscal year

⌃ *Table 1* *Create LSMW Recording*

4. **Maintain structure relations.**
   Click on the CHANGE button and the SAVE button.

5. **Maintain field mapping and conversion rules.**
   Click on CHANGE and select the menu EXTRAS • AUTO FIELD MAPPING. Press the Enter key four times, and then click on the SAVE button (💾).

Next, create an upload file. This should contain three columns: document number, company code, and fiscal year. You can enter all of the relevant data in the file and save it in the text tab-delimited format, as displayed in Figure 2.

« *Figure 2 Text Tab-Delimited File Format*

To upload the file, you need to perform the next step:

6. **Specify files.**
   Click on the CHANGE button and double-click on the LEGACY DATA – ON THE PC (FRONTEND) option. Enter your file name and choose the format TABULATOR (which, in our example, represents the text tab-delimited format). Then select the boxes FIELD NAMES AT START OF FILE and FIELD ORDER MATCHES SOURCE STRUCTURE DEFINITION. Press the Enter key and click on the SAVE button.

The next seven steps upload and validate the data:

7. **Assign files.**
   Click on the CHANGE and SAVE buttons.

8. **Read data.**
   Click on EXECUTE (⊕), and click on the BACK button (⟵) twice.

9. **Display read data.**
   Press Enter and then click on the BACK button.

10. **Convert data**
    Click on EXECUTE, and then click on the BACK button twice.

11. **Display converted data.**
    Press Enter and then click on the BACK button.

12. **Create batch session.**
    Click on EXECUTE and press Enter .

13. **Run batch input session.**
    Highlight the session, click on the PROCESS button, select DISPLAY ERRORS ONLY, and press the Enter key.

When the session is complete, you will get a message saying "Processing of Batch input session completed." This means all of the documents in the file have been posted correctly, and therefore all of the cleared documents have been reset.

Eliminating Check Printing Overflow

You can use a setting in the program variant to keep the check numbers from printing on an extra page of a payment.

Sometimes there are many line items on a check, which can then flow over to two or more pages. If you print checks on blank paper, you need to ensure that no check numbers are printed on voided checks (as will be the case with check overflow). It is important to note that if you use preprinted checks and they have been placed in sequential order in the printer, the overflow pages will be printed on check forms and, hence, the check number on the preprinted check will be out of sync with the check numbers in your SAP system.

In this tip, we will walk you through the process to make the check numbers print only on the pages that contain the check form.

✓ And Here's How...

You can use one of two options to make check numbers print in sequential order for only the first pages of a multiple-page check document:

1. In the check form, specify that the check on page FIRST is sent to the check printer, and the checks on pages NEXT and LAST are sent to another printer that contains letter paper. Then you can go to the print variant by using Transaction SE38, entering the check program, and choosing the relevant variant.

2. Your second option is to go to Transaction F110 (Payment Program), select the PRINTOUT/DATA MEDIUM tab, click on the variant in the relevant program field, and follow the menu path ENVIRONMENT • MAINTAIN VARIANTS. Then select the

Do Not Void Any Checks checkbox in the Output Control section, which is displayed in Figure 1.

Output control	
Alternative check form	
Filler for digits in words	
Number of sample printouts	
No.of items in payment summary	9999
☐ Payment Document Validation	
☐ Texts in recipient's lang.	
☐ Currency in ISO code	
☐ No Form Summary Section	
☑ Do not Void any Checks	

《 Figure 1 *Output Control of Check Variant*

Alternatively, you can choose to use only one printer, place the checks in sequential order, and let the page overflow be printed on a check page that is automatically voided based on the check form settings. Note that if you select the Do Not Void Checks checkbox in the check variant, the system will also void the check number that coincides with that check page. Therefore, do not select this checkbox.

Note that you should also be aware of this setting in other transactions that involve check printing such as Reprint Check (Transaction FCH7) and Payment with Printout (Transaction FBZ4). Figure 2 shows the output control (which means the specifications for how the check should be printed) of the transactions used for printing single checks.

Output Control		
Printer for forms	LP01	☑ Print immediately
Pmnt advice printer		☐ Recipient's lang.
		☐ Currency in ISO code
		☐ Test printout
		☑ Do not Void any Checks

⌃ Figure 2 *Output Control of Check Printing Transaction*

The Do Not Void Any Checks checkbox has been selected so that the check numbers are only printed on the initial page that contains the check form, and not on the overflow pages.

Specifying Period Texts

You can specify texts for each period in balance display reports.

Periods texts are the descriptions that are given to the financial periods (for example, January can be the text for period 1, February for period 2, and so on). The periods that are listed in balance display reports, such as in Transaction FAGLB03, are displayed numerically (normally from period 1 to 16), but do not contain the text of the period.

When you have noncalendar fiscal years, for example, April to March, it is not always obvious which month period 1 relates to. (Note: This is even more relevant if you deal with several company codes that have different fiscal year variants. Here, they may have different beginning and ending months, which may create confusion.)

This tip shows you how to display the period texts in these balance display reports.

And Here's How...

If you want the description of the periods to show in the balance display reports, you need to maintain period texts. This can be done by going to Transaction OB29 or via the IMG menu path:

> FINANCIAL ACCOUNTING (NEW) • FINANCIAL ACCOUNTING BASIC SETTINGS (NEW)
> • LEDGERS • LEDGER • MAINTAIN FISCAL YEAR VARIANT (MAINTAIN SHORTENED
> FISCAL YEAR)

Click on the fiscal year variant that is linked to the relevant company code, and click on the PERIOD TEXTS folder. Click on NEW ENTRIES, which takes you to the screen shown in Figure 1. Enter the relevant language (you can maintain texts for your periods in multiple languages), period, and short and long texts for the period.

Period texts			
Language	Period	Txt	Text
EN	1	JAN	January
EN	2	FEB	February
EN	3	MAR	March
EN	4	APR	April

« Figure 1 *Period Texts in Fiscal Year Variant*

When you use special periods, you can enter any text in the TEXT fields that would make sense to the user. In Figure 2 we have entered the texts "Q1 adjustments" for period 13, "Q2 adjustments" for period 14, and so on.

Period texts			
Language	Period	Txt	Text
EN	13	Q1	Q1 adjustments
EN	14	Q2	Q2 adjustments
EN	15	Q3	Q3 adjustments
EN	16	Q4	Q4 adjustments

« Figure 2 *Texts for Special Periods*

Once you have made these configuration settings, you can go to a report to see these texts alongside their respective periods. When you go to one of the balance display transactions (such as FAGLB03), you can pull in the description of the periods by clicking on the CHOOSE LAYOUT button and selecting CHANGE LAYOUT. Pull in the MONTH field and insert it after the PERIOD field, as we have done in Figure 3.

Period	Month	Debit	Credit	Balance	Cum. balance
Bal.Carryforw:	Bal.Carryforward				107,004,941.97-
1	January		3,235,675.73	3,235,675.73-	110,240,617.70-
2	February		3,393,363.81	3,393,363.81-	113,633,981.51-
3	March		3,322,058.60	3,322,058.60-	116,956,040.11-
4	April	104,000.36	3,449,995.72	3,345,995.36-	120,302,035.47-

⌃ Figure 3 *Period Texts in Balance Display*

Depending on your authorization, you can save the setting just for yourself or make it the default setting for everyone who uses the transaction. Note that you need to make this layout change for all of the balance display reports such as FK10N and FD10N, as a layout change in one balance report does not automatically update all reports.

Tip (29)

Defining Special Fields

You can add extra fields to line item display reports by defining special fields.

Line item display reports come with a set number of fields that exist in the Layout screen, as well as several hidden fields that can be added by changing the layout of the screen. In most cases, these fields are sufficient to analyze and report the line items in an accounting document. However, there are circumstances in which additional fields are needed. These fields exist in finance tables but are not accessible in the display reports. In this situation, you need to add special fields and pull them into the reports.

✓ And Here's How...

There are two ways of adding special fields to display reports, depending on which report you are using. If you want to add special fields to either the classic general ledger line item display (Transaction FBL3N), vendor line item display (FBL1N), or customer line item display (FBL5N), you can go to Transaction O7R3 or follow the IMG menu path:

> FINANCIAL ACCOUNTING • ACCOUNTS RECEIVABLE AND ACCOUNTS PAYABLE • CUSTOMER ACCOUNTS • LINE ITEMS • DISPLAY LINE ITEMS • DEFINE ADDITIONAL FIELDS FOR LINE ITEM DISPLAY

When you click on NEW ENTRIES, you will see the screen shown in Figure 1. You then click in the TABLE field, press the F4 button, and select the appropriate table. Then click on the FIELD field, press the F4 button, select the appropriate field you want to add, and save the transaction.

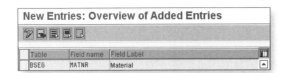

« *Figure 1 Define Special Field*

You can add as many special fields as you want, but note that the more table fields the report can access, the slower the report becomes. It is also important to note that the special field is a cross-client table, which means that any modification you make will be reflected in all clients of your SAP instance.

If you want to add special fields to the general ledger view line item display report, go to the configuration menu path:

> FINANCIAL ACCOUNTING (NEW) • GENERAL LEDGER ACCOUNTING (NEW) • MASTER DATA • G/L ACCOUNTS • LINE ITEMS • DEFINE SPECIAL FIELDS FOR LINE ITEM DISPLAY

The steps needed to add special fields to the general ledger line item display reports are exactly the same as the process you use to add to regular display reports. However, note that adding special fields in this table is independent from the special fields added in Transaction O7R3. The special fields defined here affect only the general ledger view line item display report (FAGLL03).

When you have added the special fields to the configuration table, they will be included in the respective display reports' hidden fields. You can access these by clicking on the CHANGE LAYOUT button and pulling the hidden fields from the right part of the CHANGE LAYOUT screen to the left part of the screen, as displayed in Figure 2.

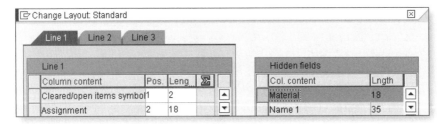

⌃ *Figure 2 Add Special Field to Line Layout*

Adding Fields to the Mass Change Option

You can add extra fields to the mass change option in line item display screens by changing the function group.

There may be cases where you need to add extra fields to the Mass Change screen. For example, you may want to add the payment term field (BSEG-ZTERM) so you can do a mass update of this field for several documents. This functionality is useful because it allows you to simultaneously change the data of several lines in documents that have already been posted.

✓ And Here's How...

To make mass changes for several documents in a line item display report, select the relevant lines and click on the MASS CHANGE button. The Mass Change screen is then shown, which is divided into three sections: PAYMENT DATA, DUNNING DATA, and ADDITIONAL DATA. You can enter the new values to which you want the fields in the documents selected to be changed. Alternatively, you can enter nothing in the field to mass delete the contents of that field.

To add extra fields to the Mass Change screen go to Transaction SE80 (you need to have a developer's access to the system), drop down on the selection box, select the option FUNCTION GROUP, and enter FI_ITEMS in the field below. Then open up the SCREENS folder and double-click on screen 0100, as it is displayed in Figure 1.

▽ 🗁 Screens	
0100	Line Items: Window for Mass Change
0200	Display Error Log for an Item
0300	Dialog: Items for Head Office/Branch

《 Figure 1 Screens Folder

Select the menu option GO TO • LAYOUT, which opens the Screen Painter of screen SAPLFI_ITEMS 0010. To modify this screen, click on the DISPLAY/CHANGE button, and click on the button at the top of the screen called DICTIONARY/PROGRAM FIELDS WINDOW. This produces a pop-up box called SCREEN PAINTER: DICT. /PROGRAM FIELDS. To add the PAYMENT TERM field, enter "BSEG-ZTERM" in the TABLE/FIELD NAME field and click on the GET FROM DICTIONARY button, as shown in Figure 2.

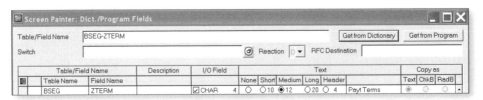

⩕ *Figure 2 Screen Painter Program Fields*

Now, select the table row line that is shown at the bottom of Figure 2 and click on the GREEN CHECK icon at the bottom of the screen. You are taken back to the screen SAPLFI_ITEMS 0010, and your cursor becomes a cross symbol that is dragging a rectangular box. Use this cursor to move the box onto the part of the screen where you want your new field to be positioned. When you have identified the appropriate position, click once on the box to place it there.

In Figure 3 the bottom-right part of the screen shows where the new PAYMENT TERMS field will be added to the Mass Change screen.

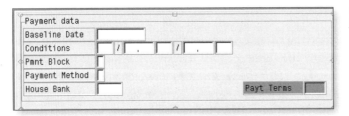

《 *Figure 3 Add Field to Screen Painter*

If you want to move the field to a different position, simply drag it again and click on the new position. When you are happy with the position, save and activate the screen. You can go back to the original screen, SAPLFI_ITEMS, and insert the following line into the source code on the FLOW LOGIC tab:

```
field *bseg-zterm module req_zterm on request.
```

Save and activate the screen.

Maintaining Worklists for FI Data

You can use worklists to combine related objects for processing and displaying data.

It is common to have several account-related objects that you want to process or display together in a transaction such as vendors, customers, the general ledger, and exchange rates. This is not normally possible unless you enter the individual values or ranges manually in the field selection. This option increases processing time and is prone to entry errors.

In this tip, we will show you how to avoid this problem and easily display and process multiple objects by using worklists.

 And Here's How...

Maintain Worklists

To create worklists for displaying and processing accounting line items, follow the menu path:

> Accounting • Financial Accounting • General Ledger • Environment • Current Settings • Maintain Worklist for Processing Open Items/Maintain Worklist for Displaying Line Items/Maintain Worklist for Displaying Balances

Next, select which object (company codes, customers, vendors, or general ledger accounts) you want to maintain worklists for.

Double-click on the customer object (KUNNR), click on the CREATE button, and give the worklist a name and description. Enter the numbers of the customers that should be grouped in the worklist, as displayed in Figure 1, and save the data. You can also use this procedure to create worklists for either of the other objects, namely vendors and general ledger accounts.

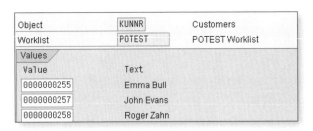

« *Figure 1 Add Customers to Worklist*

Activate Worklists

To activate the worklists in line item display reports and open item processing, you need to activate the relevant settings in the accounting editing options. To do this, go to Transaction FB00, go to the OPEN ITEMS tab, and select the USE WORKLISTS checkbox, which is shown in Figure 2.

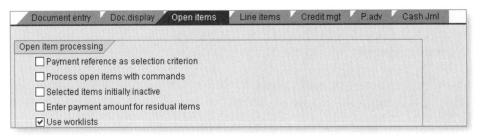

⌃ *Figure 2 Activate Worklists in Open Item Processing*

Now go to the LINE ITEMS tab, select the WORKLISTS AVAILABLE checkbox (shown in Figure 3), and save your settings.

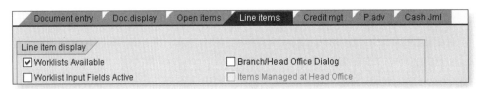

⌃ *Figure 3 Activate Worklists in Line Item Display*

When you go to the line item display Transaction FBL5N for customers, a button called ACTIVATE WORKLIST will now be displayed at the top part of the screen, as shown in Figure 4.

« *Figure 4 Worklist Button in Customer Line Item Display*

When you click on this box, a new section called CUSTOMER will appear at the top of the screen. Enter the worklist you created and click on the EXECUTE button, and the open items for the customers in the worklist are displayed. You can also perform the same steps in the customer display balance Transaction FD10N.

Clear Open Items

For the clearing of open items (Transaction F-32 for customers) you can simply enter the worklist name in the ACCOUNT field, as shown in Figure 5, and click on PROCESS OPEN ITEMS. The open items of all of the customers in the worklist are displayed for processing.

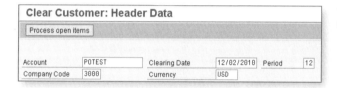

« *Figure 5 Clearing Customers Using Worklist*

You can apply this process to any open item clearing transaction for customers, such as F-28 (Process Incoming Payment), F-31 (Process Outgoing Payment), and F-26 (Incoming Payment Fast Entry).

Worklists for Exchange Rates

Worklists can be used to simplify the maintenance of exchange rates, which normally exist in table TCURR. Table TCURR contains several lines of data for different exchange rate types, validity dates, and currencies. It is usually quite cumbersome for navigating through to enter only the data that you need updated.

To define worklists for entering exchange rates, go to the IMG menu path:

> SAP NETWEAVER • GENERAL SETTINGS • CURRENCIES • DEFINE WORKLIST FOR EXCHANGE RATE ENTRY

The screen shown in Figure 6 is displayed.

You can enter a worklist name, text, and the frequency of maintenance of the exchange rates (you do not have to adhere to this interval, but it helps highlight whether the rates entered are now out-of-date).

Worklist	Text	Maint. Int	Tol. %
POTEST	Test Exch Rate Worklist	Monthly	

Exch.rate maint. Work list

⌃ *Figure 6 Maintain Exchange Rate Worklist*

You can also enter a tolerance percentage for how much the new exchange rate can deviate from the previous one. You can go to the next configuration step in the same menu path: Assign Exchange Rate to Worklist, which takes you to the screen shown in Figure 7. For each exchange rate type and currency pair, you can assign your created worklist and specify whether you will use direct or indirect maintenance.

Exch.rate maint. Assign exch. rates to work lists

ExR	From	To-C	Worklist	Quotation	
M	EUR	USD	POTEST	Direct quotation	
M	GBP	USD	POTEST	Direct quotation	

« *Figure 7 Assign Currency Pairs to Worklist*

To maintain the exchange rates using worklists follow the menu path:

> Accounting • Financial Accounting • general ledger • Environment • Current Settings • Enter Currency Exchange rates using a Worklist

You can highlight the worklist you created, click on the Change button (✏️), and enter a valid from date and exchange rate for the relevant currency pair, as shown in Figure 8.

Test Exch Rate Worklist

Worklist	ER	From	To	Rate	Relation	Valid from	Exch. Rate	Rate 1:1
POTEST	M	EUR	USD	EUR/USD	1:1	12/02/2010	1.32007	1.32007
POTEST	M	GBP	USD	GBP/USD	1:1	12/02/2010	1.55959	1.55959

⌃ *Figure 8 Maintain Exchange Rates Using Worklist*

Click on the Set Worklist to "Completed" button, which takes you to the initial screen, update the status of the worklist to show a green light, and highlight the date on which it was last maintained.

Part 4
Data Analysis

Things You'll Learn in this Section

One of the main benefits of using the SAP system is that the time you save from quicker processing of data and real-time integration of the components can be used for more data analysis. There are several transactions you can use to analyze accounting documents and processes. Most postings to accounts can be viewed and analyzed by account, line item, or document number and drilled down to the source document that generated the posting. Sometimes you may not remember what document number was posted. In this case, the system provides several fields where you can enter values that relate to the document, including entry date, company code, and username.

When line items are displayed, they are usually sorted by the assignment number field. This is a free text field that can be either populated manually or based on the sort key field, which is entered in the general ledger or vendor/customer master data. You can configure certain fields as sort keys, such as posting date, sales order, vendor, and purchase order. This means your financial line item display reports will be sorted by the defined sort key.

Sometimes the chronology of the document number ranges is broken. A typical example of this is when there is a system termination or a short dump. This can happen when you are posting a transaction and, due to some program or database error, the transaction is aborted or you lose the system connection. In this case, the document number that should have been assigned to your posting may be incorrectly assigned in the data base, even though it is not linked to a document; the next time you try to post the document, it uses the next number. To solve this potential problem, there is a report you can use to see the document number range gaps, and hence account for all of the document numbers in the system.

Account determination tables are used as the main integration point between the FI component and the other components, such as Sales and Distribution, Materials Management, and Human Resources. The Accounting Detective report allows you to analyze which accounts have been assigned to the various components. There are also reports in the components such as Purchasing and Sales and Asset Accounting, where you can analyze the invoices or asset transactions according to various criteria and trace them back to their respective accounting documents.

In this part you will find tips and tricks that will show you how to easily use the data generated from the system to analyze business results.

Tip **32**

Deriving the Assignment Number

You can populate an assignment number automatically by using sort keys.

The assignment field of a document is a free text field that you can use to sort items of an account in a line item display transaction. It is also normally used as a clearing criterion for automatic clearing. The assignment field (which has the technical name ZUONR) is a key table field in tables where open or cleared items are read (for example, in tables BSID and BSAD for customers). It can be populated manually by entering up to 18 alphanumeric characters in the field or by using a sort key, which pulls the value of a predefined accounting document field into the assignment field. However, it is better to let the system populate it automatically using a sort key, as this will save data entry time and eliminate any potential typing errors.

In this tip, we will show you how to create this sort key and use it for this purpose.

 And Here's How...

To create a sort key to enter an assignment number, go to Transaction OB16 or follow the IMG menu path:

> FINANCIAL ACCOUNTING (NEW) • ACCOUNTS RECEIVABLE AND ACCOUNTS PAYABLE • CUSTOMER (OR VENDOR) ACCOUNTS • LINE ITEMS • DISPLAY LINE ITEMS • LINE ITEMS WITHOUT ALV • DETERMINE STANDARD SORTING FOR LINE ITEMS

When the system takes you to the transaction screen, you will see a number of standard sort keys displayed with a field description. You can use any of these standard keys, modify them to suit your needs, or create new ones.

To create a new sort key, click on the NEW ENTRIES button and enter a three-digit code and description. You can choose the relevant fields from tables BKPF, BSEG, BSEC, or BSED. Pick the field names as displayed in Figure 1, and then enter the offset, if any (which specifies from what position in the original field the contents are to be transferred to the assignment field), and the length of characters of the field that you want to be populated.

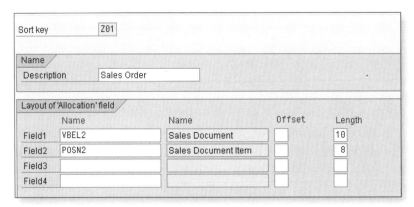

⌃ *Figure 1 Sort Key Configuration*

The fields are listed in chronological order as they are defined. This means that if you enter a sales order in FIELD 1 and a line item number in FIELD 2, the system will populate the sales number and line item as one continuous value in the assignment field.

Once you have created the sort keys, you need to enter them into the relevant master data. For the general ledger master data, go to the master data Transaction FS00 and enter the sort key in the CONTROL DATA tab, as displayed in Figure 2.

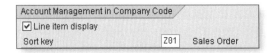

« *Figure 2 Assign Sort Key to General Ledger Master*

You can see that the assignment field is populated with the sort key you defined and the items are sorted by this field.

Note that for ALV reports such as FBL1N, even though the assignment column is initially used to sort the line items, you can manually define another column that can be used to sort the list. You can do this by clicking on the relevant column, clicking on one of the sort buttons (🖨 or 🖷), and saving it as a variant.

Tip 33

Maintaining the GR/IR Account

By using the clearing and maintenance transactions, you can clean up the items in the GR/IR Account.

You should regularly maintain the goods receipt invoice receipt (GR/IR) account, otherwise it will grow to an unmanageable size. In this tip, we will explore two transactions you can use to ensure that the lines in this account have been cleared appropriately, and also ensure that items that will never be matched are written back to their original accounts.

And Here's How...

Automatic Clearing Transaction

The first transaction you want to use is Transaction F.13 (Automatic Clearing), which matches all of the goods receipts with their related invoice receipts based on the purchase order and line item numbers. The combination of purchase order and line item number is stored in the assignment field of the GR/IR account. You should set this field as clearing criterion in the Automatic Clearing rules, either by going to Transaction OB74 or via the following configuration menu path:

> FINANCIAL ACCOUNTING (NEW) • GENERAL LEDGER ACCOUNTING (NEW) • BUSINESS TRANSACTIONS • OPEN ITEM CLEARING • PREPARE AUTOMATIC CLEARING

You can set up the clearing rules as shown in Figure 1.

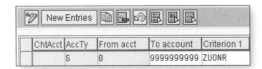

« *Figure 1* *Define Automatic Clearing Rules*

This screen indicates that for all Charts of Accounts for account type S (which stands for the general ledger), every account (0 to 9999999999) should have the assignment field (ZUONR) as an automatic clearing criteria.

Therefore, when you go to Transaction F.13, every invoice and goods receipt of equal but opposite amounts with the same purchase order and line item number will automatically be cleared from the account using the values from the assignment field.

You should enter the relevant company codes' fiscal year and any other data that will restrict the documents to be selected. Then select the SELECT G/L ACCOUNTS checkbox and enter the relevant GR/IR account(s), as we have demonstrated in Figure 2.

⌃ *Figure 2* *GR/IR Account in Automatic Clearing Program*

We recommend that you run this transaction daily, which you can do manually or by scheduling it as a background job.

GR/IR Maintenance Transaction

The next transaction you can use to maintain the GR/IR account is maintenance Transaction MR11. This transaction clears quantity discrepancies between the goods receipt and its related invoice. These quantity variances remain as balances in monetary value in the GR/IR account.

When configuring the transaction, you can choose a tolerance level (which is the maximum amount of a variance that can be written off) that the quantity variance should be equal to or less than for the variance to be cleared. The reason for this is that if the goods receipt has not been invoiced because the vendor has not yet sent the invoice, then you may not want to clear this amount, as it will be cleared at some point in the future when the invoice receipt is posted.

Figure 3 shows the settings that determine which GR/IR accounts should be maintained (if you select the relevant checkboxes for GR/IR CLEARING ACCOUNT, DELIVERY COST ACCOUNTS, or ERS-related items, this will select which type of accounts should be cleared). It also shows the latest receipt date to be considered and the tolerance percentage.

◰ *Figure 3 GR/IR Account Maintenance Settings*

We advise that you run this transaction at period end for purchase orders that are at least three months old. That way, if you do clear a goods receipt amount whose invoice was never posted, it is probably likely that the vendor was paid in some manual form.

When the documents are posted, they will create open items in the GR/IR that are the equal but opposite value to the discrepancies that are to be written off. The assignment field of these documents will contain the purchase order and line item number, so the next time you run the automatic clearing transaction, these items should be matched and cleared.

Tip 34

Finding an FI Document

You can use several selection parameters to locate an accounting document.

Sometimes a document number has been forgotten or was not recorded immediately after posting. One way of searching for the document is to go to the account that was posted to (if you remember it) and try to figure out which document is the correct one. However, depending on how many lines have been posted to that account, this process could seem similar to searching for a needle in a haystack.

In this tip, we will show you how to locate an FI document by entering other fields that relate to the accounting document so that the appropriate number is found.

✓ And Here's How...

You can display accounting documents by using Transaction FB03 or via the menu path:

ACCOUNTING • FINANCIAL ACCOUNTING • GENERAL LEDGER • DOCUMENT • DISPLAY

If you do not know the document number but have some other information that would help you track the document, click on the DOCUMENT LIST button.

You can now enter the relevant field values that relate to the document. For example, if you know that it was a journal entry and it was entered on the day you are searching for the document, enter document type SA in the DOCUMENT TYPE field (this is the standard document type for journal entries; however, this may vary depending on the document type setup in your organization) and enter the current date in the

ENTRY DATE field (shown in Figure 1). You can enter ranges and single values in these fields to add more flexibility to your search options.

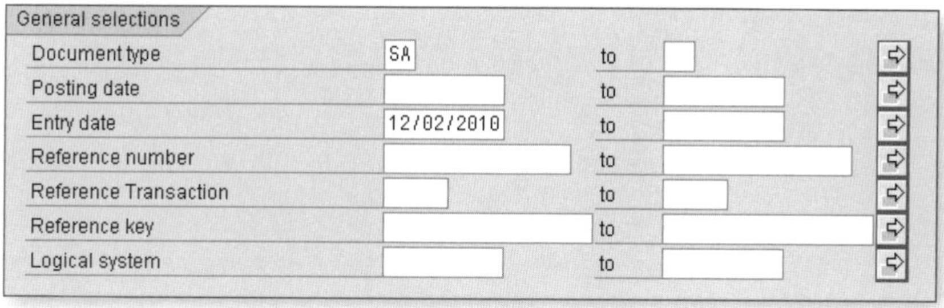

⌃ *Figure 1 General Selections for Displaying Documents*

If you want to display noted items (which are items that do not add to an account balance, but are shown in the account for informational purposes), you can select the DISPLAY NOTED ITEMS checkbox. This shows any down payment requests and bills of exchange items that exist.

You can also use this transaction to view the number of documents posted by a user on a particular date or range of dates. You can do this by clicking on the DYNAMIC SELECTIONS button (⬛) and entering the user's name in the appropriate field, as shown in Figure 2.

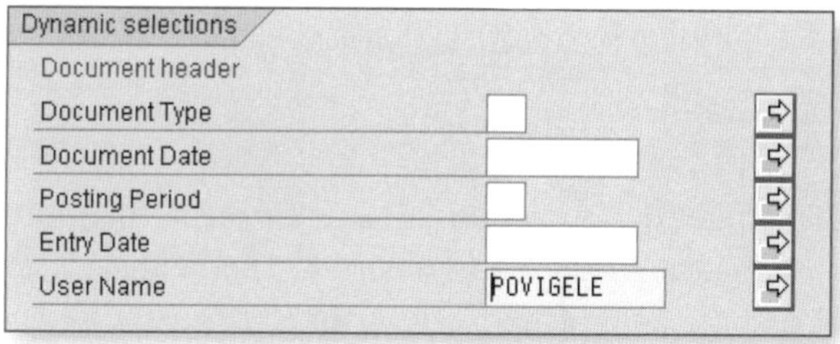

《 *Figure 2 Search by User Name*

You can save this setting as a variant (by clicking on the SAVE AS VARIANT button (🖫), giving the variant a name, and clicking on the SAVE button) if you plan to run this list regularly.

When you click on the EXECUTE (⊕) button, you will see the list of documents that are based on your selection criteria. You can then drill down into them as usual to find the source documents.

Tip **35**

Displaying Number Range Gaps

You can display gaps in document numbers across several ledgers by running a program report.

Sometimes gaps exist in the number range assignment in some documents; these can be due to buffer settings, program short dumps, or many other reasons. This situation can cause problems in some countries (for example, Italy), where it is a statutory requirement that accounting documents be in consecutive order. This is a strictly enforced requirement, as a company can expect an audit trail when the documents are not in order.

In this tip, we will explain the easiest way to expose any gaps in your document number range, so that there is a clear audit trail showing why the gaps exist.

✅ And Here's How...

To display the gaps in FI documents, go to Transaction SE38 and execute program RFBNUM00N, which takes you to the screen shown in Figure 1. Then either enter the relevant company codes or leave the field blank if you want all company codes to be considered.

Specify one fiscal year, so that in the cases where you have maintained year-dependent number ranges, you can display only number intervals for the fiscal year that you entered. You can select the specific document number or number range that you want to analyze.

⌃ *Figure 1* *Number Range Gaps Screen*

To include archived documents in the list, select the CHECK DOCUMENT ARCHIVE checkbox. If you do not use year-dependent number ranges, the system will display any gaps in the number range intervals for all years.

To display only the intervals from the year that you entered and beyond, select the DISPLAY NUMBERING GAPS STARTING WITH SPECIFIED FISCAL YEAR ONLY checkbox.

As displayed in Figure 2, the system outputs all of the intervals for every document number range, unless you select the DISPLAY GAPS ONLY checkbox, in which case only the intervals with gaps are displayed.

⌃ *Figure 2* *Display Number Range Gaps*

Tip **36**

Account Determination Analysis

You can use the Account Detective to find where accounts have been automatically assigned.

There has never been an easy way to find out where an account has been assigned without going into several configuration transactions. However, SAP recently delivered the Account Detective Report (available with SAP ERP 6.0), which changed all that.

This new report lists all of the accounts in a company code or chart of accounts, along with their master data settings, and gives you the option of finding out where they have been assigned. Let's explore this report and learn how to access it.

✅ And Here's How...

To access the Account Detective Report, go to Transaction S_ALR_87101048, which takes you to the screen shown in Figure 1.

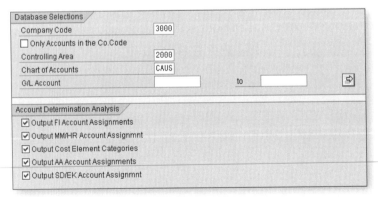

« Figure 1
Account Detective Screen

If you want to analyze the accounts in just one company code, then enter the company code and check the ONLY ACCOUNTS IN THE COMPANY CODE box. Then enter the relevant controlling area and chart of accounts. You can only enter one chart of accounts because most account determination tables are populated on a chart of accounts basis.

Figure 2 shows how the report is displayed when you click on the EXECUTE button. If you do not select any of the options in the ACCOUNT DETERMINATION ANALYSIS section, you will see a list of the accounts that you selected and their respective settings in the general ledger master record. This list is useful if all you want to do is analyze, for example, the number of accounts that are open item managed, available for line item display, or automatically posted to.

If you select any of the ACCOUNT DETERMINATION ANALYSIS checkboxes, you will see the list of master data settings as the header line and the tables (such as T095 and CSKB) where the accounts have been assigned in the item lines.

G/L acct	Name			B/S acct	AT	AcGp	Crcy
Account Assignment 1	Account Assignment 2	Account Assignment 3	Account Assignment 4				
1000	Land			X		ANL.	USD
CSKB		CE Typ: 90					
T095		01	00010000				
1010	Accumulated deprecia			X		ANL.	USD
CSKB		CE Typ: 90					
T095B		01	00010000				
2000	Buildings			X		ANL.	USD
CSKB		CE Typ: 90					
2010	Accumulated deprecia			X		ANL.	USD
CSKB		CE Typ: 90					

⌃ *Figure 2 Display Account Determination*

You can see in Figure 2 that account 00010000 is assigned to tables T095 and T095B (these are the tables for asset account determination) and to table CSKB (this is the Cost Elements table), where it is assigned to a cost element category of 90.

How to Interpret Subcontracting Account Postings

You should understand how to interpret the accounts that are posted to during the sub-contracting process.

For the subcontracting process to work, the purchasing and production teams usually make the following settings:

▶ The finished product needs to have a bill of materials (BOM) set up with the materials the subcontractor needs to create.

▶ The info record for the vendor should be set up with the subcontracting info category.

▶ The material master of the finished product should have a special procurement type of 30 in the MRP2 view.

▶ The purchase order should have an item category of L (for subcontracting).

Subcontracting is a process used in the Purchasing component of SAP ERP where an organization uses an external party to make a product by sending that party the input materials and paying a fee for the conversion to the finished product. However, from an accounting perspective, there is sometimes confusion about the accounts that are posted to when a subcontracting purchase order has been goods receipted. This tip will clarify this confusion by providing an example of the subcontracting process and detailing the accounts that are posted to and what they represent.

And Here's How...

A typical example of entries that are posted during the subcontracting process is as follows: A finished product is to be produced by a subcontractor, using one raw material that you send to him to be converted. We will assume that there is only one component in the bill of material and that the finished product is valued at the standard cost. (When there are several components, the system simply creates the additional lines for the extra raw materials' inventory and offset accounts.)

Table 1 shows how the account postings are represented in the system when the finished product is received from the subcontractor and a goods receipt has been made in the system. In this example, the finished product has a standard cost of $1000, the raw material has a standard cost of $800, the subcontracting vendor charges $200 for conversion costs, and there is a freight charge of $50.

The account key column indicates where the general ledger accounts are configured in the inventory account determination settings of Transaction OBYC.

Debit/Credit	Account	Amount ($)	Account Key
Debit	Finished product inventory	1000	BSX
Credit	Inventory change – subcontracting	1050	BSV
Credit	Price variance	50	PRD
Debit	Subcontracting services	200	FRL
Credit	GR/IR	200	WRX
Debit	Subcontracting services	50	FRL
Credit	Freight accrual	50	FR1
Debit	Raw material offset	800	GBB-VBO
Credit	Raw material inventory	800	BSX

⌃ *Table 1 Subcontracting Posting Example during Goods Receipt*

Note that the inventory change – subcontracting account is a combination of the raw material (800), the conversion cost (200), and the freight charge (50). If the value is not equal to the standard cost of the finished product (1000), then the difference (50) is posted to the price variance account.

The raw material offset account, the subcontracting services account, and the inventory change – subcontracting account should all be assigned to the same cost object (e.g., cost center) in Transaction OKB9.

Analyzing the LIV Document List

You can analyze logistics invoice verification (LIV) documents according to various statuses in a list display transaction.

Invoices that are posted with logistics invoice verification (LIV) transactions are normally analyzed by both the purchasing and accounting teams. However, these transactions normally show a list of purchase order documents or a list of accounting documents, respectively, and not the LIV documents. The LIV documents are hybrid documents of the Finance and Purchasing components and contain their own document numbers.

It is much quicker to view a LIV document directly than navigate to it from another component. In this tip, we will show you how to access and analyze this document.

✓ And Here's How...

To list the logistics invoice verification documents with the option to navigate to the purchasing or finance documents, go to Transaction MIR5 or follow the menu path:

> LOGISTICS • MATERIALS MANAGEMENT • LOGISTICS INVOICE VERIFICATION • FURTHER PROCESSING • DISPLAY LIST OF INVOICE DOCUMENTS

The screen in Figure 1 is displayed.

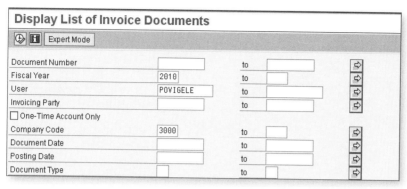

⌃ *Figure 1 Purchasing Invoice Documents Screen*

If you know the document number, you can enter it in the relevant field so that it returns only the document you want to analyze. Usually, however, you use this report when you do not know the specific document numbers but are trying to analyze which documents were posted by using certain selection criteria.

For example, you can display the list of documents that were posted for only specific users by entering the relevant user names. You can do the same for the other fields in the selection screen. If you only want to display the list for one-time vendors (vendors that do not have their own master data because you only expect to do business with them once), then you can select the ONE-TIME ACCOUNT ONLY checkbox.

If you click on the EXPERT MODE button at the top of the screen, you will see the display shown in Figure 2. You can choose to display the equivalent FI document number for the invoice (if this is different from the logistics document number) or the documents that contain postings in the G/L ACCOUNT or MATERIAL tab of the invoice.

⌃ *Figure 2 Expert Mode Screen*

109

Correcting Billing Documents with Errors

You can analyze and correct billing documents that contain accounting errors by using the release transaction.

Sometimes an accounting-related error prevents the accounting document from being created during billing document posting. When this happens, the person who posted the billing document may not necessarily notice that there was an error with the accounting interface because the billing document is still created, and the printed document (or EDI or other output) can still be sent to the customer. The system provides a message saying "Billing Document has been created (but no accounting document was generated)." However, this may not necessarily be noticed by or be relevant to a non-finance person.

This tip will show you how to display and analyze billing document errors and release the billing document when the error has been corrected.

✓ And Here's How...

One way to analyze the error for a particular billing document is to go to the Change Billing Document transaction (VF02) and click on the green flag RELEASE TO ACCOUNTING. If the error remains, the system will show you a message saying "Check the Notes in the Log".

To do so, go to the menu EDIT • LOG, where you will see a more descriptive explanation of the error message.

This process can be used when a few billing documents are processed in a period, and the person who posts the document is responsible for analyzing the error(s) and either resolving the errors or passing them to the finance department for resolution. However, the billing documents are often posted by various processes, both manual and automated, and it may not be practical to analyze every accounting error as it occurs. In such cases, we advise you to use Transaction VFX3 (Release Billing Documents to Accounting), which should be included as one of your period end closing processes.

When you go to Transaction VFX3, you will be taken to the screen shown in Figure 1, where you can enter the values that are relevant to the billing documents you want to analyze and release. In the INCOMPLETE DUE TO section, select the ACCOUNTING BLOCK and ERROR IN ACCOUNTING INTERFACE checkboxes.

Organizational Data			
Sales Organization	1000		
Creation Data			
Created By		to	⇨
Created On		to 12/31/2010	⇨
Document Info			
SD Document		to	⇨
Billing Type		to	⇨
Billing Category		to	⇨
Incomplete due to			
☑ Accounting Block			
☑ Error in accounting interface			

⌃ *Figure 1 Release Billing Documents to Accounting Screen*

Once you execute the transaction, you will see the list of billing documents that have accounting block errors. If you want to check what error is causing the block, then click on the green flag RELEASE TO ACCOUNTING. To view the detailed explanation of the message, click on the NOTES (▦) button.

Tip 40

Reconciling the General Ledger with the Asset Subledger

You can reconcile the accounts that are linked to the asset subledger with SAP General Ledger by using certain program reports.

There are situations where the balance in the asset subledger is different from the general ledger balance. For example, during a fixed assets implementation, you can post to the asset reconciliation accounts separately from their related general ledger accounts. If there is an imbalance between these two accounts, you will need to know where the difference exists so you can correct it. Therefore, you need to reconcile the two ledgers, which we will demonstrate in the following tip, as well as know how you can analyze the data to facilitate the reconciliation.

✓ And Here's How...

To reconcile the two ledgers, go to Transaction ABST2. Enter the relevant company code to be reconciled and execute the program, which takes you to the screen shown in Figure 1.

Source	CoCd	Ld	Account	Bu	Doc.no.	Period	Year	Σ 1st LC Delta GL/AA	2ndLCDelta	3rdLCDelta
AS	3000	0L	1000	1000			2010	19,900,627.00	17,304,592.09	19,900,627.00
			1010	1000			2010	1,080,448.00-	939,502.51-	1,080,448.00-
			11000	1000			2010	4,673,848.04	3,892,660.80	4,673,848.04
			11010	1000			2010	2,729,030.04-	2,376,445.80-	2,729,030.04-
			21000	1000			2010	171,838.00	149,421.75	171,838.00
			21010	1000			2010	171,838.00-	149,421.75-	171,838.00-
		0L 🛆					▪	20,764,997.00		

⌃ *Figure 1 Reconciliation of Fixed Assets to the General Ledger*

This program reads all of the transactions in the Asset Value Fields table ANLC for the current fiscal year, summarizes the values per general ledger account, and writes them to the totals table EWUFIAASUM. For this transaction to work, ensure that the current fiscal year is open (execute Transaction AJAB) and that the fiscal year change program for the previous year has been run (execute Transaction AJRW).

To analyze the difference between the value updates of a specific general ledger account in an asset account and SAP General Ledger, go to Transaction ABST. This takes you to the screen displayed in Figure 2, where you can enter the company code, fiscal year, depreciation area, and the reconciliation account to be analyzed.

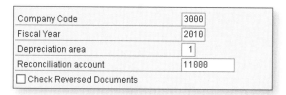

« *Figure 2 Consistency Check of SAP General Ledger to Asset Accounting*

When you execute this transaction, any inconsistencies between SAP General Ledger and asset accounting transactions will be displayed. One prerequisite for using this report is that the general ledger account needs to be set up to display line items. To configure this, select the LINE ITEM DISPLAY checkbox on the CONTROL DATA tab of the general ledger master.

You can also manually reconcile the postings between the fixed asset and general ledger accounts by using the asset history sheet and general ledger balance display reports. To do this, go to the asset history sheet Transaction AR01 and enter the relevant data, as shown in Figure 3.

Asset Balances

Company code	3000	to		
Asset number		to		
Subnumber		to		

⌃ *Figure 3 Asset History Sheet Entry Screen*

Part 5

Account Assignment

Things You'll Learn in this Section

This part of the book is dedicated to account assignments, which control how postings from other components flow into SAP General Ledger. Postings to SAP General Ledger can occur in three major ways:

▶ By assigning a general ledger account to the master record of a customer or vendor

▶ By assigning the general ledger account to a configuration table of the relevant component

▶ Directly by using a journal entry transaction

The more account assignments that are made, the fewer journal entries and manual postings need to be posted. The advantages of reducing the manual postings are that it reduces the number of tasks that are carried out at period end, and it reduces the number of potential errors from posting to incorrect accounts or cost objects. Before we delve into the account assignment tips, let's go over some of the main types of account assignment we will discuss in this part of the book:

- ▶ Customer and vendor accounts are integrated with SAP General Ledger by assigning a reconciliation account to the master data. There is only one field in the master data for the reconciliation account; however, you can also configure alternative reconciliation accounts, which can be manually selected when a posting is being made to the customer or vendor account.

- ▶ Revenue-related accounts are assigned by using access sequences that specify certain criteria on the customer master, material master, or pricing procedure to determine which accounts will be used when a sales document is posted to accounting.

- ▶ Inventory-related accounts are assigned based on the valuation class that is linked to the material master. They are also based on a transaction key and account modifier that specifies the accounts to be used depending on the type of inventory transaction posted.

- ▶ Travel expense accounts are determined based on the assignment of expense types to wage types and the subsequent assignment of wage types to account keys that control the expense, advance, or prepayment accounts to be used.

In this part of the book you will find tips on the various ways to assign accounts to source objects so that the flow of information to SAP General Ledger from other components is as seamless and automated as possible.

Assigning Alternative Reconciliation Accounts

You can choose a different reconciliation account from the one linked to the subledger account when posting an accounting document.

You can only assign one reconciliation account to the customer or vendor master, which means that any postings made to the subledger account will automatically update this one general ledger account. However, sometimes you may need more than one reconciliation account for the same customer or vendor to classify the different types of transactions you make with them.

In this tip, we will show you how to link more than one account to a single business partner.

And Here's How...

You can set up alternative reconciliation accounts by following the IMG menu path:

> FINANCIAL ACCOUNTING (NEW) • ACCOUNTS RECEIVABLE AND ACCOUNTS PAYABLE •
> BUSINESS TRANSACTIONS • POSTINGS WITH ALTERNATIVE RECONCILIATION ACCOUNT
> • DEFINE ALTERNATIVE RECONCILIATION ACCOUNTS

(Note that you can also assign alternative reconciliation accounts by using the special G/L indicator as in the case of down payments and bills of exchange. This was covered in Tip 15.)

In the resulting screen shown in Figure 1, enter the general ledger account that is directly linked to the subledger in the G/L ACC column, and enter the alternative reconciliation account in the ALT. G/L column.

G/L Acc	Alt. G/L	ID
165000	166000	AA

≪ *Figure 1* Alternative Reconciliation Accounts Configuration

If you need more than one alternative reconciliation account linked to the same general ledger account, then enter the same general ledger account in as many lines as you have alternative accounts. If you want to use a short key to represent the alternative reconciliation account (to ease document entry), you can enter any two-character alphanumeric key, such as AA, as shown in Figure 1 in the ID column.

For the reconciliation account field to be available during document entry, you have to enable this functionality in the general ledger account master. To enable the functionality, go to Transaction FS00 and select the RECON. ACCT. READY FOR INPUT checkbox in the CREATE/BANK/INTEREST tab, as shown in Figure 2.

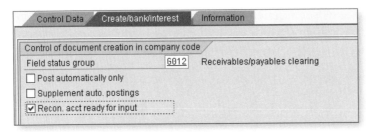

⌃ *Figure 2* Enable Entry of Reconciliation Accounts

This box may not be available in the general ledger master, so you need to enable it for the general ledger account. To do this, go to Transaction OBD4 and double-click on the account group related to the general ledger account. Then double-click on the subgroup DOCUMENT ENTRY and set the RECONCIL. ACCT READY FOR INPUT field to OPT. ENTRY. The checkbox will then be available in the general ledger master, and you can activate it for both the main reconciliation account and the alternative reconciliation account.

When you are posting to the vendor account using Transaction FB60 (or a customer account using Transaction FB70), click on the DETAILS tab, as displayed in Figure 3. You can enter either the alternative general ledger account or the ID that you set in the configuration table.

« *Figure 3* *Change Reconciliation Account during Invoice Posting*

Note that this functionality is only possible with finance-related postings to customers, vendors, and assets, such as Transactions FB60, FB70, FB01, FB02, and FB05. It cannot be used with the document entry transactions that are linked to other components such as MIRO (Logistics Invoice Verification) or VF01 (Create Billing Document).

Determining Revenue Accounts

You can maintain revenue accounts for postings from Sales and Distribution by using access sequences.

In the standard SAP system, five access sequence options are normally available in the Sales and Distribution component, and these are usually sufficient for most businesses. However, you may need to base your account assignments on fields that do not exist in the standard access sequence.

In this tip, we will show you how to create additional fields for revenue account determination.

✓ And Here's How...

You can define extra fields for determining revenue accounts by going to the following IMG menu path:

> SALES AND DISTRIBUTION • BASIC FUNCTIONS • ACCOUNT ASSIGNMENT/COSTING •
> DEFINE DEPENDENCIES OF REVENUE ACCOUNT DETERMINATION

In this transaction, define the conditions tables that the access sequence accesses. Double-click on the option ACCOUNT DETERMINATION: CREATE TABLES and enter a number between 501 and 999. When you press Enter , you will see the screen displayed in Figure 1. This shows the available fields from the field catalog, which you can double-click on to add to the condition table.

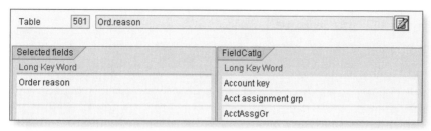

Table	501	Ord.reason	

Selected fields		FieldCatlg	
Long Key Word		Long Key Word	
Order reason		Account key	
		Acct assignment grp	
		AcctAssgGr	

⨠ *Figure 1* *Create Condition Table*

If there are fields that you want to use that are not available in the field catalog, you can add them by following the previously mentioned IMG menu path.

Double-click on the option FIELD CATALOG: ALLOWED FIELDS FOR THE TABLES. When you click on NEW ENTRIES and drop down on the FIELD column, you can double-click on the available field names to add them to the field catalog. When you have added the necessary fields to the condition table, you can save and generate the table so that all clients in this SAP instance are updated.

Now that you have defined the condition table, you need to add it to the access sequence.

Follow the same configuration menu path as above, but choose the next step, DEFINE ACCESS SEQUENCES AND ACCOUNT DETERMINATION TYPES. Double-click on the option MAINTAIN ACCESS SEQUENCES FOR ACCOUNT DETERMINATION, and the available access sequences will be shown. By selecting the KOFI access sequence and double-clicking on the ACCESSES folder, you will see the accesses that are available, as displayed in Figure 2.

No.	Tab	Description
10	1	Cust.Grp/MaterialGrp/AcctKey
20	2	Cust.Grp/Account Key
30	3	Material Grp/Acct Key
40	5	Acct Key
50	4	General

« *Figure 2* *Standard Access Sequence*

The order in which the accesses are displayed in the No. column represent the sequence the system will use to determine the account assignments.

You can now add your condition table by clicking on NEW ENTRIES. Enter the next number in the access sequence (in our example, this is 60) and enter the table number (501 in our example), as shown in Figure 3.

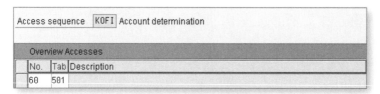

⌃ *Figure 3 Add Condition Table to Access Sequence*

Highlight your condition table and double-click on the FIELDS folder to activate the fields in this condition table that you pulled from the field catalog. Once you save your settings, the condition table will be available in the revenue account determination transaction. You can access this transaction by selecting the configuration step ASSIGN G/L ACCOUNTS, which takes you to the screen shown in Figure 4.

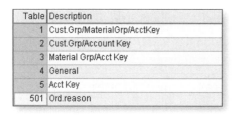

« *Figure 4 Access Sequence with New Condition Table*

Tip 43

Setting Up Revenue Recognition Accounts

Learning the proper settings for the revenue recognition process will help you to conform to the matching principle of most Accounting standards.

The most common form of revenue recognition is at the date of sale, which usually coincides with the date of shipment of inventory to the customer. For this process, the standard SAP settings for revenue account determination are sufficient. However, for noninventory sales such as services and fixed asset disposals, the revenue recognition point does not necessarily coincide with the date the customer is billed.

✓ And Here's How...

When working with noninventory sales, you can handle this type of scenario by using SAP's revenue recognition functionality in the Sales and Distribution component. You need to make the necessary configuration settings to the sales document item category and run the revenue recognition program with Transaction VF44. Because of the legal and tax implications requirements for revenue recognition, SAP recommends that you contact them via the Online Services System (OSS) to ensure that SAP's solution satisfies these requirements (see SAP Note 779366 for more information).

From a financial accounting standpoint, you need to make several settings to update the accounts related to the revenue recognition process. Table 1 describes the accounts to be used.

Account	Description
Revenue account	The account for recognized revenues
Receivables account	The customer account
Deferred revenue account	The offsetting account that is updated when the revenue recognition program is run
Unbilled receivables account	The offsetting account that is updated when the customer is billed

⌃ *Table 1 Revenue Recognition Accounts*

The revenue account is the same account that is used in the standard revenue determination process. You need to configure this revenue account in Transaction VKOA alongside the account key ERL. Assign the account key ERL to the revenue condition (PR00) in the sales pricing procedure. The receivables account is the reconciliation account, which you link to the customer master data (FD02) in the ACCOUNTING INFORMATION ACCOUNTING tab of the COMPANY CODE DATA section.

Configure the deferred revenue account in the PROVISION ACCOUNT column, shown in Figure 1. The deferred revenue account is adjacent to where the revenue account is configured in the revenue account determination table (Transaction VKOA).

App	CndTy.	ChAc	SOrg.	ActKy	G/L Account	Provision acc.
V	KOFI	CANA	0001	ERL	410000	142100

⌃ *Figure 1 Deferred Revenue Account Configuration*

The unbilled receivables account is configured in the Unbilled Receivables Account Determination table (Transaction OVUR), as shown in Figure 2. It is set up per chart of accounts and is adjacent to the receivables reconciliation account.

App	ChAc	Recon.acct	ANonBldRec
V	CAUS	140000	145500

« *Figure 2 Unbilled Receivables Account Configuration*

When you create the deferred revenue and unbilled receivables accounts, you need to make the following settings in the general ledger account master (Transaction FS00):

▶ On the Type/Description tab, select the indicator Balance Sheet Account.

▶ On the Control Data tab, do *not* select Only Balances in Local Crcy. Rather, enter the same tax category as the revenue account, select Posting Without Tax Allowed, and activate the Open Item Management and Line Item Display indicators.

▶ On the Create/Bank/Interest tab, select the Post Automatically Only indicator.

When a customer is billed (VF01/VF04), the following accounting entries are made:

▶ Debit: Receivables

▶ Credit: Unbilled receivables account

When the revenue recognition program is run (VF44), the following accounting entries are made:

▶ Debit: Deferred revenue

▶ Credit: Revenue

Tip **44**

Setting Up Material Ledger Account Determination

You can set up different accounts for single- and multilevel price determination by using special general modifiers for material ledger account keys.

The material ledger serves two purposes. First, it allows you to value your inventory in up to three currencies and valuation methods (namely legal, profit center, and group valuation). Second, it allows you to perform actual costing by rolling the variances from inventory-related transactions back into the product to establish an actual cost.

There is a lot of confusion in the material ledger regarding the accounts that these postings are made to, as well as how detailed you should be when setting up the accounts so that it is clear which postings relate to which variances. This tip will highlight the account keys you need to assign for the various material ledger functions.

✓ And Here's How...

You can assign accounts to the material ledger by going to Transaction OMWB or by following the configuration menu path:

> MATERIALS MANAGEMENT • VALUATION AND ACCOUNT ASSIGNMENT • ACCOUNT DETERMINATION • ACCOUNT DETERMINATION WITHOUT WIZARD • CONFIGURE AUTOMATIC POSTINGS

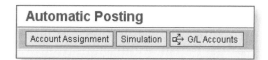

《 *Figure 1* *Automatic Posting Configuration Screen*

You can click on the ACCOUNT ASSIGNMENT button shown in Figure 1 to access the various transaction keys that contain the account determination settings. When you double-click on a transaction key, you will initially be asked to enter the relevant chart of accounts. When you have done so, you can either directly assign the relevant general ledger accounts, or specify general modification keys to differentiate general ledger accounts that belong to the same transaction key.

Where you need to define general modification keys, click on the RULES button in the transaction key, and then select the GENERAL MODIFICATION checkbox, as shown in Figure 2.

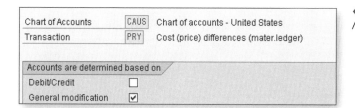

《 *Figure 2* *General Modification Checkbox*

Table 1 explains the transaction and general modification keys that are relevant to the material ledger.

Transaction Key	Description	General Modification	Description
PRY	Single-level price determination	PNL	Variance transferred to next level
PRV	Multilevel price determination	PNL	Variance transferred to next level
		PPL	Variance taken from lower level
KDM	Single-level exchange rate determination	PNL	Variance transferred to next level

⌃ *Table 1* *Material Ledger Modification Keys*

Transaction Key	Description	General Modification	Description
KDV	Multilevel exchange rate determination	PNL	Variance transferred to next level
		PPL	Variance taken from lower level
GBB	Offsetting account for inventory posting	AUI	Variances from cost center over/under absorption
COC	Revaluation of other consumables	N/A	N/A
LKW	Reserve account for nonrevaluation of inventory	N/A	N/A

⌃ *Table 1* *Material Ledger Modification Keys (Cont.)*

Setting Up Document Splitting

You can define your own active splitting scenarios if you understand the different settings for document splitting.

Of the types of document splitting that are available (active, passive, and zero-balancing), you can only configure active splitting to create balance sheet accounts for profit centers, segments, and other dimensions. SAP has a standard set of rules that contain settings for document splitting. These rules are sufficient in most cases; however, it is important to know the specific settings in case you need or want to create your own rules, or if you need to troubleshoot any issues with the standard rules.

And Here's How...

To set up document splitting you first need to identify the business transaction that you will use. Business transactions are events that lead to the update of line items in the general ledger, customer invoice, vendor invoice, and payments, for example.

You can do this by going to the following configuration menu path:

> FINANCIAL ACCOUNTING (NEW) • GENERAL LEDGER ACCOUNTING (NEW) • BUSINESS TRANSACTIONS • DOCUMENT SPLITTING • EXTENDED DOCUMENT SPLITTING • DEFINE BUSINESS TRANSACTION VARIANTS

Highlight the relevant business transaction and double-click on the ACCOUNTING TRANSACTION VARIANT folder to see the screen shown in Figure 1.

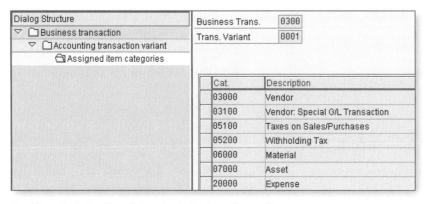

⤊ *Figure 1 Business Transaction Variant*

Here you can see the business transaction 0300 (which stands for Vendor Invoice), which is assigned to the standard business transaction VARIANT 0001.

Next, assign the business transaction and variant to the appropriate item category. Item categories characterize the items of an accounting document based on the account type of the line item; for example, vendor, customer, or asset. To assign the item categories, highlight the standard variant 0001 and double-click on the ASSIGNED ITEM CATEGORIES folder to access the screen shown in Figure 2.

⤊ *Figure 2 Assign Item Categories to Business Transaction*

Now you can see the item categories that have been assigned to the business transaction for vendor invoices (0300) in the standard variant (0001).

Next, assign general ledger accounts to these item categories by going to the following configuration menu path:

> FINANCIAL ACCOUNTING (NEW) • GENERAL LEDGER ACCOUNTING (NEW) • BUSINESS TRANSACTIONS • DOCUMENT SPLITTING • CLASSIFY G/L ACCOUNTS FOR DOCUMENT SPLITTING

This takes you to a screen similar to the one in Figure 3, which shows general ledger account ranges that are assigned to the account assignment categories VENDOR (03000) and EXPENSE (20000).

| Chart of Accts | CAUS | Chart of accounts - United States |

Acct from	Account to	Overrd.	Cat.	Description
160001	160001	☐	03000	Vendor
169900	169900	☐	03000	Vendor
202000	202000	☐	20000	Expense
211100	211200	☐	20000	Expense

≫ **Figure 3** *Assigned GL Account Ranges*

Now, classify the document types for document splitting by going to the following configuration menu path:

FINANCIAL ACCOUNTING (NEW) • GENERAL LEDGER ACCOUNTING (NEW) • BUSINESS TRANSACTIONS • DOCUMENT SPLITTING • CLASSIFY DOCUMENT TYPES FOR DOCUMENT SPLITTING

The resulting screen in Figure 4 shows the assignment of document type KR (for vendor invoices) to the above business transaction and variant.

Type	Description	Transactn.	Variant	Description	Name
KR	Vendor invoice	0300	0001	Vendor invoice	Standard

≫ **Figure 4** *Classify Document Types for Document Splitting*

Next, define a splitting method, which defines how an account assignment is inherited during document splitting. To do this, access the configuration menu path:

FINANCIAL ACCOUNTING (NEW) • GENERAL LEDGER ACCOUNTING (NEW) • BUSINESS TRANSACTIONS • DOCUMENT SPLITTING • EXTENDED DOCUMENT SPLITTING • DEFINE DOCUMENT SPLITTING METHOD

Use the standard splitting method (0000000012) shown in Figure 5.

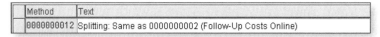

Method	Text
0000000012	Splitting: Same as 0000000002 (Follow-Up Costs Online)

« *Figure 5* *Document Splitting Method*

The next step is to define the document splitting rule, which brings all of the prior steps together. To do this, access the prior configuration menu path.

In the screen that appears, highlight the line that contains document splitting method 0000000012 and business transaction 0300 (vendor invoice), and then double-click on the folder on the left part of the screen called ITEM CATEGORIES TO BE EDITED. Highlight the item category 03000 (vendor) and double-click on the folder BASE ITEM CATEGORIES to get to the screen shown in Figure 6.

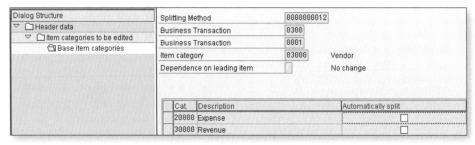

« *Figure 6* *Document Splitting Rule*

This splitting rule shows that for standard splitting method 0000000012, business transaction 0300 (vendor invoice), and business transaction variant 0001 (standard), the item category 03000 (customer) derives its account assignment from base item categories 20000 (expense) and 30000 (revenue). Simply put, it means that if you post a document that contains a vendor line and an expense (or revenue) line, the vendor line will inherit the profit center from the expense (or revenue) line.

Finally, you need to activate the document splitting in order for it to work. To do so, go to the following configuration menu path:

> FINANCIAL ACCOUNTING (NEW) • GENERAL LEDGER ACCOUNTING (NEW) • BUSINESS TRANSACTIONS • DOCUMENT SPLITTING • ACTIVATE DOCUMENT SPLITTING

This takes you to the screen shown in Figure 7.

⋀ *Figure 7 Activate Document Splitting*

You can see that document splitting has been activated for splitting method 0000000012. By selecting the INHERITANCE checkbox, you ensure that lines without an account assignment in a document will inherit the lines in the document that contain account assignments.

To deactivate document splitting for a company code, you can double-click on the folder on the left part of the screen called DEACTIVATION PER COMPANY CODE and select the INACTIVE checkbox (not shown) for the relevant company code.

Tip 46

Performing Foreign Currency Valuation

You can perform foreign currency valuation for different accounting principles by using valuation areas.

Foreign currency valuation is a process in which you compute the unrealized exchange rate gains or losses (between the local currency and the document currency) of the open items and balances of certain accounts at a key date. This functionality has always been available in SAP R/3 (using Transaction F.05). However, with the introduction of SAP General Ledger in SAP ERP, there is now the option to revalue currencies according to different accounting principles that are represented by different ledger groups.

✓ And Here's How...

The first step in configuring foreign currency valuation is to set up (or choose) a valuation method. You can do this by following the IMG menu path:

> FINANCIAL ACCOUNTING (NEW) • GENERAL LEDGER ACCOUNTING (NEW) • PERIODIC PROCESSING • VALUATE

Step 1

Choose the first step: DEFINE VALUATION METHODS. This step helps you define how the data is selected for valuation—under what conditions the valuation should be carried out (e.g., only when there are exchange rate losses or only gains, or all the time) and what document type and exchange rate type should be used for the valuation.

Step 2

Once you have defined the valuation method, continue on to the next step of the configuration menu: DEFINE VALUATION AREAS. Here you assign a valuation area, which is usually a two-character key, to the valuation method that you defined and select the local currency to be used as a basis for valuation. If you want to have different valuation areas depending on which accounting principle is used, you can define unique keys to represent each accounting principle. For example, Figure 1 shows that the legal valuation area US is assigned to the company code currency, and group valuation area IA is assigned to the group currency.

Valuation	Valuation method	Crcy type	
US	DEMO	Company code currency	
IA	DEMO	Group currency	

« Figure 1 *Define Valuation Areas*

You need to assign these accounting principles to a ledger group (refer to Part 2 for more information on ledger groups) by going to the step CHECK ASSIGNMENT OF ACCOUNTING PRINCIPLE TO LEDGER GROUP. Note that you must first have defined the accounting principles. If you still need to complete this, follow the IMG menu path to define the principles:

FINANCIAL ACCOUNTING (NEW) • FINANCIAL ACCOUNTING GLOBAL SETTINGS (NEW) • LEDGERS • PARALLEL ACCOUNTING • DEFINE ACCOUNTING PRINCIPLES

Enter the name and description of the accounting principles, such as GAAP (Generally Accepted Accounting Principles) and IAS (International Accounting Standards), as shown in Figure 2.

Accounting Principle	Name/Description of Accounting Principle
GAAP	Generaly Accepted Accounting Practices (USA)
IAS	International Accounting Standards

Figure 2 Define Accounting Principles

Step 3

In the next configuration step, ASSIGN VALUATION AREAS AND ACCOUNTING PRINCIPLES, you assign the valuation areas to the accounting principles. This enables you to update the different ledger groups, depending on which valuation area you use.

Tip 47

Specifying Third-Party Orders Account Assignment

You can specify the offsetting account to be used on third-party purchase orders by modifying the account assignment category.

You use third-party purchase orders, also known as drop-ship or drop-shipment orders, when the vendor (manufacturer or wholesaler) ships the purchased product directly to the customer. Because the purchase requisition (and hence purchase order) is automatically processed, there is no process for manually entering the general ledger account in the line item of the purchase order.

Also, as the third-party process does not involve receiving the product into inventory, the usual account assignment based on the valuation class of the material does not apply here. Instead, the account is derived from the account modification that is assigned to the account assignment category. You need to understand where this account is defined if you want to specify a particular account for drop-shipments, which is separate from your cost of sales account.

✔ And Here's How...

To understand how the third-party account assignment process works, follow the IMG menu path:

MATERIALS MANAGEMENT • PURCHASING • ACCOUNT ASSIGNMENT • MAINTAIN
ACCOUNT ASSIGNMENT CATEGORIES

Double-click on the account assignment category that is used for third-party orders, which takes you to the screen shown in Figure 1. (Note: If you do not know what account assignment category this is, go to Transaction VOV5 and look at the schedule line category that is linked to item category TAS; then go to Transaction VOV6 and double-click on this schedule line category to see which account assignment category it uses. You will see which general modification this account assignment category uses.)

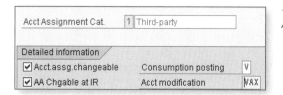

« Figure 1 Third-Party Account Assignment Category

In the standard SAP system, the general modification (this is the key that specifies which account is posted to for inventory movements) that is used is normally VBR, which means the offsetting account used is the cost of sales account. However, if you want to use a special account for third-party orders, you need to configure this different account in the account determination table for Materials Management (Transaction OBYC).

Double-click on account key GBB (offsetting entry for inventory posting) and copy one of the lines that use the general modification in the account assignment category. Then change the general modification to any three-character key that you want (for example, VAZ, as shown in Figure 2) and enter the new account to which you want the drop-shipment order posted.

Account assignment				
Valuation modif.	General modification	Valuation class	Debit	Credit
US01	VAZ	7900	893010	893011
US01	VAZ	7920	893010	893011

⏫ Figure 2 Create New Account Modification

Once you save your settings, you can go back to the account assignment category and change the general modification to the new one you created. Note that if the account assignment category is being used for other purposes, you may want to copy it to a new category and then change the general modification. If this is the case, then you also need to assign the new account assignment category to the purchasing item category for third-party orders. You can do this using configuration Transaction OMG0.

Tip **48**

Using the Debit/Credit Shift Setting

You can assign an account to two different nodes in the financial statement version depending on whether it has a positive or negative balance by using the debit/credit shift functionality.

The financial statement version is a structure that represents the way you can group the general ledger accounts (for a specific chart of accounts) in the balance sheet and profit and loss statements. One requirement that external parties sometimes request (such as tax authorities, banks, or the relevant accounting standards board of your region) is that you represent certain asset accounts in the liability section if the accounts have a negative balance. A typical example involves a bank account that is managed as an overdraft account with a debit or credit balance. This account may need to be assigned as a liability if it has a negative balance and an asset if it has a positive balance.

✅ And Here's How...

You can access the financial statement versions by going to Transaction OB58 or accessing the IMG menu path:

> FINANCIAL ACCOUNTING (NEW) • GENERAL LEDGER ACCOUNTING (NEW) • PERIODIC PROCESSING • DOCUMENTS • DEFINE FINANCIAL STATEMENT VERSIONS

Double-clicking on the relevant financial statement version takes you to the screen shown in Figure 1.

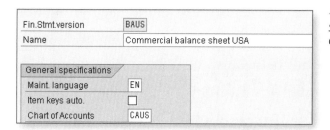

« *Figure 1* *Financial Statement Version Configuration*

Click on the Fin.statement items button, which takes you to the hierarchy structure where you can create items and assign accounts.

To set up the debit/credit shift functionality using the bank account example from the previous page, select the lowest node that the bank account is assigned to in the assets section and ensure that only the Debit checkbox is selected for the account group, as shown in Figure 2.

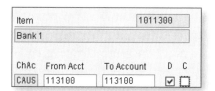

« *Figure 2* *Debit Checkbox for Bank Account*

You then assign exactly the same range of accounts to a node as we did in the liabilities section. Ensure that only the Credit checkbox is selected. Now click on the node in the Assets section, click on the Select button (), and click once on the node in the Liabilities section.

Go to the menu Edit • Debit/Credit Shift • Define, and the pop-up box shown in Figure 3 will appear, indicating which node will be the debit item and which will be the credit item.

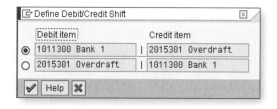

« *Figure 3* *Define Debit/Credit Shift*

If you agree with the proposed setting, click on the green check box, and you will see the contra items highlighted next to their corresponding nodes.

Setting Up Travel Management Account Determination

You can set up expense types for normal expense prepayments and advance payments by using wage type assignments to symbolic accounts.

The Travel Management submodule involves all activities that relate to planning and booking trips, as well as recording travel expenses for reimbursement. If you spend a certain amount on a trip expense, such as a hotel, the general ledger account that represents hotel expenses should eventually be updated. You may also need to record advance payments and company-paid expenses in some scenarios, which involve slightly different settings when configuring travel expenses. You should know how these expense types are configured to post to the respective general ledger accounts; incorrect assignments lead to a variety of general ledger journal corrections during the month-end process.

✓ And Here's How...

You can set up the account determination for travel expenses via the following IMG menu path:

> FINANCIAL ACCOUNTING (NEW) • TRAVEL MANAGEMENT • TRAVEL EXPENSE • MASTER DATA • TRAVEL EXPENSE TYPES • CREATE TRAVEL EXPENSE TYPES FOR INDIVIDUAL RECEIPTS

Select the relevant trip provision variant (which in essence holds the trip accounting rules for a particular country) and either copy an existing expense type, or create a new one. Depending on whether the expense is to be paid up front by the company or reimbursed to the employee, select the appropriate option, PAID BY COMPANY or

REIMBURSED TO EMPLOYEE, in the AMOUNTS ARE field. The screen in Figure 1 shows an expense type that is to be paid up front by the company.

Travel Expense Types for Receipt : US accounting (docs)		
Travel Expense Cat.	Accommodations	
Provider Category	Hotel Chain	
ExpTy.Permissibility	123456789	
Amounts are	Paid by Company	

« *Figure 1 Expense Type Configuration*

You can now assign a wage type to the expense type by going to the configuration step in the TRAVEL EXPENSE menu:

WAGE TYPES FOR INTERFACES • ASSIGN WAGE TYPES TO TRAVEL EXPENSE TYPES FOR INDIVIDUAL RECEIPTS

Assign at least one existing wage type to the travel expense type.

In the configuration step TRANSFER TO ACCOUNTING • DEFINE ASSIGNMENT OF WAGE TYPE TO SYMBOLIC ACCOUNT, you assign the wage type to a symbolic account assignment. If the symbolic account assignment has a positive sign in front of the number, then the expense amount you enter is debited to the general ledger account. If it has a negative sign, then the expense amount credits the general ledger account.

If a balance sheet account is to be updated (as in the case of prepayments and advance payments), the W/O CO RECEIVER checkbox should be selected, as shown in Figure 2.

Wage	Text	Key	Start Date	End Date	Symb.Ex	W/o
4090	Advance		01/01/1995	12/31/9999	+X7	☑
4095	CashAdv.		01/01/1995	12/31/9999	-X8	☑

« *Figure 2 Wage Type Assignment to Symbolic Account*

Next, go to the configuration step CONVERSION OF SYMBOLIC ACCOUNT TO EXPENSE ACCOUNT and double-click on the transaction key HRT (trip costs postings, expense accounts). Assign the relevant expense, prepayment, and travel advance accounts to the general modification, which has the same last two digits as the symbolic account that is assigned to the wage type. The screen in Figure 3 shows the account assignments to the general modification.

« *Figure 3 Account Assignment to General Modification*

General modification	Account
1X7	474290
1X8	474295

Part 6

Environment

Things You'll Learn in this Section

The environment section of the Financial Accounting component relates to the default settings that can be made either on a user-specific or system-wide basis, which helps minimize the time needed to process a transaction. The day-to-day processing of finance transactions normally involves performing the same tasks in a somewhat repetitive manner. You can make various settings that are either specific to a particular submodule or that span the entire financials landscape. These settings can include activities such as:

▶ Entering exchange rates

▶ Maintaining posting periods

▶ Storing user parameters

▶ Maintaining worklists

▶ Controlling document numbers

You can save a lot of processing time by defaulting known values in specific fields so that users do not have to enter them over and over again. Also, as different users have different functions that require specific default settings only for that function, you might find it more practical to customize the screen on a user-specific basis, rather than a system-wide basis.

This part of the book provides several unique tips and tricks that show you how to streamline the tasks users need to perform a transaction for both user-specific and global settings. There are settings that can be made in the accounting editing options that are specific to individual users. For example, you may want to default only the company code for which you are responsible. Or you may want to be able to park only a document that has all of the complete information in it.

Alternatively, there are also settings that can be made on a global basis, such as the document types and posting keys that are used in an Enjoy Transaction or the activating barcode entry for incoming invoices.

Establishing Default Settings for Enjoy Transactions

You can preset the document types and posting keys to be used in Enjoy Transactions.

When processing a document with an Enjoy Transaction such as FB50 for general ledger documents, FB60 for vendor invoices, or FB70 for customer invoices, you do not need to enter the posting keys or document types that need to be used, as they are already preset in the system. However, you may need to use different document types and posting keys than the ones that are predefined in order to distinguish specific transactions. For example, you may want a document type for intercompany transactions to be distinguished from those to external parties so that you can easily identify them separately in a particular account.

✅ And Here's How...

Default Document Types

To set up default document types for Enjoy Transactions, go to Transaction OBZO. When you click on the NEW ENTRIES button, you can enter the relevant COMPANY CODE, ACCOUNT TYPE, which determines the transaction that this setting is relevant for (general ledger, customer, or vendor), BUSINESS TRANSACTION (invoice or credit memo or blank for general ledger documents), and related DOCUMENT TYPE you want to be used, as shown in Figure 1.

Document Types for Enjoy Transactions			
CoCode	Acct type	Trans.	Document Type
3000	G/L accounts		SB
3000	Customers	Invoice	DA
3000	Vendors	Invoice	KA

« Figure 1 *Document Types for Enjoy Transactions*

If you do not define any document type, the system will propose the standard document types: vendor invoice (KR), vendor credit memo (KG), customer invoice (DR), customer credit memo (DG), and general ledger document (SA).

You can override these document types in the Enjoy Transaction (for example, FB50) by clicking on the EDITING OPTIONS button. Next, go to the SPECIAL OPTIONS FOR SINGLE SCREEN TRANSACTIONS section and change the DOC TYPE OPTION to DOCUMENT TYPE READY FOR INPUT, as shown in Figure 2.

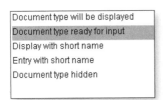

《 *Figure 2* *Setting the Document Type Option*

Click on the SAVE button (▨) and the BACK button (◀), which will take you to the original screen. The document type field is now blank and available for you to enter the relevant document type you want to use.

Default Posting Keys

To set up default posting keys for incoming invoices and credit memos, follow the IMG menu path:

> FINANCIAL ACCOUNTING • ACCOUNTS RECEIVABLE AND ACCOUNTS PAYABLE • BUSINESS TRANSACTIONS • INCOMING INVOICES/CREDIT MEMOS • INCOMING INVOICES/CREDIT MEMOS – ENJOY • DEFINE POSTING KEYS FOR INCOMING INVOICES/CREDIT MEMOS

Double-click on the description VENDOR ITEM IN INCOMING INVOICE (Transaction EGK) to view or enter the posting keys you want to be used for vendor invoices, as shown in Figure 3.

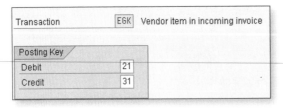

《 *Figure 3* *Define Posting Keys for Incoming Invoices*

You can go back to the initial screen by clicking on the BACK button and double-clicking on the description G/L ITEM IN INCOMING INVOICE (Transaction EGS) to view or enter the posting keys you want used for the offsetting general ledger accounts on vendor invoices.

For outgoing invoices and credit memos, follow the IMG menu path:

FINANCIAL ACCOUNTING • ACCOUNTS RECEIVABLE AND ACCOUNTS PAYABLE • BUSINESS TRANSACTIONS • OUTGOING INVOICES/CREDIT MEMOS • OUTGOING INVOICES/CREDIT MEMOS – ENJOY • DEFINE POSTING KEYS FOR OUTGOING INVOICES/CREDIT MEMOS

Double-click on the description CUSTOMER ITEM IN INCOMING INVOICE (Transaction AGD) to view or enter the posting keys that will be used for customer invoices, as shown in Figure 4.

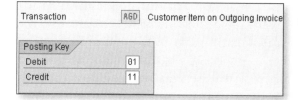

« *Figure 4 Define Posting Keys for Outgoing Invoices*

Go back to the initial screen by clicking on the BACK button, and then double-click on the description G/L ITEM IN OUTGOING INVOICE (Transaction AGS) to view or enter the posting keys that will be used for the offsetting general ledger accounts on customer invoices.

For general ledger postings, go to the following IMG menu path:

FINANCIAL ACCOUNTING • GENERAL LEDGER ACCOUNTING (NEW) • BUSINESS TRANSACTIONS • G/L ACCOUNT POSTING – ENJOY • DEFINE POSTING KEY FOR G/L ACCOUNT POSTING

You can view or enter the posting key for general ledger account postings in Transaction SAK.

Customizing Fields with Accounting Editing Options

You can use accounting editing options to customize certain fields when displaying and processing accounting documents.

When you process and display finance transactions, you usually want the transaction screens to have only the preset fields and settings that are relevant to you. One way to accomplish this is for the Basis team to make these default settings for all users. However, many of these settings are user specific, which may be cumbersome to maintain, as there could be thousands of system users that require different settings. Therefore, there is a way to customize the screens in certain transactions to suit your individual requirements.

✅ And Here's How...

To customize the user-specific settings in finance transactions, you can go to Transaction FB00 or access the menu path:

ACCOUNTING • FINANCIAL ACCOUNTING • GENERAL LEDGER • ENVIRONMENT • USER PARAMETERS

This takes you to the screen shown in Figure 1.

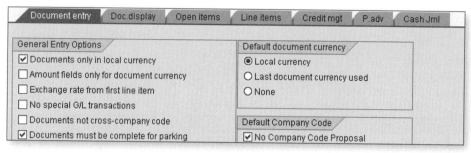

⇧ *Figure 1 Document Entry Editing Options*

There are various settings in each tab that represent different processes in the Financial Accounting component.

If you select the DOCUMENT ENTRY tab, some of the settings you can make are as follows:

▶ DOCUMENTS ONLY IN LOCAL CURRENCY
Select this checkbox to enter the values in the company code currency. This means you can only enter documents where the currency is equal to the local currency. The foreign currency amount fields are hidden.

▶ DOCUMENT MUST BE COMPLETE FOR PARKING
By selecting this checkbox, you can park a document only if all of the required fields have been validated and the balance of the document comes to zero.

▶ NO COMPANY CODE PROPOSAL
Select this checkbox to make the system issue a pop-up box (for Enjoy Transactions only) asking you to enter a company code rather than defaulting a company code.

If you select the OPEN ITEMS tab (not shown), some of the settings you can make are as follows:

▶ SELECTED ITEMS INITIALLY INACTIVE
Select this checkbox so that the items that are proposed for clearing are not automatically selected. Instead, you need to double-click on the proposed item to select it.

▶ SORTING BY AMOUNT WITHOUT +/- SIGN
Select this box to sort the open items by treating the values as absolute amounts, that is, without taking the +/- signs into account.

When you save these settings, you will see a message saying "The options were saved in the user master record." This means the settings are only applicable to the user that made them. You can view the settings that have been made by going to your user profile in Transaction SU3 and clicking on the PARAMETERS tab. This takes you to the screen shown in Figure 2.

Parameter		
Parameter ID	Parameter value	Short Description
F02	XXX XXX X X	Accounting Options / Part 2
F03	X XXX X X	Accounting User Options (Single-Screen Transactions
FOP	XXXX X XX XX	Financial Accounting Options

⮝   *Figure 2 User Parameters for Accounting Options*

The X marks in the PARAMETER VALUE column coincide with the checkboxes that are activated in the DOCUMENT ENTRY tab of Transaction FB00. Parameter IDs FOP and FO2 represent the settings that are made in the GENERAL ENTRY OPTIONS section, and Parameter ID FO3 represents the settings that are made in the SPECIAL OPTIONS FOR SINGLE SCREEN TRANSACTIONS section. This latter section is only available if you click on the EDITING OPTIONS button in an Enjoy Transaction, which takes you to the screen shown in Figure 3.

Special options for single screen transactions	
☑ Hide transaction	Doc.type option Document type hidden 🗈
☑ Propose final amount	☑ Document date equals pstg date
☑ D/C indicator as +/- sign	☑ Complex Search for Business Partner

⮝   *Figure 3 Special Options for Single Screen Transactions*

The settings you make here enable or disable certain fields in the Enjoy Transactions such as FB50, FB60, and FB70.

Displaying LIV and Finance Document Numbers

You can display both the accounting and logistics invoice verification numbers when a purchasing invoice is posted.

When you post a logistics invoice verification (LIV) document, the standard system is set up to display the logistics number in the message bar at the bottom of the screen. This can sometimes be confusing because the accounting document number that relates to that posting is different from the number that the logistics team uses, and this is the number that is usually referenced by the finance team. This issue relates to the logistics invoice verification transactions such as MIRO (Enter Incoming Invoice), MIR7 (Park Incoming Invoice), MR8M (Cancel Invoice Document), and MRRL (Evaluated Receipt Settlement).

In this tip, we will show you how to display the logistics and account numbers at the same time when a logistics invoice verification posting is made.

And Here's How...

To display both the logistics and accounting documents, you need to go to the PARAMETERS tab of your user profile. You can access these either by going to Transaction SU3 or via the top menu path SYSTEM • USER PROFILE • OWN DATA and then clicking on the PARAMETERS tab.

This takes you to the screen shown in Figure 1.

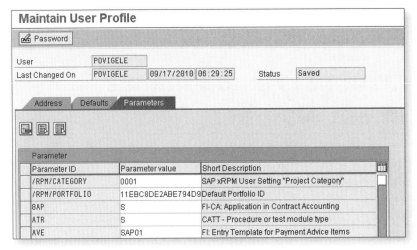

Maintain User Profile

| Password |

| User | POVIGELE |
| Last Changed On | POVIGELE | 09/17/2010 | 06:29:25 | Status | Saved |

Address   Defaults   Parameters

Parameter

Parameter ID	Parameter value	Short Description	
/RPM/CATEGORY	0001	SAP xRPM User Setting "Project Category"	
/RPM/PORTFOLIO	11EBC8DE2ABE794D9	Default Portfolio ID	
8AP	S	FI-CA: Application in Contract Accounting	
ATR	S	CATT - Procedure or test module type	
AVE	SAP01	FI: Entry Template for Payment Advice Items	

▲ *Figure 1 Maintain User Profile*

Scroll to the bottom of the screen until you get to a blank line, and enter Parameter ID "IVFIDISPLAY." Enter "X" (upper case) in the PARAMETER VALUE column, as shown in Figure 2, and click on the SAVE button.

Parameter

Parameter ID	Parameter value	Short Description
IVFIDISPLAY	X	

▲ *Figure 2 Parameter ID for Invoice FI Display*

The changes only take effect after you have logged off the SAP system and logged back on. The next time you post a logistics invoice verification document, such as with Transaction MIRO, you will see a message in the status bar, as shown in Figure 3.

Invoice document 5105608884 was posted (Accountng Documnt: 5100000002)

▲ *Figure 3 Message Including Accounting Document Number*

The system will now display both the logistics and accounting documents. You can access both documents by using Transactions MIR4 and FB03 and navigate from one to the other.

Display the logistics document using Transaction MIR4 (Display Invoice Document). Enter the logistics document number and the fiscal year and press ⌜Enter⌝ to view the document. To navigate from here to the accounting document, click on the

Follow-On Documents button, and you will see the accounting document, as shown in Figure 4.

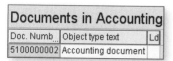

« *Figure 4 Navigate to Accounting Document from MIR4*

You can also display the accounting document by using Transaction FB03, where you enter the document number, company code, and fiscal year and press Enter to view the document. You can navigate to the logistics document by selecting the menu option:

Environment • Document Environment • Original Document

Note that the logistics and accounting document number range statuses do not change in the same increments. The logistics number range applies to all company codes, whereas the accounting number range is only for one company code.

Mass Change for Fixed Assets

To make mass changes to fixed assets, you can create substitution rules and worklists.

Changing master data on a mass basis is very common with finance data. There are several situations where the data that you originally entered in a master record is incorrect or where an organizational change has been made and requires you to update certain records. For other finance data such as general ledger, vendors, and customers, you can use Transaction MASS and choose the appropriate object type (such as G/L account, customers, or vendors). However, this transaction does not have an option for fixed assets. You therefore need to have an alternative way to perform a mass change without having to modify the master records individually.

✓ And Here's How...

You can change mass data for fixed assets through the following processes:

▶ Create a substitution rule

▶ Create a worklist

▶ Release the worklist

Create a Substitution Rule

Creating a substitution rule enables you to define certain prerequisites for the field you want to change and specify what new value you want to populate the field with (for instance if you can state—as a prerequisite—that all assets that belong to plant 1000 should have a cost center of 100ABC). The system will then take all of the assets in that plant (regardless of what cost center they currently have) and substitute their cost center field with 100ABC. You can create substitution rules by accessing Transaction OA02 or following the menu path:

> ACCOUNTING • FINANCIAL ACCOUNTING • FIXED ASSETS • ENVIRONMENT • MASS CHANGE RULE

Click on the SUBSTITUTION button, and in the following screen, click on the new SUBSTITUTION (☐ Substitution) button. On the right-hand part of the screen, give the SUBSTITUTION a name and a description, as shown in Figure 1, and click on the SAVE button.

Substitution	TESTSUB	Fixed Asset substitution
Applicatn area	AM	Asset Accounting
Callup point	4	AM - Master data mass change

« Figure 1 Fixed Asset Substitution Creation

You can create a substitution rule to change all of the assets that are assigned to cost center 1000 to cost center 2000. To do this, click on the STEP button (☐ Step), and a pop-up box entitled SUBSTITUTABLE FIELDS will appear. Scroll down the list until you get to TABLE-FIELD ANLZ-KOTSL with the description COST CENTER.

Select the checkbox to the left of this field and press ⌈Enter⌉, which makes another pop-up box appear, entitled ENTERING THE SUBSTITUTION METHOD. Select CONSTANT VALUE and press ⌈Enter⌉. You can now define the prerequisite for this substitution.

Using the above cost center numbers, the prerequisite will be cost center 1000 (because this is the field to be substituted). Double-click on the PREREQUISITE button on the left part of the screen, and you will see a listing of tables appear on the right part of the screen, as shown in Figure 2.

List of structures	
Techn. Name	Short Descript.
Structure ANLA	Asset Master Record Segment
Structure ANLB	Depreciation terms
Structure ANLV	Insurance data
Structure ANLZ	Time-Dependent Asset Allocations

« Figure 2 Available Table Structures for Substitution

Double-click on STRUCTURE ANLZ and scroll down the list until you find the cost center technical name (ANLZ-KOSTL). When you double-click on this value, it will appear in the top-right part of the screen.

Click on the equals sign, click on the CONSTANT button, and enter cost center 1000 in the pop-up box. Press ⎡Enter⎤, and the formula ANLZ-KOSTL = '1000' will appear in the top-right part of the screen. Now double-click on the SUBSTITUTIONS button (⎡ Substitutions   ⎤) on the left part of the screen, enter cost center 2000 in the CONSTANT VALUE field, and click on the SAVE button.

You now need to activate the substitution for a company code. To do this, click on the BACK button four times to go back to the original screen, and click on the NEW ENTRIES button to enter the relevant company code and substitution rule, as shown in Figure 3.

CoCd	Company Name	No.	Subst.	Substitution text
3000			TESTSUB	

⏶ *Figure 3 Activating Substitution for Company Code*

Create a Worklist

You can create the worklist (to specify for which assets the substitution rule is relevant) by going to Transaction AR01, or follow the menu path:

> ACCOUNTING • FINANCIAL ACCOUNTING • FIXED ASSETS • ENVIRONMENT • WORKLIST
> • GENERATE

Enter the company code and cost center, as shown in Figure 4, and click on the EXECUTE button (⊕).

Company code	3000	to	⇨
Asset number		to	⇨
Subnumber		to	⇨
Selections			
Asset class		to	⇨
Business area		to	⇨
Cost center	1000	to	⇨

⏶ *Figure 4 Generate Fixed Assets Worklist*

You can now see a list of all of the assets that are assigned to cost center 1000. To include these assets in a worklist, click on the CREATE WORKLIST button (⎡ WL ⎤).

This takes you to the pop-up box shown in Figure 5. Give the worklist a name in the WL NAME field, and then highlight the task CHANGE ASSET W/O DIALOG (BULK CHANGE).

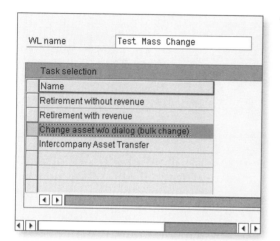

« **Figure 5** Naming the Worklist

When you press Enter, another pop-up box will appear titled MASS CHANGE: SELECT SUBSTITUTION. Enter the substitution that you created (for example, TESTSUB, created above) and press Enter again. You will receive a system message such as the one in Figure 4.6.

« **Figure 6** Message from Creating Worklist

Release the Worklist

You can release the worklist (so that the substitution rule can be carried out for the affected assets) by going to Transaction AR31 or via the following menu path:

> ACCOUNTING • FINANCIAL ACCOUNTING • FIXED ASSETS • ENVIRONMENT • WORKLIST • EDIT

This takes you to the screen shown in Figure 7.

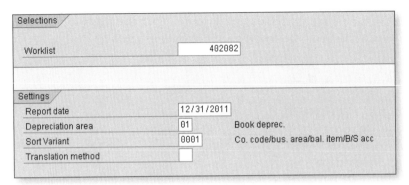

When you click on the EXECUTE button, you will see the list of assets in cost center 1000 with the WORK ITEM STATUS set to READY. Click on the RELEASE button and you will see the message shown in Figure 8.

Work queue 000000402082 released

《 *Figure 8 Message from Releasing Worklist*

Note that the next time you execute this worklist the assets will be displayed with a WORK ITEM STATUS of "Completed". This tells you the mass change has been carried out.

Modifying Message Control Settings

By modifying the settings in the application area of the message number, you can control the severity of a message the systems issues to the user.

When you process finance transactions, the system sometimes issues a message to prevent you from doing something that may cause a conflict in the system or to alert you of the consequences of carrying out the process. With the standard system, an information message is simply displayed at the bottom of the screen, a warning message prevents you from further processing until you press the [Enter] key, and an error message stops you from continuing with the transaction altogether.

Based on business requirements, you may want to lessen the severity of a message so that processing is not held up.

 ## And Here's How...

A typical example of a system message that occurs is when you are posting a document to a previous fiscal year. If you enter a posting date of a prior fiscal year, the system issues a warning message saying "Posting takes place in previous fiscal year." As this is only a warning message, you can press [Enter] to carry on with the transaction.

However, if you are processing many documents, pressing [Enter] each time you get this message may be an extra step that increases the time it takes to process the transaction. To deal with this, you first need to double-click on the message bar when it appears. This takes you to the long text of the message, as shown in Figure 1.

> **Posting takes place in previous fiscal year**
>
> Message no. F5202

« *Figure 1 Long Text on the Message Bar*

The important thing to note from the screenshot is the message number (F5202). This number is a combination of the application area (the first two digits: F5) to which the message belongs and the number (202) on which the message text and system settings are based. To change the settings of the message, you can go to Transaction OBA5 or access it via the following configuration menu path:

> CROSS APPLICATION COMPONENTS • BANK DIRECTORY • CHANGE MESSAGE CONTROL

This takes you to the pop-up box shown in Figure 2, where you enter the relevant APPLICATION AREA from the message and press Enter.

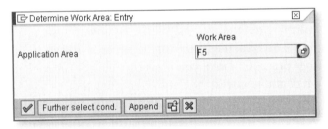

« *Figure 2 Enter Application Area*

Usually the standard messages do not show up in the configuration table, and you will have to include the message number in the message control table in order to modify it. However, note that not all of the standard messages can be entered in this table, as some of SAP's messages (particularly the ones that are critical to the system functioning properly) cannot be modified.

To modify a standard message, first click on the NEW ENTRIES button. Enter the message number in the MSGNO column, enter a hyphen sign in the ONLINE and BATCHL columns, and press Enter. The screen should now look like the one shown in Figure 3.

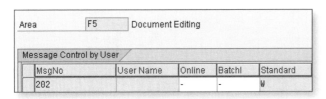

« *Figure 3* *Make Settings to Message Number*

The columns shown in Figure 3 are explained as follows.

► ONLINE
The message settings made here affect any postings that you make directly on the screen. Some of the setting options (which are the same for all of the columns) are "E" for ERRORS, "W" for WARNING, and "-" for SWITCH OFF MESSAGE.

► BATCHL
The message settings made here affect any postings made by a batch input session.

► STANDARD
This is the standard system-delivered message setting.

The settings we have made in Figure 3 will turn off the message so that it does not appear the next time you enter a posting date from a previous year.

Tip 55

Maintaining Text Determination Configuration

By using text IDs, you can store information regarding vendors and customers in their master records.

The information that is entered in the customer and vendor master is sufficient to transact reports and issue output on the system. Often, however, you may want to add extra information in the respective master records. This data usually represents general information about the business partner or specific information on the business that you do with them.

✓ And Here's How...

To add texts to the customer or vendor master, you need to set up text IDs. These text IDs can be set up at the central and accounting levels of the customer and vendor master records. We will use customers as an example here, as the settings are essentially the same for vendors.

You can define text IDs centrally for customers by going to Transaction OBT1 or following the configuration menu path:

> FINANCIAL ACCOUNTING (NEW) • ACCOUNTS RECEIVABLE AND ACCOUNTS PAYABLE • CUSTOMER ACCOUNTS • MASTER DATA • PREPARATIONS FOR CREATING CUSTOMER MASTER DATA • DEFINE TEXT IDS FOR CENTRAL TEXTS (CUSTOMERS)

Click on the CREATE button (🗋) and enter a text ID and description in the pop-up box that appears, as shown in Figure 1.

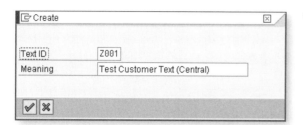

« *Figure 1 Create Central Text ID*

Press the [Enter] button, and your text ID will appears in the list on the screen. Ensure that you select the RELEVANT TEXT box, as this is the only way this text will be made available in the customer master. You can create as many text IDs as you want to represent different classifications of text that you want to maintain. For example, you can create a text ID called "Sales Notes" that could represent any relevant sales-related information for the customer.

Once you have done that, go to the customer master record in Transaction FD02. When you enter the customer number and company code, go to the GENERAL DATA section and select EXTRAS • TEXTS from the top menu. You will see the text ID you created, as shown in Figure 2.

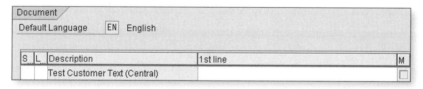

⌄ *Figure 2 Choose Text ID in Customer Master*

Double-click on the ID line, which takes you to a blank page in Microsoft Word format, where you can enter as much text as you require for this customer. When you have finished, click on the SAVE button. Anytime you want to access the text you entered, simply navigate to the text ID in the customer master and double-click on the relevant line. The text that was entered above is stored centrally in the customer master.

If you want to store text for the customer in only specific company codes, go to Transaction OBT2 or access it via the following configuration menu path:

FINANCIAL ACCOUNTING (NEW) • ACCOUNTS RECEIVABLE AND ACCOUNTS PAYABLE • CUSTOMER ACCOUNTS • MASTER DATA • PREPARATIONS FOR CREATING CUSTOMER MASTER DATA • DEFINE TEXT IDS FOR ACCOUNTING TEXTS (CUSTOMERS)

Click on the CREATE button (□) and enter a text ID and description in the pop-up box that appears, as shown in Figure 3.

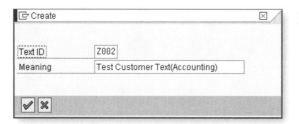

« *Figure 3 Create Accounting Text ID*

The rest of the process works exactly like the setup for central texts. However, when you go to the customer master record in Transaction FD02, you need to go to the COMPANY CODE DATA section and select EXTRAS • TEXTS from the top menu.

Activating Barcode Entry for Non-PO Invoices

You can enable the barcode dialog box in invoice processing screens by making several configuration settings.

You can scan accounts payable paper invoices so that the images can be retrieved when the invoice is displayed in the system. This way, you will always have access to the invoice image by looking on the system, and you will no longer need to wade through loads of paper to find a particular invoice (which will also reduce your company's carbon footprint).

To set this up, you need a barcode to be attached to the paper invoice prior to it being scanned. The barcode number can then be input in a dialog box when the invoice is being entered. To activate this dialog box, you need to make several configuration settings.

In this tip, we will look at the settings you need to make for non-purchase order invoices.

✓ And Here's How...

There are three steps you need to follow to activate the barcode dialog box for incoming invoices:

- ▶ Edit document type
- ▶ Maintain document types for barcode entry
- ▶ Specify control parameters for barcode entry

First, edit the document types, which groups similar stored documents together (for example, incoming invoices without verification). To do this, you can either use Transaction OAC2 or follow the configuration menu path:

> SAP NETWEAVER • APPLICATION SERVER • BASIS SERVICES • ARCHIVELINK • CUSTOM-IZING INCOMING DOCUMENTS • EDIT DOCUMENT TYPES

You can use one of the standard document types (for non-PO invoices this would be FIIINVOICE) or create a custom one. In this example we will create a custom document type.

To do this, click on the NEW ENTRIES button and enter a document type name, a description, and a document class FAX (this is the standard format for scanned incoming documents), as shown in Figure 1.

Global document types		
Document type	Description	Document Class
ZTESTBC	Incoming invoice	FAX

⩘ *Figure 1 Edit Document Type*

Next, assign the document type you created to a company code and the document type for non-PO invoices. You can do this by going to Transaction OBD5 or via the following configuration menu path:

> FINANCIAL ACCOUNTING (NEW) • FINANCIAL ACCOUNTING GLOBAL SETTINGS (NEW) • DOCUMENT • BAR CODE ENTRY • MAINTAIN DOCUMENT TYPES FOR BAR CODE ENTRY

Click on the NEW ENTRIES button, enter the relevant company code and non-PO invoice document type (KR), and assign the document type you created in the first step, as shown in Figure 2.

CoCd	Type	Doc. type
1000	KR	ZTESTBC

« *Figure 2 Assign Document Type*

The last step is to activate the barcode entry function. You can do this by going to Transaction OAC5 or via the following configuration menu path:

FINANCIAL ACCOUNTING (NEW) • FINANCIAL ACCOUNTING GLOBAL SETTINGS (NEW) • DOCUMENT • BAR CODE ENTRY • SPECIFY CONTROL PARAMETERS FOR BAR CODE ENTRY

Click on the NEW ENTRIES button, where you can enter the Object Type BKPF (for accounting documents) and the document type you created in the first step, and select the BAR CODE ACTIVE checkbox, as shown in Figure 3.

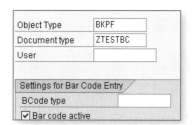

« *Figure 3 Activate Bar Code Entry*

The next time you process a non-purchasing order invoice using Transaction FB60 and you click on the SAVE button, you will see a dialog box appear (as shown in Figure 4). When you see this dialog, enter the barcode number and press ⌜Enter⌟.

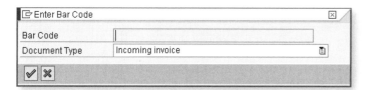

⌃ *Figure 4 Bar Code Dialog Box for non-PO Invoice*

To retrieve the archived image of the invoice, go to Transaction FB03, enter the invoice number, and press ⌜Enter⌟ to display the document. Next, click on the SERVICES FOR OBJECTS button (🖥️ 📄) and select ATTACHMENT LIST. This will show a line that represents the barcode entry. By double-clicking on this line you can see the image of the invoice.

Activating Barcode Entry for PO Invoices

You can enable the barcode dialog box in invoice processing screens by making several configuration settings.

Similar to the previous tip, you can scan accounts payable invoices so that the images can be retrieved when the document is displayed. This way you always have access to the invoice image by looking on the system, and you do not have to wade through loads of paper to find a particular invoice.

This requires a barcode to be attached to the paper invoice prior to it being scanned. The barcode number can then be input in a dialog box when the invoice is being entered.

To activate this dialog box, you need to make several configuration settings.

✓ And Here's How...

There are three steps you need to follow to activate the barcode dialog box for incoming invoices:

- ▶ Edit document type
- ▶ Maintain document types for barcode entry
- ▶ Specify control parameters for barcode entry

First, you need to edit the document types, which groups similar stored documents together. To do this, you can either use Transaction OAC2 or follow the configuration menu path:

SAP NETWEAVER • APPLICATION SERVER • BASIS SERVICES • ARCHIVELINK • CUSTOM-
IZING INCOMING DOCUMENTS • EDIT DOCUMENT TYPES

In this example we will choose the standard document type for PO invoices, which is MMILOGINV. The configuration is already set in the standard system, as shown in Figure 1, so you do not need to do anything here.

Global document types		
Document type	Description	Document Class
MMILOGINV	Incoming invoice log. invoice verific.	FAX

✖ *Figure 1 Edit Document Type*

Next, assign the document type you created to a company code and the document type for creating PO invoices (RE). You can do this by going to Transaction OBD5, clicking on the NEW ENTRIES button, and entering the relevant information, as shown in Figure 2.

CoCd	Type	Doc. type
1000	RE	MMILOGINV

« *Figure 2 Assign Document Type*

You can then check which object type the document type is assigned to. You do this by going to Transaction OAC3 or via the configuration menu path:

SAP NETWEAVER • APPLICATION SERVER • BASIS SERVICES • ARCHIVELINK • CUSTOM-
IZING INCOMING DOCUMENTS • EDIT LINKS

Double-click on the first activity line that reads LINK INFORMATION FOR OPTICAL ARCHIVE and scroll down the list until you get to document type MMILOGINV, as shown in Figure 3.

Links for Content Repositories					
ObjectType	Doc. Type	L	Cont.Rep.ID	Link	Retent.Period
BUS2081	MMILOGINV	X	D3	TOA01	0

✖ *Figure 3 Check Object Type Assignment*

The final step is to activate object type BUS2081. To do this, go to Transaction OAC5, click on the CHANGE button (✐), click on the NEW ENTRIES button, and enter the information as shown in Figure 4.

« *Figure 4 Activate Barcode Entry*

Next, process a purchasing invoice using Transaction MIRO. Click on the SAVE button. In the dialog box that appears (as shown in Figure 5), enter the barcode number and press ⌈Enter⌋ to confirm its attachment to the invoice.

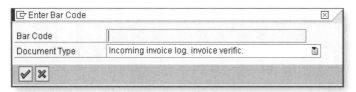

≫ *Figure 5 Barcode Dialog Box for PO Invoice*

To retrieve the archived image of the invoice, go to Transaction MIR4, enter the invoice number, and press ⌈Enter⌋ to display the document. Click on the SERVICES FOR OBJECTS button (🔧📄) and select ATTACHMENT LIST. This displays a line that represents the barcode entry. By double-clicking on this line, you can see the invoice image.

Defining Payment Groupings

You can use grouping keys to select similar items for payment.

When you make a payment to a customer or vendor, the system automatically selects all of the open items that are due and groups them together in one payment (this is the case if the SINGLE PAYMENT checkbox is not selected in the vendor or customer master record).

If there are credit memos in a vendor's account, for example, the system will not match the credit memo with the specific invoice that it relates to during the automatic payment. Instead, it will net it off with all of the other open invoices in the account. This treatment is acceptable to most businesses; however, sometimes you may need to group common open items together so that they are grouped together in a single payment.

In this tip we will show you how to group similar items so they are paid together.

✓ And Here's How...

You can set up grouping keys to group similar items for payment. Do this by going to Transaction OBAP or by following the menu path:

> FINANCIAL ACCOUNTING (NEW) • ACCOUNTS RECEIVABLE AND ACCOUNTS PAYABLE •
> BUSINESS TRANSACTIONS • INCOMING PAYMENTS • AUTOMATIC INCOMING PAYMENTS
> • DEFINE PAYMENT GROUPINGS

Click on the NEW ENTRIES button and enter a two-character grouping key and a text in the DESCRIPTION section, as shown in Figure 1.

↟ *Figure 1 Define Grouping Key*

In the APPLICATION OF RULE section, select the necessary checkboxes FOR CUSTOM-ERS and FOR VENDORS, which determines whether the fields you are defining will be pulled from the BSID table (open items for vendors), the BSIK table (open item for customers), or both.

In the FIELDS FOR GROUPING PAYMENTS section, you can define up to three fields, which can be used as grouping criteria. You then define the number of characters in the field that should be determined by using the OFFSET and LENGTH fields. In the example shown, we have entered the technical name for the ASSIGNMENT field (ZUONR) and a character length of 18, as this is the maximum number of characters this field can take.

Now you need to add the grouping key you created to the vendor or customer master. We will use the vendor master in this example, as the settings are basically the same as the customer master. Go to Transaction FK02, and on the PAYMENT TRANSACTIONS ACCOUNTING tab of the COMPANY CODE section, enter the grouping key in the appropriate field, as shown in Figure 2.

Automatic payment transactions				
Payment methods	C	Payment block		Free for payment
Alternat.payee		House Bank		
Individual pmnt	☐	Grouping key	Z1	Assignment Field
B/exch.limit		USD		
Pmt adv. by EDI	☐			

⌃ *Figure 2* Add Grouping Key to Vendor Master

The settings you make in this screen ensure that any invoices created for this vendor that have the same value in the assignment field will be grouped together for payment. If the payment grouping does not work the way you expect and you have followed the instructions specified above, refer to OSS Note 305414 for troubleshooting help.

Setting Up Payment Tolerance Groups

When you set up tolerance groups, you can define the maximum amounts that you can write off during a clearing process.

When you clear open items against each other, you can set a tolerance limit. This allows you to write off differences up to a certain amount to a separate general ledger account. There is sometimes confusion about where to define these tolerance groups, as SAP has a number of tables (for general ledger accounts, customers and vendors, and employees) where tolerance groups are defined.

In this tip, we will show you how to set up tolerance limits so that if you have a clearing difference that is less than the tolerance limit, the system will still allow the document to be posted.

✅ And Here's How...

First, it is important to distinguish the tolerance groups that are used for clearing differences from the ones that are used for logistics invoice verification. The tolerance groups for logistics invoice verification deal with the differences between the amount on the goods receipt and the amount on the invoice receipt, which are determined when you post a purchasing invoice.

You set the configuration for this tolerance group in Transaction OMR6. We will only discuss the tolerance groups related to those clearing differences in this section, which are determined when you perform a clearing transaction. There are three types of tolerance groups for this purpose:

- ▶ Tolerance groups for employees
- ▶ Tolerance groups for general ledger accounts
- ▶ Tolerance groups for customers/vendors

Employees

You can configure the tolerance groups for employees by going to Transaction OBA4 or using the following configuration menu path:

FINANCIAL ACCOUNTING (NEW) • GENERAL LEDGER ACCOUNTING (NEW) • BUSINESS TRANSACTIONS • OPEN ITEM CLEARING • CLEARING DIFFERENCES • DEFINE TOLERANCE GROUPS FOR EMPLOYEES

Probably, your company code is already configured by a consultant in this table with a blank tolerance group (as this is the only way any user can post to this company code). Therefore, you can select the company code and click on the COPY button (🖺) to copy the blank tolerance group. You can then assign your new tolerance group to the company code and local currency, as shown in Figure 1.

« *Figure 1* *Assign Tolerance Group to Company Code*

Next, adjust the tolerance limit settings as required in the PERMITTED PAYMENT DIFFERENCES section, which is shown in Figure 2.

« *Figure 2* *Set Tolerance Limits for Employees*

The REVENUE line on this screen indicates that when the credit amount is greater than the debit amount, you can still post the document if the amount is below whichever amount is less: $1000 or 10% of the debit line.

The EXPENSE line indicates that when the debit amount is greater than the credit amount, you can still post the document if the amount is below whichever amount is less: $1000 or 10% of the credit line.

The CASH DISCNT ADJ.TO column shows that if the difference between the debit and credit amount is up to $10, it will be adjusted with the cash discount posting.

Next, assign the tolerance group to the relevant users. To do this, go to Transaction OB57 or access the configuration screen via the following configuration menu path:

> FINANCIAL ACCOUNTING (NEW) • GENERAL LEDGER ACCOUNTING (NEW) • BUSINESS TRANSACTIONS • OPEN ITEM CLEARING • CLEARING DIFFERENCES • ASSIGN USERS TO TOLERANCE GROUPS

Click on the NEW ENTRIES button and assign the user(s), as shown in Figure 3.

User name	Tolerance group
POVIGELE	EE

《 Figure 3 Assign Tolerance Group to Employee

General Ledger Accounts

To set up the tolerance group for general ledger accounts, go to Transaction OBA0 or access the configuration screen via the configuration menu path:

> FINANCIAL ACCOUNTING (NEW) • GENERAL LEDGER ACCOUNTING (NEW) • BUSINESS TRANSACTIONS • OPEN ITEM CLEARING • CLEARING DIFFERENCES • DEFINE TOLERANCE GROUPS FOR G/L ACCOUNTS

Click on the NEW ENTRIES button and enter the company code and tolerance group details, as shown in Figure 4.

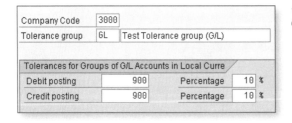

《 Figure 4 Set Tolerance Limits for General Ledger Accounts

The DEBIT POSTING field indicates that when the credit amount is greater than the debit amount (and hence there is a debit difference to be posted), you can still post the document if the amount is below whichever amount is less: $900 or 10% of the debit line.

The CREDIT POSTING line indicates that when the debit amount is greater than the credit amount (and hence there is a credit difference to be posted), you can still post the document if the amount is below whichever amount is less: $900 or 10% of the credit line.

The next step is to assign this tolerance group to one or more general ledger accounts. You can do this by going to the general ledger master data maintenance transaction (FS00), selecting the CONTROL DATA tab, and entering the tolerance group you created in the TOLERANCE GROUP field, as shown in Figure 5.

Figure 5 Assign Tolerance Group to General Ledger Account

If this field does not appear in your general ledger master record, you need to enable the field status for the account group of the general ledger in Transaction OBD4.

When you are clearing this general ledger account and there is a difference between the debit and credit open items, the system looks at the tolerance limits set up for the user that is making the posting (set up in Transaction OBA4), as well as the tolerance set up for the general ledger (set up in Transaction OBA0), and picks the more restrictive setting of the two. It posts the difference to the account that is configured in Transaction OBXZ.

Customers/Vendors

To set up the tolerance groups for customers/vendors, go to Transaction OBA3 or access the configuration screen via the configuration menu path:

FINANCIAL ACCOUNTING (NEW) • ACCOUNTS RECEIVABLE AND ACCOUNTS PAYABLE • BUSINESS TRANSACTIONS • OPEN ITEM CLEARING • CLEARING DIFFERENCES • DEFINE TOLERANCES FOR CUSTOMERS/VENDORS

Click on the NEW ENTRIES button and assign your tolerance group to the relevant company code and local currency, as shown in Figure 6.

Company Code	3000	IDES US INC	New York
Currency	USD		
Tolerance group	3000	Test Tolerance (cust/vend)	

« *Figure 6* Assign
Tolerance Group to Company Code

Enter the tolerance limit settings as required in the PERMITTED PAYMENT DIFFERENCES section, which is shown in Figure 7.

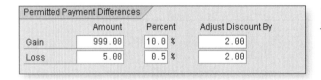

Permitted Payment Differences			
	Amount	Percent	Adjust Discount By
Gain	999.00	10.0 %	2.00
Loss	5.00	0.5 %	2.00

« *Figure 7* Set Tolerance Limits
for Customers/Vendors

For selected customers and vendors to use this tolerance group, you need to include it in their master records. To do this (for customers, for example), go to Transaction FD02 (Customer Master Maintenance) and on the PAYMENT TRANSACTIONS TAB of the COMPANY CODE DATA section, enter the tolerance group you created, as shown in Figure 8.

Payment data			
Terms of payment	0001	Tolerance group	3000

≫ *Figure 8* Assign Tolerance Group to Customer Master

When you are clearing this customer's account and there is a difference between the debit and credit open items, the system looks at the tolerance limits set up for the user that is making the posting (set up in Transaction OBA4), as well as the tolerance set up for the customer (set up in Transaction OBA3), and picks the more restrictive setting of the two. It then posts the difference to the account that is configured in Transaction OBXL.

Part 7

Integration

Things You'll Learn in this Section

Integration between the Financial Accounting component and the other components is a key part of the SAP ERP design. It ensures that data flows seamlessly between the components. Because the FI component depends on data that is fed from other areas, the configuration that relates to the integration points is normally embedded in those areas either as part of a preconfigured client or as part of the customizing activities carried out during a project. Therefore, the person that is responsible for customizing the FI component should also be aware of the settings in these other components that will affect finance data. The components or functionalities and their descriptions that are most commonly integrated with the FI component are:

▶ **Materials Management**

Posting logistics invoice verification creates entries in the vendor, inventory, tax, and expense accounts.

▶ **Sales and Distribution**

Posting a billing document can generate financial postings for the customer, revenue, accrual, surcharge, tax, and rebate accounts.

▶ **Production Planning**

The settlement of manufacturing orders posts work in process or variances to the relevant balance sheet and profit and loss (P&L) accounts.

▶ **Inventory Management**

Inventory transactions using movement types create accounting entries in the inventory-related accounts such as raw materials, finished goods, and scrap.

▶ **Cost Element Accounting**

Profit and loss accounts are usually set up as cost elements (with the exception of accounts that are posted to during production settlement). Balance sheet accounts can be set up as statistical cost elements if they are fixed asset reconciliation accounts that are used to post a budget to the asset.

In this part of the book, we will provide ideas that are mainly based on settings made in other components that influence financial postings. For example, we will show you how to optimally align logistics and finance document numbers, handle delivery costs on purchase and sales orders, and set up the accounts to be posted to during manufacturing order settlement.

Aligning FI and Logistics Document Numbers

By changing the document number range settings, you can synchronize your accounting document numbers with your logistics invoice verification document numbers.

The document numbers that are generated from logistics invoice verification transactions, which in turn post to finance, do not correspond to their ensuing accounting document numbers. This is because the configuration of the document numbers in the Logistics components is different from what is done in the FI component. This sometimes causes confusion when the finance team is working with the logistics team on a specific document, as each team references a different document number. It also means the accounting team cannot easily display a purchasing invoice using an accounting transaction without navigating through different screens to get to the appropriate document.

In this tip, we will show you how to synchronize your logistics document numbers with your accounting document numbers for purchasing invoices.

And Here's How...

First, go to the configuration logic for deriving the logistics invoice verification document number ranges by following the configuration menu path:

> MATERIALS MANAGEMENT • LOGISTICS INVOICE VERIFICATION • INCOMING INVOICE
> • NUMBER ASSIGNMENT • MAINTAIN NUMBER RANGE FOR LOGISTICS DOCUMENTS
> • TRANSACTION - ASSIGN NUMBER RANGE

This takes you to the screen shown in Figure 1.

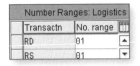

Number Ranges: Logistics		
Transactn	No. range	
RD	01	▲
RS	01	▼

« *Figure 1 Assign Number Range to Logistics Transaction*

TRANSACTION TYPE RD relates to invoices and TRANSACTION TYPE S relates to cancellations made in logistics invoice verification. They are both assigned to No. RANGE number 01. Take a note of this number and go to the following configuration menu path to see which number range interval is assigned to it:

MATERIALS MANAGEMENT • LOGISTICS INVOICE VERIFICATION • INCOMING INVOICE • NUMBER ASSIGNMENT • MAINTAIN NUMBER RANGE FOR LOGISTICS DOCUMENTS • MAINTAIN NUMBER RANGE INTERVALS FOR INVOICE DOCUMENTS

In the screen that appears, click on the INTERVALS button to take you to the screen shown in Figure 2.

Intervals					
No	Year	From number	To number	Current number	Ext
01	9999	5105600101	5105699999	5105608891	☐

≈ *Figure 2 Display Number Range Intervals*

You can now see the interval and current number that is assigned to number range number 01. This is the number range that is used when you post a purchase order invoice using Transaction MIRO. The CURRENT NUMBER status in this range is 510560891. Take note of these numbers so that you can align the accounting number accordingly.

You now need to look at which accounting number range is used for the accounting document number that is generated from Transaction MIRO. To do this, go to the following menu path:

MATERIALS MANAGEMENT • LOGISTICS INVOICE VERIFICATION • INCOMING INVOICE • NUMBER ASSIGNMENT • MAINTAIN NUMBER RANGE FOR LOGISTICS DOCUMENTS • MAINTAIN NUMBER ASSIGNMENTS FOR ACCOUNTING DOCUMENTS

In the screen that appears, click on the DOCUMENT TYPES IN INVOICE VERIFICATION button and double-click on Transaction MIRO to access the screen shown in Figure 3.

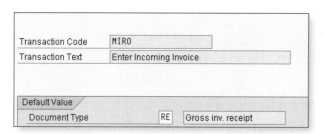

« **Figure 3** Document Type for Invoice Verification

You can see that Transaction MIRO is assigned to the accounting DOCUMENT TYPE RE. Now click on the BACK button (↩) twice to take you back to the original screen, where you click on the DOCUMENT TYPE button. Scroll down, and when you reach DOCUMENT TYPE RE (Gross Inv. Receipt), double-click on it. This takes you to the screen shown in Figure 4.

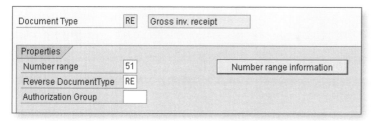

⌃ **Figure 4** Number Range Assignment to Document Type

You can see that accounting document type RE is assigned to NUMBER RANGE 51. To see which number range interval is assigned to number range 51, click the BACK button twice to take you back to the original screen, where you click on the NUMBER RANGE FOR DOCUMENT TYPE IN FI button. Enter the relevant company code, click on the INTERVALS button, and scroll down to number range 51, where you can make the entries shown in Figure 5.

No	Year	From number	To number	Current number	Ext
51	9999	5105600101	5105608891		☑

Intervals

⌃ **Figure 5** Maintain Number Range Interval

Number range 51 (for accounting documents) has been given exactly the same interval as the number range number 01 (for logistics invoice verification), and the EXT column (for external number assignment) has been flagged. This is necessary so that the system does not use an internally derived number for the accounting document, but instead accepts whatever number is generated from the logistics invoice verification. This way, both numbers (for accounting and logistics) will never be out of synch.

If the original accounting number interval had a current number, you would need to make this current number zero before the system would allow you to check the EXT column. Do this by clicking on the STATUS button in the previous screen and deleting the current number for that number range. The current number needs to be set exactly the same as the logistics invoice number status (5105608891), shown previously in Figure 2.

Aligning FI and Billing Document Numbers

By changing the document number range settings you can synchronize your accounting document numbers with your billing document numbers.

The document numbers that are generated from billing transactions, which in turn post to finance, do not correspond to their ensuing accounting document numbers. This is because the configuration of the document numbers in the Sales and Distribution components is different from that done in the FI component. This sometimes causes confusion when the finance team is liaising with the billing team about a specific document, as each team references a different document number.

Additionally, payments from a customer normally reference the billing document number on the customer's remittance advice, which may not be immediately linked with the accounting document referenced in the customer's account.

In this tip, we will show you how to synchronize your billing document numbers with your accounting document numbers. Note that if you work with a country that requires chronological FI number ranges, the cancellation of a billing document that has not been passed to FI will lead to a gap in the number ranges. In these cases, you need to release all billing documents to accounting before cancelling them.

And Here's How...

First, go to the configuration logic for deriving billing document number ranges following the configuration menu path:

SALES AND DISTRIBUTION • BILLING • BILLING DOCUMENTS • DEFINE BILLING TYPES

Scroll down to BILLING TYPE F2 (which is the standard billing type for billing documents) and double-click on that line to take you to the screen shown in Figure 1.

Billing Type	F2	Invoice (F2)		Created by	SAP

Number systems

No.range int.assgt.	19		Item no.increment	10

General control

SD document categ.	M	Invoice	☐ Posting Block
Transaction group	7	Billing documents	☑ Statistics
Billing category			
Document Type			

⌃ *Figure 1 Define Billing Type*

There are two things to note in Figure 1:

▶ The NO.RANGE INT.ASSGT is 19. This is the document number range that holds the interval from which the billing document numbers are generated.

▶ The DOCUMENT TYPE field is blank. When this is the case, the system uses the default document type RV for the FI document.

To check this number range interval, go to the following configuration menu path:

SALES AND DISTRIBUTION • BILLING • BILLING DOCUMENTS • DEFINE NUMBER RANGE FOR BILLING DOCUMENTS

In the screen that appears, click the INTERVALS button and scroll down to number range 19, which is shown in Figure 2.

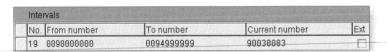

Intervals				
No.	From number	To number	Current number	Ext
19	0090000000	0094999999	90038083	☐

⌃ *Figure 2 Display Number Range Intervals*

You now need to find the number range assignment for the FI document. To do this, go to the configuration for the FI document type RV by either using Transaction OBA7 or following the configuration menu path:

FINANCIAL ACCOUNTING (NEW) • FINANCIAL ACCOUNTING GLOBAL SETTINGS •
DOCUMENT TYPE • DOCUMENT HEADER • DEFINE DOCUMENT TYPES

In the screen that appears, scroll down until you reach DOCUMENT TYPE RV and double-click on that line to get to the screen shown in Figure 3.

Document Type	RV	Billing doc.transfer	
Properties			
Number range	14		Number range information

⌃ *Figure 3 Number Range Assignment to Document Type*

You can see that NUMBER RANGE 14 is assigned to DOCUMENT TYPE RV. To edit the number range interval, click on the NUMBER RANGE INFORMATION button, then enter the relevant company code and click on the STATUS button. Scroll down to NUMBER RANGE 14, delete the value in the CURRENT NUMBER column, and save the settings.

Now click on the BACK (⟲) button, click on the INTERVALS button, enter the same interval as the one in the billing document number range shown in Figure 3, and select the EXT checkbox. Finally, click on the STATUS button again to change the current number to the one in the billing document number range (90038083 in our example).

Once you have made all of the above settings, the next time a billing document is posted, it will have the same document number as its resulting accounting document.

Accruing Freight on Sales Orders

You can automatically accrue the freight costs that you charge to a customer during billing to a balance sheet and expense account.

When you invoice a customer for a product, depending on the freight terms specified in the contract, either your business or the customer could be responsible for paying the freight costs. If the customer is responsible, then you normally charge them for the product and freight and then pay the freight vendor separately once the invoice is received.

However, depending on the timing, the freight vendor's invoice may not come in until the next period, so your balance sheet will not reflect the liability and expense in the period that the delivery cost was incurred. In this tip, we will show you how to automatically accrue these freight costs at the same time the customer is invoiced.

✅ And Here's How...

You need to follow several steps to set up a freight accrual automatically when you bill a customer. First, set up an access sequence on which the freight condition type will be based. Do this by going to Transaction V/07, clicking on the NEW ENTRIES button, and giving the access sequence a value and description, as shown in Figure 1.

Overview Access Sequence			
AS	Description	Ty.	Description
ZD00	Freight Cost		

⌃ *Figure 1* Define Access Sequence

Next, double-click on the ACCESSES folder, click on the NEW ENTRIES button, and enter the information, as shown in Figure 2.

No.	Tab	Description	Requiremnt	Exclusive
1	350	Sales org.		☑

Overview Accesses

⌃ **Figure 2** *Define Accesses*

We want the freight condition type to be based only on the sales organization in the access sequence. You create the freight condition type by going to Transaction V/06.

The easiest way to create a new condition type is to copy an existing one. Select the standard freight condition HD00, click on the COPY (▣) button, and enter the details, as shown in Figure 3.

Condit. type	ZD00	Freight Accrual		Access seq.	ZD00	Freight Cost

Records for access

Control data 1

Cond. class	A	Discount or surcharge		Plus/minus		positive a
Calculat.type	A	Percentage				
Cond.category	F	Freight				
Rounding rule		Commercial				
StrucCond.						

⌃ **Figure 3** *Create Condition Type*

You now need to make the following changes:

▸ Enter the access sequence we created (ZD00) in the ACCESS SEQ. field.

▸ Set the CALCULAT.TYPE to A (percentage).

▸ Select the ITEM CONDITION checkbox (not shown in the screenshot).

▸ Select the ACCRUALS checkbox (not shown in the screenshot).

Now you need to create and assign an account key to the relevant general ledger accounts. To do this, go to the following configuration menu path:

> SALES AND DISTRIBUTION • BASIC FUNCTIONS • ACCOUNT ASSIGNMENT/COSTING •
> REVENUE ACCOUNT DETERMINATION • DEFINE AND ASSIGN ACCOUNT KEYS

In the screen that appears, double-click on DEFINE ACCOUNT KEYS, click on the NEW ENTRIES button, and give the key a description, as shown in Figure 4.

« *Figure 4 Define Account Key*

To assign this account key to the relevant general ledger accounts, go to the following configuration menu path:

> SALES AND DISTRIBUTION • BASIC FUNCTIONS • ACCOUNT ASSIGNMENT/COSTING • REVENUE ACCOUNT DETERMINATION • ASSIGN G/L ACCOUNTS

Now double-click on ACCT KEY and enter the relevant information, as shown in Figure 5.

Acct Key						
App	CndTy.	ChAc	SOrg.	ActKy	G/L Account	Provision acc.
V	KOFI	CAUS	3000	ZF1	31204001	476901

⌃ *Figure 5 Assign Account Key to General Ledger Account*

Note that the accrual account is entered in the G/L ACCOUNT column, and the expense account is entered in the PROVISION ACC. column.

If you have Controlling Profitability Analysis (CO-PA) implemented in your organization, then you need to assign the condition type ZD00 to a value field in CO-PA. This is the only way that a billing document that contains this condition can be posted to accounting. To do this, go to Transaction KE4I and make the necessary assignment, as shown in Figure 6.

| CTyp | Name | Val. fld | Description | Transfer +/- |
| ZD00 | Freight Accrual | VV110 | Accrued freight | ☐ |

⌃ *Figure 6 Assign Condition Type to Value Field*

Next, assign the condition type (ZD00, in our example) and account key (ZF1, in our example) to the relevant pricing procedure. To do this, go to Transaction V/08, select the relevant pricing procedure, and double-click on the CONTROL folder on the left part of the screen. You now click on the NEW ENTRIES button and add condition type ZD00, as shown in Figure 7.

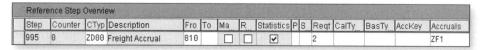

	Step	Counter	CTyp	Description	Fro	To	Ma	R	Statistics	P	S	Reqt	CalTy	BasTy	AccKey	Accruals
Reference Step Overview																
	995	0	ZD00	Freight Accrual	810		☐	☐	☑			2				ZF1

⌃ *Figure 7 Add Condition Type to Pricing Procedure*

The key columns to note are as follows:

▸ STEP: We entered 995 because it is the next available step number in the pricing procedure.

▸ CTYP: Enter the new condition type (ZD00) in this field.

▸ FRO: 810 is the step number for the freight revenue condition ZF00. This is what the freight accrual condition (ZD00) will be based on.

▸ STATISTICS: Select this box, as this condition is statistical and therefore will not affect the price to the customer.

▸ REQT: Set this field to 2 (item with pricing).

▸ ACCRUALS: Enter the account key that was created above (ZF1).

The last step is to create a condition record for your newly created condition type. To do this, go to Transaction VK11, enter condition type ZD00, click on the KEY COMBINATION button, and click on the CHECK button. Now enter the relevant sales organization and 100%, as shown in Figure 8, and save your entries.

	Sales Org.	S	Description	P	Amount	Unit
Sales org.						
	3000		USA Philadelphia		100.000	%

⌃ *Figure 8 Maintain Condition Record*

When you create a sales order and enter the price (PR00) and freight revenue (ZF00) conditions, you will see that the freight accrual condition (ZD00) is automatically derived with the same value as the freight revenue condition. This is shown in Figure 9.

Pricing Elements									
Non-Active	CnTy	Name	Amount	Crcy	per	U		Condition value	Curr.
☐	PR00	Price	1,000.00	USD		1	EA	1,000.00	USD
		Gross	1,000.00	USD		1	EA	1,000.00	USD
		Discount Amount	0.00	USD		1	EA	0.00	USD
		Rebate Basis	1,000.00	USD		1	EA	1,000.00	USD
		Net Value for Item	1,000.00	USD		1	EA	1,000.00	USD
☐	ZF00	Freight	0.00	USD		1	LB	50.00	USD
		Net value 2	1,050.00	USD		1	EA	1,050.00	USD
		Total	1,050.00	USD		1	EA	1,050.00	USD
		Total	1,050.00	USD		1	EA	1,050.00	USD
☐	ZD00	Freight Accrual	100.000	%				50.00	USD

⌃ *Figure 9 Conditions Tab of Sales Order*

The accounting document that is generated from the sales document when it is billed looks like the screen shown in Figure 10.

CoCd	Itm	PK	S	Account	Description	Amount	Curr.
3000	1	01		8010	Acme Industries	1,050.00	USD
	2	50		800000	Sales revenues - dom	1,000.00-	USD
	3	50		809000	Sales rev.- Freight	50.00-	USD
	4	50		31204001	Freight accruals	50.00-	USD
	5	40		476901	Freight Expense	50.00	USD

⌃ *Figure 10 Billing Accounting Document with Freight Accrual*

The freight accrual and expense amounts are posted to their relevant accounts to reflect the amount of freight that was billed to the customer. When the freight vendor's invoice arrives, it can be matched with the freight accrual account (31204001 in this example), and any difference can be written off to the expense account (476901 in this example).

Handling Planned Delivery Costs

You can accrue planned delivery costs on a purchase order by utilizing the accrual key in the calculation schema.

When a product is purchased from a vendor, there are normally delivery costs associated with it. Sometimes the delivery costs are known at the time of purchase (planned delivery costs) and sometimes they are not (unplanned delivery costs). When the costs are known, it is prudent to accrue them when the product has been received into the system. This way, if the freight vendor's invoice does not arrive in the same period that the goods were received, there will be an estimate in the system that reflects the cost of delivering the product.

In this tip we will show you how to set up planned delivery costs so that you can record a delivery accrual when the goods receipt transaction is made.

✅ And Here's How...

To set up planned delivery costs, you need to assign an accrual key to the relevant condition in the calculation schema. First, you need to establish which calculation schema is relevant for your purchase order document type. You can do this by going to the following configuration menu path:

> MATERIALS MANAGEMENT • PURCHASING • CONDITIONS • DEFINE PRICE DETERMI-
> NATION PROCESS • DEFINE SCHEMA DETERMINATION

Double-click on DETERMINE CALCULATION SCHEMA FOR STANDARD PURCHASE ORDERS to access the screen shown in Figure 1.

Schema GrpPOrg	Sch.Grp Vndr	Proc.	Description
		RM0000	Purchasing Document (Big)

⌃ *Figure 1 Display Calculation Schema*

Because the first two columns are blank, the standard calculation schema used will be RM0000 for all purchase organizations and all types of vendors. You can go to the following configuration menu path to see where the accrual key is assigned in this calculation schema:

> MATERIALS MANAGEMENT • PURCHASING • CONDITIONS • DEFINE PRICE DETERMI-
> NATION PROCESS • DEFINE CALCULATION SCHEMA

Now you highlight calculation schema RM0000 and double-click on CONTROL DATA on the left part of the screen. To look at the standard freight condition types, scroll down to condition type FRA1, as shown in Figure 2.

Step	Counter	CTyp	Description	Fro	To	Ma	R	Stat	P	SuTot	Reqt	C	Ba	AccKey	Accruals
31	1	FRA1	Freight %	20		☑	☐	☑						FRE	FR1
31	2	FRB1	Freight (Value)	20		☑	☐	☑						FRE	FR1
31	3	FRC1	Freight/Quantity	20		☑	☐	☑						FRE	FR1

⌃ *Figure 2 Freight Conditions in Calculation Schema*

The three freight condition types shown on the screen differ by whether they are percentage based, fixed values, or based on quantity. However, they all contain the same accrual account key (FR1) and hence will generate the same type of account postings. Note that only the accrual key is relevant for these conditions. The account key that is shown (FRE) is only relevant if you have activated purchase account management.

Now that you know which accrual key is linked to the freight condition in the calculation schema, you can see which account has been assigned to this key. To do this, go to Transaction OBYC and double-click on transaction key FR1. This takes you to the screen shown in Figure 3.

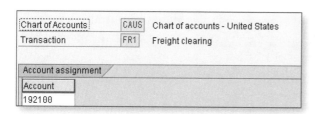

« *Figure 3* Account Assignment
for Freight Transaction Key

You can enter the freight condition either in the purchasing info record (in which case it will default to the purchase order for that vendor and product) or directly into the purchase order. Figure 4 shows an example of a freight amount of $10 entered in freight condition FRB1 on the line item CONDITIONS tab of a purchase order.

Material Data	Quantities/Weights	Delivery Schedule	Delivery	Invoice	Conditions

Qty		1 EA	Net		250.00 USD

Pricing Elements

N	CnTy	Name	Amount	Crcy	per	U.	Condition value	Curr.
☐	PBXX	Gross Price	250.00	USD	1	EA	250.00	USD
		Net incl. disc.	250.00	USD	1	EA	250.00	USD
		Net incl. tax	250.00	USD	1	EA	250.00	USD
☐	FRB1	Freight (Value)	10.00	USD			10.00	USD

⌃ *Figure 4 Conditions Tab of a Purchase Order*

When the goods receipt is posted for this purchase order, the freight accrual of $10 is posted to the account (192100) configured in accrual key FR1. This is shown in Figure 5.

CoCd	Itm	PK	S	Account	Description	Amount	Curr.
3000	1	81		400000	Raw Materials - Othe	60.00	USD
	2	96		191100	Goods Rcvd/Invoice R	50.00-	USD
	3	50		192100	Freight Clearing Acc	10.00-	USD

⌃ *Figure 5 Goods Receipt Accounting Document Including Freight Accrual*

When the freight invoice is received, go to Transaction MIRO. Ensure that you select the option PLANNED DELIVERY COST (if the freight vendor sends a separate invoice) or GOODS/SERVICE ITEMS + PLANNED DELIVERY COSTS (if the product vendor includes the freight in their invoice). You can find this setting on the right part of the MIRO screen, titled LAYOUT.

In the example shown in Figure 6, we assume that the freight vendor has sent a separate invoice. We therefore select the PLANNED DELIVERY COST option, which brings up only the freight amount of $10.

⌃ *Figure 6 Planned Delivery Cost Line Item*

If the vendor's freight amount is different from the one entered in the purchase order, then the difference will be posted to the account that is linked to the product you purchased.

Handling Unplanned Delivery Costs

You can add unplanned delivery costs to a purchase order invoice and configure how they are posted.

When a product is purchased from a vendor, there are normally delivery costs associated with shipping the product. Sometimes the delivery costs are known at the time of purchase (planned delivery costs), but sometimes they are not (unplanned delivery costs). When they are not known, you have the option of entering these costs when the invoice is received. However, you need to decide where these costs should be posted and how (or if) they are split among several purchase order lines.

✓ And Here's How...

To configure how unplanned delivery costs are posted, go to the following configuration menu path:

> MATERIALS MANAGEMENT • LOGISTICS INVOICE VERIFICATION • INCOMING INVOICE • CONFIGURE HOW UNPLANNED DELIVERY COSTS ARE POSTED

This takes you to the screen shown in Figure 1.

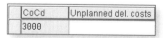

« *Figure 1 Configure Unplanned Delivery Cost*

If you want to see the options in the UNPLANNED DEL. COSTS column, click on the field and press F4. The options that appear here are:

▶ **Blank**: This means the unplanned costs are distributed among the invoice items in the ratio of the monetary value of the invoice items

▶ **2**: This posts the unplanned delivery cost to a separate general ledger account. You specify this general ledger account by going to Transaction OBYC and then double-clicking on transaction key UPF to see the screen shown in Figure 2.

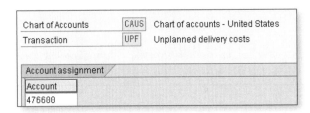

« *Figure 2* General Ledger Account for Unplanned Delivery Costs

▶ **1**: This means the unplanned costs are distributed among the invoice items, but when determining the ratio of each item it takes into account the monetary value of the item and the planned delivery costs.

Note that if you want to use your own logic to distribute the unplanned delivery costs, you need to utilize the Business Add-In (BAdI) MRMBADI_UDC_DISTRIBUTE.

To enter unplanned delivery costs, go to Transaction MIRO, enter the basic data and purchase order information as usual, and go to the DETAILS tab. As shown in Figure 3, you enter the amount of the unplanned delivery cost in the UNPL. DEL. CSTS field.

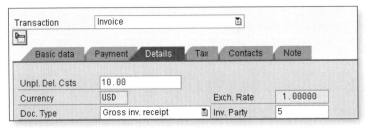

⌃ *Figure 3* Entering Unplanned Delivery Costs in Transaction MIRO

If the unplanned delivery cost comes from a different vendor from the one that provides the product (for example, the freight vendor), then you need to do a couple of things. First, at the top of the MIRO screen, change the TRANSACTION to "Subsequent debit". Then go to the DETAILS tab and enter the total amount of the invoice in the UNPL. DEL. CSTS. field, and enter the freight vendor in the INV. PARTY field, as shown in Figure 4.

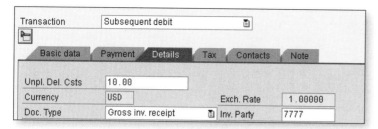

⌃ **Figure 4** *Entering Unplanned Delivery Costs with Different Vendor*

In this example, the invoicing party has been changed from 5 (which is the product vendor) to 7777 (which is the freight vendor).

Creating Statistical Cost Elements

To control expenditure on fixed assets, you can use internal order budgeting, which requires the asset balance sheet accounts to be created as statistical cost elements.

When you procure fixed assets externally, you may need to track the expenditure against a budget to prevent overspending and to signal whether you are getting close to the spending limit.

Budgets can be created by using internal orders or work breakdown structure (WBS) elements, which are tied to the fixed assets. However, because internal orders and WBS elements are controlling objects that require cost elements, you need to set up your fixed asset balance sheet accounts as cost elements for this linkage to be made. Note that the general SAP rule is that only profit and loss accounts are to be created as cost elements. Therefore, in this special situation you need to set up the balance sheet accounts as statistical cost elements so you can create budgets for your fixed assets. (Note that amounts posted to statistical cost elements cannot be allocated in CO like the other cost element categories).

✓ And Here's How...

You need to follow a few steps to make this process work. We will use internal orders in our example, as they have the same type of settings as WBS elements.

The first step is to link all of the internal orders to the assets as statistical. You can do this in Transaction KO02 (or Transaction KO01 when creating the order) by going to the CONTROL DATA tab and selecting the STATISTICAL ORDER checkbox, as shown in Figure 1.

« Figure 1 *Flagging Internal Order as Statistical*

You now need to assign this internal order to the asset master (Transaction AS02) on the ORIGIN tab and in the INVESTMENT ORDER field.

To create the fixed asset balance sheet accounts in the next step (which are configured in Transaction AO90), go to the following configuration menu path:

FINANCIAL ACCOUNTING (NEW) • ASSET ACCOUNTING • TRANSACTIONS • BUDGET MONITORING WITH STATISTICAL ORDERS/WBS ELEMENTS • CREATE STATISTICAL COST ELEMENTS

In the screen that appears, double-click on CREATE COST ELEMENTS FOR PROJECT/ORDER ACCOUNT ASSIGNMENT. This takes you to the screen shown in Figure 2.

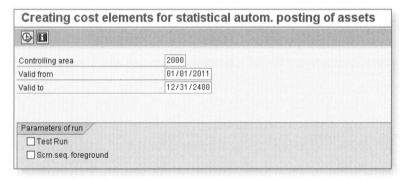

⌃ Figure 2 *Create Cost Elements for Internal Orders*

Now enter the relevant details as necessary, and click on the EXECUTE button (), which gives you a list of the asset balance sheet accounts that have been created as cost elements. This list is illustrated in Figure 3.

Cost elem.	Type	Description
160000	90	Land + Land Improvements
160010	90	Buildings
160020	90	Machinery + Equipment
160030	90	Leasehold Improvements
160040	90	Motor Vehicles
160060	90	Furnitureftware
160070	90	Computer Hardware
160080	90	Computer Software
160090	90	Assets under Construction
160200	90	Low Value Assets

« *Figure 3* *List of Statistical Cost Elements*

The system has assigned a cost element category (or type) of 90 to these balance sheet accounts. This is the only cost element category that can be used for balance sheet accounts. All of the others are for profit and loss accounts or secondary cost elements.

Now that you have made the necessary settings, you can enter a budget on the internal order ($28,000 in this example) by going to Transaction KO22 and clicking on the ORIGINAL BUDGET button, which takes you to the screen shown in Figure 4.

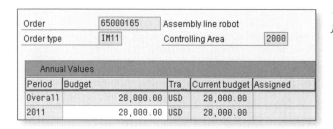

« *Figure 4* *Entering a Budget for an Internal Order*

The amount ($28,000 in this example) that is entered on the screen controls the amount that can be spent on any assets that are assigned to this order. Depending on the availability control settings in your system, you will see a warning or error message if a purchase order or invoice is within a certain tolerance limit of this budget. You can find the availability control in the configuration menu path:

> CONTROLLING • INTERNAL ORDERS • BUDGETING AND AVAILABILITY CONTROL

You can also report on the actual costs made on the asset against the budget by going to Transaction S_ALR_87013019, entering the order, and executing the report to see the screen shown in Figure 5.

| Order group   65000165   Assembly line robot | | | | |
Fiscal Year *				
Orders	Budget	Actual	Commitment	Assigned
65000165 Assembly line robot	28,000.00	25,680.00		25,680.00
* Total	28,000.00	25,680.00		25,680.00

≫ *Figure 5* *Budget/Actual Report for Internal Order*

The BUDGET column represents the budget that was entered in Transaction KO22, while the ACTUAL column represents the purchases that have been made on the asset, which is assigned to the internal order. Double-clicking on the ACTUAL line makes a pop-up box appear. In this box, double-click on ORDERS: ACTUAL LINE ITEMS, which shows you the statistical cost elements that make up the actual costs.

Tip 66

Configuring Production Settlement Accounts

You should know how to make the settings for accounts that are posted to upon settling manufacturing orders.

Settlements are made at period end so that the costs that exist in a manufacturing order can be transferred to a receiving object such as a cost center, material, or profitability segment. Usually, the settlement process also creates a posting to a general ledger account that is associated with the receiving object. You need to know where these general ledger accounts are configured and how to exclude them from being created as cost elements so that they do not create a double posting in the Controlling component.

And Here's How...

Two profit and loss accounts are associated with manufacturing order settlements. They are configured in different parts of the system. We will walk you through each one.

Production Variance Account

The production variance account is posted to when a manufacturing order has either been fully delivered or marked as technically complete at period end. To configure this account, go to Transaction OBYC, double-click on transaction key PRD (COST (PRICE) DIFFERENCES), and enter the accounts for each valuation modifier and class, as shown in Figure 1.

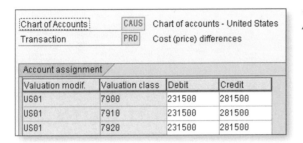

 Figure 1 *Production Variance Account Configuration*

The DEBIT column represents the account posted to for an unfavorable variance, while the CREDIT column represents the account for a favorable variance. If the variance accounts were set up as cost elements, then they would also require a cost object. This would therefore create a double posting in the Controlling component, and therefore cause an imbalance with the FI component.

Work in Process Account

The system posts to the work-in-process (WIP) account when a manufacturing order has not been fully delivered or marked as technically complete at period end. This account represents the balance of the debits and credits on the manufacturing account. To configure this account, go to the following configuration menu path:

> CONTROLLING • PRODUCT COST CONTROLLING • COST OBJECT CONTROLLING • PRODUCT COST BY ORDER • PERIOD END CLOSING • WORK IN PROCESS • DEFINE POSTING RULES FOR SETTLING WORK IN PROCESS

This takes you to the screen shown in Figure 2, where you assign a profit and loss and balance sheet account to the relevant controlling area, company code, and results analysis category.

CO Ar	Company Code	RA Version	RA category	B	Cost Ele	Record	P&L Acct	BalSheetAcct
1000	1000	0	WIPR			0	893000	793000

⌃ **Figure 2** *Work-in-Process Account Configuration*

When there is a debit balance on the manufacturing order, a settlement process debits the balance sheet account and credits the P&L account. The P&L account should not be set up as a cost element, as it is the offsetting amount of the balance on the manufacturing order. If the P&L account was a cost element, then it would appear on the manufacturing order and bring its balance to zero. This should not be the case until the order has been completed and variances have been calculated.

Tip 67

Posting to a General Ledger Account and a Material in MIRO

Activating the G/L ACCOUNT and MATERIAL tabs allows you to make direct postings during logistics invoice verification.

When an invoice is received and needs to be matched to a purchase order, there are sometimes extra items that need to be booked to an account different from the one that was on the purchase order. The screen in the logistics invoice verification transaction normally contains only one tab, called PO REFERENCE, where you can enter the purchase order number and inherit its line items. However, you cannot enter any other accounts that are not part of the purchase order.

To avoid this problem, in this tip we will show you how to activate two extra tabs for either posting to a general ledger account or directly to a material.

And Here's How...

To enable direct posting during logistics invoice verification, go to the following configuration menu path:

> MATERIALS MANAGEMENT • LOGISTICS INVOICE VERIFICATION • INCOMING INVOICE • ACTIVATE DIRECT POSTING TO G/L ACCOUNTS AND MATERIAL ACCOUNTS

This takes you to the screen shown in Figure 1, where you can see the relevant checkboxes.

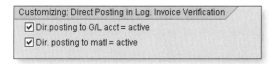

《 Figure 1 Activate Direct Posting to General Ledger and Material Accounts

If you select the DIR.POSTING TO G/L ACCT = ACTIVE checkbox, the tab for posting directly to a general ledger account will be enabled and appear on the Logistics Invoice Verification screen. If you select the DIR.POSTING TO MATL = ACTIVE checkbox, the tab for posting directly to a material will be enabled.

The next time you post go to the logistics invoice verification transaction (MIRO), the lower part of the screen will look like the screen shown in Figure 2.

《 Figure 2 Activated Tabs in MIRO Transaction

If you want to post directly to a general ledger account, click on the G/L ACCOUNT tab and enter the relevant line item details as you would in a normal accounting posting (such as in Transactions FB50, FB60, or FB70). Figure 3 shows an example of this entry.

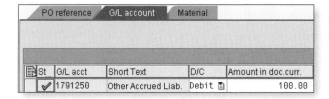

《 Figure 3 Posting to a General Ledger Account in MIRO

If you want to post directly to a material, click on the MATERIAL tab and enter the material number, plant, amount, and quantity, as shown in Figure 4.

	Material	Plnt	Valuation ty	D/C		Amount	Quantity	Base Unit
	US-BULK2	3100		Debit	🗐	100.00	10	LB

⌃ Figure 4 Posting to a Material Account in MIRO

Note that when you make a posting directly to a material, the system will debit or credit the material's valuation price with the amount and quantity that you post.

If the material is valued at the moving average price (that is, with price control V), this amount will be posted to the general ledger account, which is linked to the valuation class of the material (this general ledger account is stored in Transaction OBYC under transaction key BSX). If the quantity you enter is more than the quantity of inventory on hand, then the difference will be posted to the price variance account (this general ledger account is stored in Transaction OBYC under transaction key BSX). If the material is valued at the standard price (that is, with price control S), this amount will be posted to the price variance account.

Referencing Sales Document Numbers

You can populate the assignment and reference fields of an accounting document with the sales document number.

When you post a billing document, an accounting document is created. You can set up this document so that the REFERENCE and ASSIGNMENT NUMBER fields can be populated with values from the sales document, such as the sale order, delivery, or billing document number. You can use the REFERENCE and ASSIGNMENT NUMBER fields to sort, analyze, and clear the lines in the accounting document. This helps you easily see the sales order number that is linked to a general ledger account posting without needing to drill down into the document to access this information.

And Here's How...

To pull the relevant sales document numbers into the accounting reference fields, you need to make the relevant settings in the copy control functionality in the Sales and Distribution component. There are three levels of copy control for billing documents, depending on the source document type. They are as follows:

▶ **Order to bill copying control**
This controls the data of the document flow from sales orders to billing documents.

▶ **Delivery to bill copying control**
This controls the data of the document flow from delivery documents to billing documents.

▶ **Bill to bill copying control**

This controls the data of the document flow from billing documents to billing documents.

You can access the copy control settings for sales orders to billing documents by going to Transaction VTFA or via the following configuration menu path:

> Sales and Distribution • Billing • Billing Documents • Maintain Copying Control for Billing Documents

In the screen that appears, double-click on the line Copying Control: Sales Document to Billing Document to get to the screen Display View: Header Overview. Scroll down until you reach the relevant billing document type in the Tgt column that is assigned to the relevant sales document in the Source column, as shown in Figure 1.

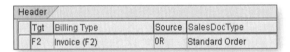

« *Figure 1 Copy Control from Sales Order to Billing Type*

In this example, we have selected standard billing document type F2, which is derived from sales document type OR. This means that this is not a delivery-related billing document, but instead is created directly from the sales order. You can click on the Display -> Change button (🖉) and double-click on the Billing Type line to see the screen shown in Figure 2.

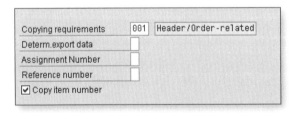

« *Figure 2 Assignment and Reference Number Fields in the Copy Control Screen*

To find out which sales-related number can be populated in the assignment or reference number field of the accounting document, click on the corresponding field (for example, the Assignment Number field) and press the ⌨F4 key to display the options shown in Figure 3.

Assignment Number	Short Descript.
A	Purchase order number
B	Sales order number
C	Delivery number
D	External delivery number
E	Actual billing document number
F	External delivery no. if avaialable, otherwise delivery no.

« *Figure 3* Assignment Number Copying Options

Selecting any of the options shown populates the assignment field of the accounting document with that value. The same logic applies to the REFERENCE NUMBER field, except that the assignment number is transferred to the line item of the accounting document, while the reference number is transferred to the header item of the accounting document.

If you want to define your own rules for the fields that are transferred to accounting, you can use the following user exits:

▶ EXIT_SAPLV60B_001: Changes the header data in structure ACCHD

▶ EXIT_SAPLV60B_002: Changes the line item data in structure ACCIT

Assigning Accounts for Non-Stock PO Items

You can use material groups to assign accounts automatically to non-stock items on a purchase order.

One of the biggest headaches for the finance team when using SAP software has to do with correcting the accounts that are posted to when a purchase order is goods receipted or invoiced. Usually, the accounts on a purchase order are automatically derived from the material (through the valuation class) or the fixed asset (through the asset class).

However, for purchased items such as services, supplies, and other expenses, the purchasing team needs to enter the account manually on the ACCOUNT ASSIGNMENT tab of the purchase order line item. This leads to cases where incorrect accounts entered by the purchasing team are not identified until the goods receipt or invoice receipt has been posted, and several correcting journals will need to be made.

One way to avoid manual entry of accounts in non-stock purchase orders is to use material groups.

And Here's How...

You can create material groups by going to Transaction OMSF or by following the configuration menu path:

> LOGISTICS • GENERAL • PRODUCT LIFECYCLE MANAGEMENT (PLM) • MATERIAL MASTER • SETTINGS FOR KEY FIELDS • DEFINE MATERIAL GROUPS

Click on the New Entries button, and enter a material group number and description, as shown in Figure 1.

Matl Group	Material Group Desc.
Z1000	Bulbs
Z2000	Pallets
Z3000	Bottles

« *Figure 1 Create Material Groups*

The next step is to create a valuation class, which enables you to assign the material group to a general ledger account. You can create valuation classes by going to Transaction OMSK or via the configuration menu path:

> Materials Management • Valuation and Account Assignment • Account Determination • Account Determination without Wizard • Define Valuation Classes

Click on the Valuation Class button and the New Entries button, and enter a four-digit valuation class, an account category reference (which you can choose from the drop-down list in the ARef column), and a suitable description. Figure 2 shows an example of this setting.

Valuation Classes		
ValCl	ARef	Description
Z001	0002	Purchasing Supplies

« *Figure 2 Define Valuation Class*

You now need to assign the material group to this valuation class. You can do this by going to Transaction OMQW or via the following configuration menu path:

> Materials Management • Purchasing • Material Master • Entry Aids for Items without a Material Master

This takes you to the screen shown in Figure 3, where you can assign the material group to the valuation class we just created.

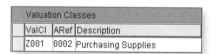

Mat. Grp	Mat. Grp Descr.	ValCl
Z1000	Bulbs	Z001
Z2000	Pallets	Z001
Z3000	Bottles	Z001

« *Figure 3 Assign Valuation Class to Material Groups*

The final step is to assign the valuation class to the relevant general ledger account that you want the purchased items to be posted to. You first need to find out which account modification key the account assignment category uses. This account assignment category is entered on the purchase order for non-stock purchases. For example, account assignment category K (cost center) is normally used for purchases that relate to expenses or supplies. If you go to Transaction OME9 and double-click on account assignment category K, you will see (as shown in Figure 4) that it is assigned to account modification VBR.

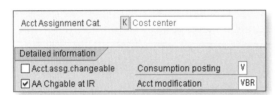

« *Figure 4 Account Modification Assignment*

You can now assign the valuation class to a general ledger account using account modification key VBR. To do this, go to Transaction OBYC, double-click on transaction key GBB, and click on the NEW ENTRIES button (□). Enter "VBR" in the GENERAL MODIFICATION field, and assign the valuation class to a general ledger account, as shown in Figure 5.

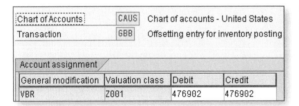

« *Figure 5 Automatic Account Determination Screen*

If you also want the cost center to be defaulted from the material group, you can assign the automatically configured general ledger account above to a cost center by using Transaction OKB9.

Setting Up a Goods-in-Transit Account

If you want to identify the shipments that have been made but have not yet reached the customer, you can configure a separate account for goods in transit.

When a post goods issue (PGI) transaction is done, it usually reflects the issuing of your inventory that is to be delivered to the customer. The standard accounting postings for this transaction are for the inventory account to be credited and the cost of sales account to be debited.

The billing document is then sent out almost immediately to the customer. However, in some scenarios (particularly with long haul shipments), it may take days, or even months for the product to reach the customer. In these cases, we recommend setting up a goods-in-transit account for shipments that have not yet been billed. This will rectify the issue of having to reverse the postings to the cost of sales account (every month end) for items that have been shipped but have not yet been billed to the customer.

✓ And Here's How...

To set up the goods-in-transit account, use the standard SAP transaction for creating new accounts (FS00). Note that the following indicators should be set as part of creating the account:

- ▶ BALANCE SHEET ACCOUNT
- ▶ OPEN ITEM MANAGEMENT
- ▶ LINE ITEM DISPLAY

You need to configure this account to be the offsetting account to inventory when the PGI function is carried out. Note that the usual offsetting account to inventory is the cost of sales account. However, we do not want the cost of sales account to be posted to until the customer is billed.

To make this setting, go to Transaction OBYC, double-click on transaction key GBB, and scroll down until you see GENERAL MODIFICATION VAX (shown in Figure 1).

Account assignment					
Valuation modif.	General modification	Valuation class	Debit	Credit	
US01	VAX	7900	893010	893010	
US01	VAX	7920	893010	893010	

《 Figure 1 Display Cost of Sales Account Assignment

You can now overwrite the entries in the DEBIT and CREDIT columns (in this example, we use overwrite account 893000) with the goods-in-transit account that you created.

The next step is to create an account key for your cost of sales condition type. The cost of sales condition type is normally not set up to post to accounting. However, by assigning it to an account key, which in turn is assigned to a general ledger account, you enable the cost of sales condition to be posted to this account. Tip 62 covered setting up and assigning account keys, so please refer to that tip for more information on these procedures.

The important thing to note is that when assigning the general ledger accounts to the account key in Transaction VKOA, the first general ledger account column should be the goods-in-transit account, and the second should be the cost of sales account. Figure 2 shows this configuration.

Acct Key							
	App	CndTy.	ChAc	SOrg.	ActKy	G/L Account	Provision acc.
	V	KOFI	CAUS	3000	VPR	194002	893010

《 Figure 2 Assign General Ledger Accounts to Account Key

You now need to assign the account key (VPR in our example) to the cost of sales condition type VPRS. Before you do this, you need to flag the condition type as an accrual condition. To do this, go to Transaction V/06 and double-click on the VPRS condition. Go to the CONTROL DATA 2 section and select the ACCRUALS checkbox, as shown in Figure 3.

⤊ **Figure 3** *Accruals Checkbox in Cost Condition Type*

Now you can go to the relevant pricing procedure (Transaction V/08) and enter account key VPR in the ACCRUALS column, as shown in Figure 4.

	Reference Step Overview														
Step	Counter	CTyp	Description	Fro	To	Ma	R	Stat	P	SuTot	Reqt	CalTy	Ba	A	Accruals
940	0	VPRS	Cost			☐	☐	☑	B	4					VPR

⤊ **Figure 4** *Assign Accrual Key to Condition Type*

Based on the above setup, the following accounting entries will be posted:

- When the post goods issue function is carried out:
  - Debit: Goods-in-transit account
  - Credit: Inventory account
- When the customer is billed:
  - Debit: Customer
  - Credit: Revenue
  - Debit: Cost of sales account
  - Credit: Goods-in-transit account

As you can see, the goods-in-transit account is a clearing account that only has a balance when an order has been shipped and not billed. The function of this account is very similar to that of the goods receipt/invoice receipt (GR/IR) account, except that it relates to sales transactions, while the GR/IR account relates to purchasing transactions.

Just like the GR/IR account, the goods-in-transit account can become unmanageable if not maintained regularly. One way to do this is by populating the assignment field of this account with the sales order and line item number. To do this, go to the configuration for creating a sort key (Transaction OB16), click on the NEW ENTRIES button, and enter the details as shown in Figure 5.

⋀ *Figure 5 Define Sales Order Sort Key*

You now need to assign the sort key on the CONTROL DATA tab in the general ledger master record of the goods-in-transit account (Transaction FS00). This setting only populates the assignment field of the goods-in-transit account during the PGI posting, not the billing document posting. To populate the assignment field with the sales order and item during billing, you need to utilize user exit EXIT_SAPLV60B_002.

For regular maintenance, you can use the Automatic Clearing transaction (F.13) to regularly clear out the items that have the same sales order and line item number and whose total balance comes to zero.

Part 8

Reporting

Things You'll Learn in this Section

A key element of the Financial Accounting component is the process of extracting data from the system and into a report in both a timely manner and a user-friendly format. Due to the real-time nature of the SAP system, most reports are immediately updated once a transaction has been carried out.

SAP provides many reports in the Financial Accounting area, which you can mostly use without the need to customize them. It is important that you are aware of the available reports so you do not end up creating a custom report when a standard report exists that does the same thing. In many cases, you only need to tweak the standard reports a little for them to work the way you want.

Some reports are more flexible than others. For example, classical reports (the older, non-interactive SAP R/3 reports), are not flexible, as they present all of the information on a single screen, and you usually cannot navigate beyond what is displayed. With drill-down reports, however, you can display the reports for single or multiple characteristics, so you can change the report totals depending on the combination of characteristics you choose. With line item display reports, you can see the details of every document that was posted for the selected object and can usually drill into the line to display the source document. With ABAP List Viewer reports, you can add, hide, subtotal, filter, and sort columns, among other things.

You can download most reports to Microsoft Excel to further manipulate the data. If the standard SAP reports do not meet certain reporting requirements for your business, you can create custom reports that do not require programming, such as SAP Query and Report Painter reports.

In this part of the book, we will show you how to make the most of the standard reports to get extra information from them or improve their layout. For example, we will show you how to add extra fields to reports that do not exist in the layout variant. We will also show you how to improve the formats of the user-unfriendly aging reports. Additionally, we will introduce a few ideas on creating and using drill-down reports (which are not normally used in Financial Accounting) for more flexible reporting.

Adding Fields to Fixed Asset Reports

You can add extra fields to the standard fixed asset reports by using sort versions.

The Fixed Assets component contains a variety of standard reports. These standard reports come with preset columns that are based on certain fields in the asset master record, such as company code and asset class. You may need to add other fields that are not available in these reports but that are utilized by your business. You can do this by creating custom sort versions, which specify the fields that are sorted and subtotaled in the asset reports.

✔ And Here's How...

To create sort versions in the Fixed Assets component, go to Transaction OAVI or follow the configuration menu path:

> FINANCIAL ACCOUNTING • ASSET ACCOUNTING • INFORMATION SYSTEM • DEFINE SORT VERSIONS FOR ASSET REPORTS

In the screen that appears, click on the NEW ENTRIES button and enter a sort version key and description, as shown in Figure 1. Note that your custom sort version should begin with either X, Y, or Z.

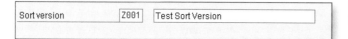

« Figure 1 *Define Sort Version*

In the SORT LEVELS section, click on the first field in the TABLE column and press the F4 key to see the table options from which you can choose. Choose the relevant fields you want to display from the table in the FIELD NAME column. In our example (shown in Figure 2) we have chosen the fields EVALUATION GROUP 1 (ORD41) and ORIGINAL ASSET (AIBN1) from the asset reporting table ANLAV.

| Sort version | Z001 | Test Sort Version | | | | | | |

Sort levels								
Table	Field name	Description	Offs	Lng	Total		Statistics	Page
ANLAV	ORD41	Eval.group 1			☐		☐	○
ANLAV	AIBN1	Original asset			☐		☐	○

⌃ **Figure 2** Define Sort Levels

If you want to control the values and lengths of the fields, you can use the OFFS and LNG columns. In the OFFS column (which stands for offset), you can specify from what position (from the first character of the field value) you want to display the field value. In the LNG (which stands for length) column, you can specify how many characters from the offset position you want to display for the field.

To subtotal the fields in the report, select the TOTAL checkbox. You can also add a page break to the printed version of the report any time there is a new value in the field list. To do this, select the radio button for the relevant field under the PAGE column. The page break can only be made for one field in the sort version.

Once you have created the sort version, you need to insert it in one of the fixed asset reports. To demonstrate this process, we will go to the asset balances report, which you can access with Transaction AR01. Enter the custom sort version in the SORT VARIANT field of the SETTINGS section, as shown in Figure 3.

Settings		
Report date	12/31/2011	
Depreciation area	01	Book deprec.
Sort Variant	Z001	Test Sort Version

« **Figure 3** Insert Sort Variant in Asset Report

When you execute the report, the list shown will not initially show the columns you added to the sort version. You need to manually add them by clicking on the CHANGE LAYOUT button (▦) and clicking on the SHOW SELECTED FIELDS button (◀) to pull in the hidden fields.

Adding Fields to Customer/ Vendor Address Lists

You can add more fields to the customer and vendor address list reports by making changes to the underlying query.

The customer and vendor address list reports (Transactions S_ALR_87012180 and S_ALR_87012087, respectively) provide the business partners' address information in an easy-to-read tabular format. You will find, however, that the number of fields in this report is quite limited and not suitable for sufficient master data analysis and reporting. When you click on the CHANGE LAYOUT button (▦), you will not find any extra fields to add to the report. In this tip, we will show you how to insert additional fields into this report without having to do any ABAP programming or other complex modification.

 And Here's How...

Using the customer address list report as an example, you can find the underlying source of the report by going to Transaction SE93, entering "S_ALR_87012180" in the TRANSACTION CODE field, and clicking on the DISPLAY button. At the bottom of the screen, in the DEFAULT VALUES section, are the screen fields and values as shown in Figure 1.

Default Values	
Name of screen field	Value
D_SREPOVARI-REPORTTYPE	AQ
D_SREPOVARI-REPORT	/SAPQUERY/FDG
D_SREPOVARI-EXTDREPORT	F1

« *Figure 1* Default Values for Transaction Code

The value of screen field D_SREPOVARI-REPORTTYPE indicates that it is an SAP Query (AQ); the value of screen field D_SREPOVARI-REPORT specifies which SAP Query is being used in the report (/SAPQUERY/FDG); the value of screen field D_SREPOVARI-EXTDREPORT specifies to which user group the query belongs (F1).

With this information, you can go to the SAP Query Transaction to modify this query accordingly by accessing Transaction SQ01 and going to the menu ENVIRONMENT • QUERY AREAS. Select the GLOBAL AREA (CROSS CLIENT) option, as shown in Figure 2.

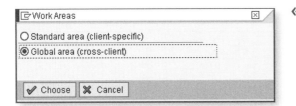

« Figure 2 Set Query Area

Click on the OTHER USER GROUP button (⊞) and double-click on the user group /SAPQUERY/FD. This displays query F1, as shown in Figure 3.

Queries of user group /SAPQUERY/FD: FI Accounts Receivable Evaluat	
Name	Title
F1	List of customer addresses

« Figure 3 Query of User Group

To modify this query, click on the CHANGE button, and in the screen that appears click on the BASIC LIST button to see the screen titled QUERY F1 LAYOUT DESIGN. In our example we will add the INDUSTRY key to this query. You can do this on the left part of the design screen (which you may have to expand to see the fields and their descriptions). Open the folder called KNA1, and open the GENERAL DATA IN CUSTOMER MASTER section to select the INDUSTRY KEY field (KNA1-BRSCH) in the LIST FIELDS column. This is shown in Figure 4.

Data fields	List fields	Selection Fields	Technical Name
▽ ☐ KNA1	6	21	
▽ ▦ General Data in Customer Master	6	3	KNA1
Authorization group	☐	☐	KNA1-BEGRU
Industry key	☑	☐	KNA1-BRSCH

⌃ Figure 4 Enable Industry Key Field in Table KNA1

Once you have saved your query, the next time you go to the List of Customer Addresses report, you will see that the field you added (in our case, the INDUSTRY KEY field) is included in the report (shown as INDUSTRY SECTOR), as shown in Figure 5.

List of customer addresses					
Customer	Name 1	Street name	Postal code	Location	Industry sector
1010	Becker Berlin (Versand)	Beatestrasse 4	13505	Berlin	MBAU
1176	Waffeln & Oblaten GmbH	Am Reisenbrook 17	22359	Hamburg	FOOD
1172	CBD Computer Based Design	Schillerstrasse 85	22767	Hamburg	HITE
1171	Hitech AG	Goethestrasse 137		Hamburg	HITE

⌃ *Figure 5 List of Customer Addresses Report*

Note that to mitigate any issues that may occur with upgrades or enhancements, you should not directly modify the SAP standard query. Instead, you should create a custom transaction code based on Transaction S_ALR_87012180, create a custom query based on /SAPQUERY/FDG, make the changes to this query, and assign it to your custom transaction code.

Improving the Format of Aging Reports

You can display the standard aging reports in a much more user-friendly format by changing your system settings.

SAP ERP has always come with predelivered customer and vendor aging reports (the reports that classify the open items of vendors and customers according to the number of days they are overdue in different intervals such as 1-30, 31-60, 61-90, etc.).

There is, however, a lot of confusion about which reports should be used for aging purposes (none of the reports has the word *aging* in them) and how to improve the format of these reports for better usability. In this little-known tip, we will focus on how to improve the aging reports for customers.

✓ And Here's How...

To access the customer aging report, go to Transaction S_ALR_87012176 or use the following menu path:

> ACCOUNTING • FINANCIAL ACCOUNTING • ACCOUNTS RECEIVABLE • INFORMATION SYSTEM • REPORTS FOR ACCOUNTS RECEIVABLE ACCOUNTING • CUSTOMER ITEMS • CUSTOMER EVALUATION WITH OI SORTED LIST

Enter the intervals you want to display in the DUE DATE SORTED LIST section of the report, as shown in Figure 1.

« *Figure 1* Open Item Due
Date Intervals

When you execute this report, you will see the relevant information of your customers' items in the intervals (for example 30, 60, 90, 120) that you specify in the Due Sorted List part of the selection screen.

The problem with this report is that the format is not very user-friendly and cannot easily be downloaded. The system displays an address block for each customer, as shown in Figure 2.

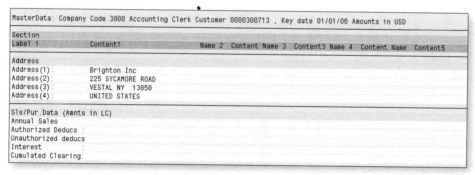

⌃ *Figure 2* Standard Customer Evaluation Report Layout

To make this report more user-friendly and convert it into an ABAP List Viewer (ALV) format, click on the Start button on your computer desktop. Go to the Control Panel, and double-click on the SAP Configuration icon (⬛). Now go to the Design Selection tab, select the Use Classic Design radio button, and select the Use Accessibility Mode checkbox, as shown in Figure 3.

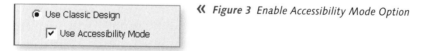

« *Figure 3* Enable Accessibility Mode Option

Now you can save the settings shown in the screenshot in your computer. Note that depending on the version of Windows or Macintosh that you are using, the options you can select may be slightly different. In this example, we are using Windows XP.

You need to log off and then back on to the SAP system for the changes to take effect. When you do, you can go back to Transaction S_ALR_87012176 and execute the report to see the layout shown in Figure 4.

CoCd	Customer	Address (2)	Address (4)	Cty	Crcy	Total balance in LC	To 0	1 - 30	From 31 To 60	From 61 To 90	From 91 To 120	From 121
			Open Item Sorting on Key Date 01/01/2006 in Local Currency									
3000	255	Emma Bull	DENVER CO 80216	US	USD	2,207.00	2,207.00					
3000	257	John Evans	NEDERLAND CO 804	US	USD	2,299.00	2,299.00					
3000	258	Roger Zahn	ALBUQUERQUE NM 8	US	USD	1,912.00	1,912.00					
3000	260	Chelsa Quinn Yates	ALBUQUERQUE NM 8	US	USD	2,124.00	2,124.00					
3000	262	Robert Jensen	CANON CITY CO 812	US	USD	3,720.00	3,720.00					
3000	266	Charles Scott	TORREY UT 84775	US	USD	2,995.00	2,995.00					
3000	272	Joe Masson	SALINA UT 84654	US	USD	748.00	748.00					
3000	281	Tracy Collins	VAIL CO 81658	US	USD	1,567.50	1,567.50					

⌃ *Figure 4 Customer Report with New Layout*

This list shows a much better display than the one using the standard settings. You can perform the usual ALV functions (which you can't do in the standard report) such as sort, filter subtotal, and download to Excel. You can double-click on each line to see the details that make up the amount, which is not possible with the standard report.

For certain versions of Windows, you may find that the next time you log off and on to your computer, your SAP screen has the older "classic" format. If this is the case, deselect the settings that you made in this tip, and only reset them when you need to display the aging reports.

Financial Statements by Functional Areas

By activating the cost of sales accounting scenario, you can view your income statement by functional areas and by general ledger accounts.

Most financial statement reports use a period-based accounting approach. This means you use revenue and cost elements to report transactions that have occurred in that period. This method of reporting is useful for analyzing the activities that took place in a period.

However, it does not show the functional areas where the activities occurred. For example, an account called "Salaries" tells you how much was paid in salaries for the month, but it does not tell you if the salaries are related to production, sales, research, and so on. One workaround to this issue is to create different salary accounts to represent different functions, but this could lead to an unmanageable number of accounts and may create issues with account determination.

The SAP solution to this issue is to activate cost of sales accounting and use functional areas in parallel with general ledger accounts in your financial statements. In this tip, we will show you the only way you can use functional areas for reporting.

✓ And Here's How...

You must follow a few steps to use functional areas. First, before making any postings (in the period in which you want to start using cost of sales accounting) you need to assign the cost of sales scenario to your leading ledger. To do this, go to the following configuration menu path:

> FINANCIAL ACCOUNTING (NEW) • FINANCIAL ACCOUNTING GLOBAL SETTINGS (NEW)
> • LEDGERS • LEDGER • ASSIGN SCENARIOS AND CUSTOMER FIELDS TO LEDGERS

In the screen that appears, highlight the leading ledger and double-click on the SCE-
NARIOS folder on the left part of the screen. Click on the NEW ENTRIES button and
enter scenario "FIN_UKV," as shown in Figure 1.

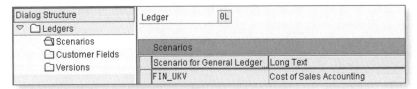

⌃ *Figure 1 Assign Scenario to Ledger*

Next, activate cost of sales accounting for the relevant company code. You can do
this by going to the following configuration menu path:

> FINANCIAL ACCOUNTING (NEW) • FINANCIAL ACCOUNTING GLOBAL SETTINGS (NEW)
> • LEDGERS • LEDGER • ACTIVATE COST OF SALES ACCOUNTING

Change the COS STATUS to "Active" for the relevant company code, as shown in
Figure 2.

≪ *Figure 2 Activate Cost of Sales Accounting*

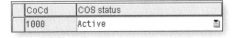

Now define the functional areas you want to use for reporting. To do this, go to the
following configuration menu path:

> FINANCIAL ACCOUNTING (NEW) • FINANCIAL ACCOUNTING GLOBAL SETTINGS (NEW)
> • LEDGERS • FIELDS • STANDARD FIELDS • FUNCTIONAL AREAS FOR COST OF SALES
> ACCOUNTING • DEFINE FUNCTIONAL AREA

Click on the NEW ENTRIES button and enter a functional area key (up to 16 characters) and description, as shown in Figure 3.

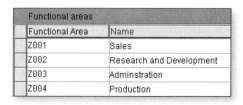

« Figure 3 Define Functional Areas

Now that you have defined the functional areas, you need to derive them when postings are made. The most common way of deriving functional areas is through a cost center category, because cost centers are normally logically grouped into areas where costs occur, and cost center categories reflect groups of similar cost centers. To assign functional areas from cost center categories, go to the following configuration menu path:

CONTROLLING • COST CENTER ACCOUNTING • MASTER DATA • COST CENTERS • DEFINE COST CENTER CATEGORIES

This takes you to the screen shown in Figure 4, where you can assign the functional areas you defined to the relevant cost center categories.

	CCtC	Name	ActPri	ActSec	ActRev	PlnPri	PlnSec	PlnRev	Cmmt	Func
	E	Development	☐	☐	☑	☐	☐	☑	☑	Z002
	F	Production	☐	☐	☑	☐	☐	☑	☑	Z004

☆ Figure 4 Assign Functional Areas to Cost Center Categories

Other ways of deriving functional areas are as follows (in order of which takes priority when there is more than one assignment):

▶ **Manual entry**

By enabling the FUNCTIONAL AREA field in the field status group (Transaction OBC4) that is assigned to a general ledger account, you can enter a functional area directly when making postings to this account.

▶ **Substitution**

You can create a substitution rule (Transaction OBBH) to derive a functional area using certain prerequisites.

▶ **General ledger account**

You can directly assign a functional area in the general ledger account master record (Transaction FS00).

▶ **Cost objects**

You can enter a functional area in the master data of most cost objects such as cost centers, internal orders, WBS elements, and cost collectors. You may need to make some or all of the above assignments depending on the data flows and processing requirements of your business. Once you make them, you can then use the standard general ledger reports to view the financial statements by functional area. You can access one of these reports through Transaction S_PL0_86000028 or by following the menu path:

> FINANCIAL ACCOUNTING • GENERAL LEDGER • INFORMATION SYSTEM • GENERAL LEDGER REPORTS (NEW) • FINANCIAL STATEMENT/CASH FLOW • GENERAL • ACTUAL/ ACTUAL COMPARISONS • FINANCIAL STATEMENT: ACTUAL /ACTUAL COMPARISON

The resulting report is the same as the one you would use for the general ledger financial statements. As the cost of sales ledger is now part of the general ledger, the functional area is simply a different reporting dimension that you can now use in your financial statements. This eliminates any reconciliation issues that could occur between the general ledger financial statements and other cost of sales reports, such as those based on costing-based profitability analysis.

Report on Vendors and Customers with No Activity

The vendor and customer business reports allow you to display the business partners that have not had any activity within a specified period.

There are some vendors and customers that you have done business with in the past but are not likely to do so in the future. In these situations, it is prudent to block these accounts so they are not accidentally posted to. You may also want to have a list of vendors and customers you have not transacted with for a while in order to consider them for archiving.

By using the vendor or customer business report, you can display the business partners that do not have any purchases or sales within a certain period.

✓ And Here's How...

To access the vendor business report, use Transaction S_ALR_87010043 or follow the menu path:

> ACCOUNTING • FINANCIAL ACCOUNTING • ACCOUNTS PAYABLE • INFORMATION SYSTEM • REPORTS FOR ACCOUNTS PAYABLE ACCOUNTING • VENDOR BALANCES • VENDOR BUSINESS

This takes you to the screen shown in Figure 1. Enter the company code(s) to be used in the analysis.

⌃ **Figure 1** *Vendor Business Report Initial Screen*

In the FURTHER SELECTIONS section (shown in Figure 2), you can enter the periods of the fiscal year that you want to evaluate. The system's default setting chooses all of the periods specified in your fiscal year variant (including any special periods), but you can change this to the period range that is relevant for your analysis. Double-click on the PURCHASES FOR ACCT field. In the pop-up box that appears, double-click on the SINGLE VALUE icon (⊟). Leave this field blank, as shown in Figure 2.

⌃ **Figure 2** *Enter Further Selections*

Now enter the fiscal year in the OUTPUT CONTROL section. This report is normally used to show the value of the transactions made with vendors during the specified period and year. However, if you want to display the vendors that have had no purchases during this period, select the ACCOUNTS WITH NO PURCHASES checkbox, as shown in Figure 3.

Output control
☐ Corporate group version
☐ Display Totals Only
Fiscal year 2011
☐ Display one-time account data
☑ Accounts with no purchases

« **Figure 3** *Specify Accounts with No Purchases*

When you click on the EXECUTE button, you will see the list of vendors with no activity in the period. This is symbolized by the fact that the PURCHASING column has a zero amount for all of the vendors in the list (see Figure 4).

Vendor	Name 1	Cty	PostalCode	City	Street	Rg	Crcy	Purchasing
8	Jose Fernandez	MX	11111	Mexico City	Via Rioja 1		USD	0.00
TM_US_L_01	Carrier Land US 01	US	10019	New York	200 Madison Avenue	NY	USD	0.00
TM_US_L_02	Carrier Land US 02	US	02215	Boston	152 Bay State Road	MA	USD	0.00
TM_US_L_03	Carrier Land US 03	US	02118	Boston	735 Harrison Avenue	MA	USD	0.00
TM_US_R_01	Carrier Rail US	US	20002	Washington	60 Massachusetts Ave NE		USD	0.00
TP_AIR_MX	Airport Mexico DF	MX		Mexico City		DF	USD	0.00
TP_AIR_WI	Airport Wichita	US		WICHITA		KS	USD	0.00
TP_PORT_MX	Port Veracruz-Mexico	MX		Veracruz		VER	USD	0.00
TP_TRN_MX	Train Station Mexico	MX		Mexico City		DF	USD	0.00
TP_TRN_WI	Train Station Wichita	US		Wichita		KS	USD	0.00
TS_CHICAGO	Train Station Chicago	US	60606	Chicago	255 South Canal Street	IL	USD	0.00
TS_LA	Train Station Los Angeles	US	90012	Los Angeles	800 N. Alameda Street	CA	USD	0.00
							USD	0.00

⌃ **Figure 4** *Display Vendors with No Activity*

There is a similar report for customers, which you can access with Transaction S_ALR_87012186 or by going to the following menu path:

ACCOUNTING • FINANCIAL ACCOUNTING • ACCOUNTS RECEIVABLE • INFORMATION SYSTEM • REPORTS FOR ACCOUNTS RECEIVABLE ACCOUNTING • CUSTOMER BALANCES • CUSTOMER SALES

You can enter exactly the same settings we just discussed for vendors if you want to display the customers that do not have any transactions within the specified period.

Display Offsetting Account for FI Documents

By using a specific SAP Query report, you can view both the originating and offsetting accounts in an accounting document.

When you view an accounting document line item report, it is normally difficult to pull in the offsetting account for a line that has been posted. For example, if a vendor invoice posting is made that credits the vendor and debits an expense account, you cannot see the vendor account when you look at the expense line item report. Instead, you have to drill into the document and display the document overview before seeing the offsetting account. To view the offsetting account directly in a report, you can use a predelivered SAP Query report.

✅ And Here's How...

To access the query report that displays the offset account, go to Transaction SQ01, select ENVIRONMENT • QUERY AREAS, select GLOBAL AREA (CROSS-CLIENT), and click on the CHOOSE button, as shown in Figure 1.

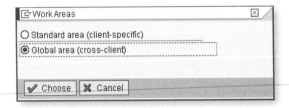

« Figure 1 *Specify Global Query Area*

Click on the OTHER USER GROUP button (🔄) and select the user group /SAPQUERY/ AU: AUDIT INFORMATION SYSTEM (AIS). There are three finance reports you can use (for customers, vendors, and general ledger accounts) that display the offsetting account (shown in Figure 2).

Queries of user group /SAPQUERY/AU: Audit Information System (AIS)		
Name	Title	InfoSet
OD	*** A I S *** Customer Account Analysis	/SAPQUERY/FIDD
OK	*** A I S *** Vendor Account Analysis	/SAPQUERY/FIKD
OS	*** A I S *** G/L Account Analysis	/SAPQUERY/FISD

☆ *Figure 2 Queries from AIS User Group*

In our example we will use the general ledger analysis report. Click on query OS and click on the EXECUTE button (⊕), which takes you to the screen shown in Figure 3. Here, you can enter the relevant information in the CHART OF ACCOUNTS, G/L ACCOUNT, and COMPANY CODE fields.

G/L account selection				
Chart of accounts	CAUS	to		⇨
G/L account	415000	to		⇨
Company code	3000	to		⇨

☆ *Figure 3 General Ledger Account Analysis Initial Screen*

In the PROGRAM SELECTIONS section, enter offsetting account type "K" (for vendors), as shown in Figure 4. The offsetting account type indicates which type of account (vendors, customers, fixed assets, general ledger, or material) you want to display as the offsetting account. If you leave this field blank, it will display all of the offsetting accounts that were posted to for documents that contain the general ledger account you specified.

OA posting key		to		⇨
OA account type	K	to		⇨
OA account no.		to		⇨

☆ *Figure 4 Specify Offsetting Account Type*

In the REF. CURRENCY (OPTIONAL) field (not shown in the screenshot) enter the currency of the company code in which you are reporting. Otherwise, the report will be shown in German Deutsche Mark (DEM). To view the screen in a better layout, click on the SAP LIST VIEWER output format. When you click on the EXECUTE button, you will see the report, as shown in Figure 5.

Offsetting Account - Overview							
Acct type	G/L Acct	Customer	Vendor	Account name	D/C	∑ Amount in LC USD	∑ Absolute Amount USD
K	160000		424	Sedona Suppliers	H	200.00-	200.00
			3755	Bellevue Plant 4000		328.50-	328.50
			3801	Acme Industrial Supplies	S	61,767,922.54	61,767,922.54
				Acme Industrial Supplies	H	17,748,128.12-	17,748,128.12
			4910	D. & P. Forbes		2,190.00-	2,190.00
	161000		3940	Mitch & Collins		40,000.00-	40,000.00
K						▪ 43,977,075.92 ▪	79,558,769.16
						▪▪ 43,977,075.92 ▪▪	79,558,769.16

⌃ *Figure 5 Display Line Items with Offsetting Accounts*

The report shows the vendors that were posted to for documents that contained the specified general ledger account (415000). You can also see which reconciliation general ledger account (in the G/L AcctT column) is linked to the offsetting vendor account.

Creating Report Painter Reports for SAP General Ledger

You can create report painter reports that are based on the totals tables of SAP General Ledger.

Before SAP General Ledger was introduced, there were several different ledgers you could use to create Report Painter reports for general ledger accounts, profit centers, and functional areas. However, with the introduction of SAP General Ledger, which now encompasses different ledgers such as the cost of sales and profit center ledger, you may be confused about which library to use in order to create Report Painter reports for SAP General Ledger. Additionally, if you used Report Painter reports with the classic General Ledger, you would need to know how to convert these reports to read SAP General Ledger tables. In this tip, we will show you how to do just that.

✅ And Here's How...

To create a Report Painter report, go to Transaction GRR1 and click on the LIBRARY field. Press the F4 button and select LIB (library) 0FL, as shown in Figure 1.

Lib	Description	Table	Author	Date
0F1	Income Statement (Cost of Sales)	GLFUNCT	SAP	11/06/1995
0FA	GASB 34/35: Commitmt/Actl w. Budget	FMRFA	SAP	07/03/2001
0FL	New General Ledger	FAGLFLEXT	SAP	02/25/2004
0M1	Library for Table Group GLFUNC	GLFUNCT	SAP	04/04/1996

≪ *Figure 1 Choose SAP General Ledger Library*

Notice from Figure 7.1 that library 0FL is based on SAP General Ledger totals table FAGLFLEXT. This means all of the characteristics that are available in the new general ledger table will be available in the report.

Select library F1, enter a report name and description, and click on the CREATE button. Select EDIT • GEN. DATA SELECTION to see how the characteristics transfer in the screen shown in Figure 2.

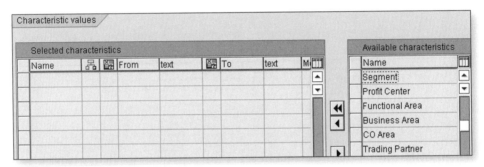

⌃   *Figure 2 Available Characteristics for SAP General Ledger Report*

The available characteristics on the right part of the screen, such as profit center and functional area, are now part of SAP General Ledger even though they previously existed in their own ledgers.

The other steps for creating the Report Painter report can be followed as normal. The main difference with creating Report Painter reports in SAP General Ledger involves the library that you choose and the characteristics that are available to report on.

Convert Existing Reports

If you already had reports that you created that are based on the classic ledgers (for example, using library 8A2 for profit centers), you can convert these reports to the SAP General Ledger library 0FL. To do this, go to Transaction FAGL_RMIGR and enter the source library, report, and the destination library, as shown in Figure 3.

⌃   *Figure 3 Transfer Classic Profit Center Accounting Report to SAP General Ledger*

When you click on the EXECUTE button, you will see a screen that looks like the one shown in Figure 4. Select the line that is displayed and click EXECUTE again.

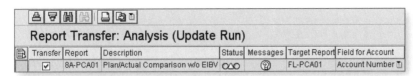

❯ **Figure 4** *Analysis of Transferred Report*

Now you see a log telling you whether the transfer was successful or not. If it was successful, you need to add the report (FL-PCA01 in our example) to a report group. To do this, go to Transaction GR51, give the report group a name, and enter "0FL" into the general ledger library in the LIBRARY field, as shown in Figure 5.

≪ **Figure 5** *Create Report Group*

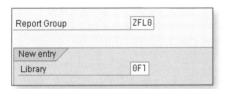

Press ⌈Enter⌉, give the report a description, and click on the REPORTS button. Enter the new report "FL-PCA01" and click on the SAVE button. You can now execute your report from Transaction GR55 or by assigning it to a custom transaction code.

Tip 78

Creating Drill-Down Reports

You can easily create drill-down reports in SAP General Ledger by copying standard reports.

With the introduction of new characteristics into SAP General Ledger such as profit center, functional area, and segment, some new standard reports are now three-dimensional in nature. This means you can report on multiple dimensions, such as all the accounts posted to for a particular profit center in a segment. This is much more flexible than the previous general ledger reports, where the general ledger account was the only object on which you could report.

However, these new drill-down reports may not have all of the elements that satisfy your reporting needs. Let's look at how we can create customized versions of these drill-down reports.

✓ And Here's How...

To create a drill-down report for SAP General Ledger, you first need to create a form to define the rows, columns, and formulas to be used in the report. To create a form, go to the following configuration menu path:

> FINANCIAL ACCOUNTING (NEW) • GENERAL LEDGER ACCOUNTING (NEW) • INFORMATION SYSTEM • DRILLDOWN REPORTS (G/L ACCOUNTS) • FORM • SPECIFY FORM

In the screen that appears, double-click on CREATE FORM and ensure that the FORM TYPE is set to REPORTING FOR TABLE FAGLFLEXT. Enter a form name and description, as shown in Figure 1.

Form type	Reporting for Table FAGLFLEXT	
Form	ZGLFORM	Test G/L Form

Create

⌃ *Figure 1 Create Form Initial Screen*

The easiest and most expedient way to create a form is to copy a standard one and amend it. You can enter the relevant form that you want to copy in the COPY FROM section, as shown in Figure 2.

Copy from	
Form	0SAPBSPL-01

« *Figure 2 Copy From*

Now click on the CREATE button, and either change the rows and columns as required or leave them as they are and click on the SAVE button. Assign the form you created to a report by following the configuration menu path:

> FINANCIAL ACCOUNTING (NEW) • GENERAL LEDGER ACCOUNTING (NEW) • INFORMATION SYSTEM • DRILLDOWN REPORTS (G/L ACCOUNTS) • REPORT • DEFINE REPORT

In the screen that appears, double-click on CREATE REPORT and ensure that the REPORT TYPE is set to REPORTING FOR TABLE FAGLFLEXT. Now enter a report name and description. Specify the form you created in the WITH FORM field, as shown in Figure 3.

Report type	Reporting for Table FAGLFLEXT	
Report	ZGLFORM	Test GL report
With form	ZGLFORM	

⌃ *Figure 3 Create Report from Form*

Click on the CREATE button, which takes you to a screen where you can add all of the characteristics you want to include in the report. You can simply select the relevant characteristics on the right part of the screen (as shown in Figure 4) and click on the ◀ button to pull them into the left part of the screen.

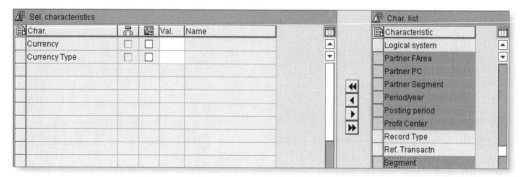

⌃ *Figure 4 Select Characteristics for Report*

When your report has been created, you can either assign it to a custom transaction code (explained in Tip 95 of Part 10) or access it (and all other SAP General Ledger drill-down reports) using Transaction FGI3.

Tip 79

Using Drill-Down Reports

By using general ledger drill-down reports, you can perform multidimensional reporting of the characteristics that exist in the SAP General Ledger totals table.

Drill-down reports are now available in SAP General Ledger. They are very similar to the reports used in Controlling Profitability Analysis (CO-PA), where you can sort different characteristics to display key figures for those characteristics. You can use the system-delivered drill-down reports or create your own.

However, unless you know how to navigate these reports, you may not realize the full benefit of their three-dimensional reporting capabilities.

✓ And Here's How...

To access one of the standard drill-down reports for SAP General Ledger, go to the following menu path:

> ACCOUNTING • FINANCIAL ACCOUNTING • GENERAL LEDGER • INFORMATION SYSTEM • GENERAL LEDGER REPORTS (NEW) • FINANCIAL STATEMENT / CASH FLOW • GENERAL • ACTUAL/ACTUAL COMPARISON • FINANCIAL STATEMENT: ACTUAL/ACTUAL COMPARISON

This takes you to the screen shown in Figure 1, where you enter the currency type and company code.

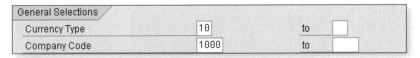

General Selections			
Currency Type	10	to	
Company Code	1000	to	

⌃ *Figure 1 Enter General Selections*

You can also enter values in the other fields of the GENERAL SELECTIONS section if you want to restrict the report by other characteristics. Otherwise, leave these fields blank and go to the REPORT SELECTIONS section. Enter the necessary values, as shown in Figure 2.

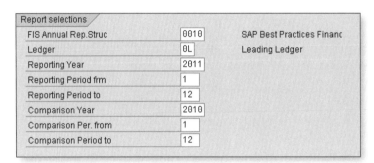

Report selections		
FIS Annual Rep.Struc	0010	SAP Best Practices Financ
Ledger	0L	Leading Ledger
Reporting Year	2011	
Reporting Period frm	1	
Reporting Period to	12	
Comparison Year	2010	
Comparison Per. from	1	
Comparison Period to	12	

« *Figure 2 Enter Report Selections*

Click on the EXECUTE button to display the report. The top-left part of the screen shows the available characteristics for sorting (see Figure 3).

Navigation			
Profit Center	⊠ Currency Type ▲ ▼ 🔍 10	Company code currenc	
Account Number	⊠ Currency ▲ ▼ 🔍 USD	US Dollar	
Segment			
Functional Area			
🔲 ♻ ✖			

FS Item/Account			
◇─ Commercial balance sheet	0.00	0.00	0.00
◇└─◆ Accounts not assigned	0.00	0.00	0.00

⌃ *Figure 3 Drill-Down Report Layout*

You can expand the line called ACCOUNTS NOT ASSIGNED by clicking on the diamond (◆) icon to give a full list of accounts in the financial statement version. If you click once on one of the characteristics (for example, PROFIT CENTER) and click on the line FS ITEM/ACCOUNT, the system will be displayed by profit center, as shown in Figure 4.

Profit Center				
◇2000/3000	Motorcycles	0.00	181,709.27	181,709.27-
◇2000/3005	Vehicles	0.00	304,731.29	304,731.29-
◇2000/3010	High Speed Pumps	0.00	179,198.60	179,198.60-
◇2000/3060	Food Products	0.00	87,381.38	87,381.38-
◇2000/3070	Pharm. & Cosmetics	0.00	94,926.90	94,926.90-
◇2000/3100	Chemical products	10,000.00-	101,571.81	111,571.81-

≫ *Figure 4* Sort by Profit Center

If you want to display the report by another characteristic (for example, segment), click once on SEGMENT and click on the PROFIT CENTER line. This switches the display from profit centers to segments. If you want to use two characteristics in the report (for example, all of the accounts posted to in profit center 3100), click on ACCOUNT NUMBER and the diamond icon (◊) that appears to the left of profit center 3100. This displays a list of accounts that make up the amount in profit center 3100, as shown in Figure 5.

Segment	Currency Type	▲ ▼ ⊜ 10	Company code currenc	
Functional Area	Currency	▲ ▼ ⊜ USD	US Dollar	
FS Item/Account	Profit Center	▲ ▼ ⊜ 2000/3100	Chemical products	
⊜ ⟳ ✖				

Account Number				
◇CAUS/1010	Accumulated deprecia	60,914.00-	95,719.00-	34,805.00
◇CAUS/191100	Goods Rcvd/Invoice R	11,300.00-	0.00	11,300.00-
◇CAUS/231500	Expense from price d	999.15	0.00	999.15
◇CAUS/400000	Raw Materials - Othe	300.00	0.00	300.00
◇CAUS/417000	Purchased services	10,000.00	0.00	10,000.00
◇CAUS/470000	Purchase of interco	0.00	52,815.61	52,815.61-
◇CAUS/476000	Office supplies	0.00	18,745.80	18,745.80-
◇CAUS/476300	External Services	0.00	22,268.13	22,268.13-
◇CAUS/476900	Other general expens	0.00	7,742.27	7,742.27-
◇CAUS/481000	Depreciation Expense	8,703.00	52,211.00	43,508.00-
◇CAUS/790000	Work in process inve	0.85	0.00	0.85
◇CAUS/811000	Income from activate	10,000.00-	0.00	10,000.00-
◇CAUS/900000	Retained Earnings	52,211.00	43,508.00	8,703.00
◆Result		10,000.00-	101,571.81	111,571.81-

≫ *Figure 5* Sort by Profit Center and Account Number

Because the currency type selected in the selection screen was the company code currency, the values of the report are displayed in this currency (USD in this example). However, you can display this report in any currency that you have maintained in the currency tables by clicking on the CURRENCY button (🔲) at the top part of the screen, entering a currency and translation key (as shown in Figure 6), and clicking on the EXECUTE button.

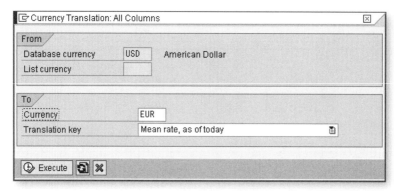

⤒ *Figure 6 Change Display Currency*

You can also drill into any of the lines on the report by clicking once on the line and selecting the top menu GOTO • LINE ITEMS. This gives you a list of the general ledger documents that make up the amount on the report. The line item view that is displayed is in the same format and layout as the FAGLL03 (G/L Account Line Item Display) report. You can further navigate from that view to see the document overview, source document, and other assignments to the document.

Quick Access to FI Reports

You can use a single transaction to access the available SAP standard reports within a given FI submodule.

Navigating to FI reports normally involves either going to several different transactions or following long menu paths from SAP's application menu. However, there are single transactions you can use to access the general ledger, accounts receivable, and accounts payable submodules.

And Here's How...

To quickly access reports in the general ledger submodule, use Transaction F.97 to see the screen shown in Figure 1.

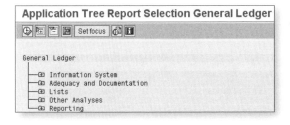

**« *Figure 1* Application Tree for General Ledger Reports*

Now navigate to the report you need by expanding the relevant section. For example, if you want to access a tax report for the United States, navigate the application tree as follows:

REPORTING • TAXES REPORTS • USA • USE AND SALES TAXES

To display the report, click on the report line and then click on the EXECUTE button.

You can display the programs the reports are based on by selecting the top menu SETTINGS • TECHNICAL NAMES ON/OFF.

If you want to set a specific node as the starting point when you go to this transaction, click on the node that you want to set and click on the SET FOCUS button. For example, if you perform this process for the INFORMATION SYSTEM node, the screen will look like the one shown in Figure 2.

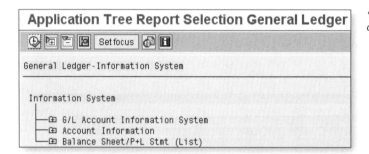

« Figure 2 *Set Focus on Specific Node*

If you want to save the setting so that this is the only node that shows up when you go to Transaction F.97, click on the node once and select the menu option SETTINGS • DEFINE INITIAL POSITION. If you want to reset the starting node, select the menu option SETTINGS • RESET INITIAL POSITION.

For quick access reports in the accounts payable submodule, go to Transaction F.98 to access the screen shown in Figure 3.

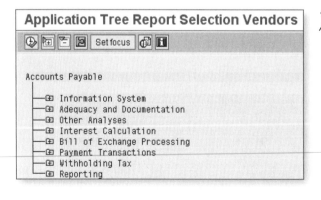

« Figure 3 *Application Tree for Accounts Payable Reports*

For quick access reports in the accounts receivable submodule, go to Transaction F.99 to access the screen shown in Figure 4.

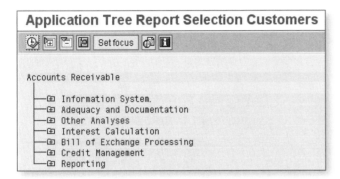

« *Figure 4 Application Tree for Accounts Receivable Reports*

The navigation and settings you can configure in the accounts payable and receivable application tree reports are similar to those we described previously regarding the general ledger.

Part 9
Data Update

Things You'll Learn in this Section

Updating data in the SAP system is usually carried out once a transaction is posted or a record is processed. Due to the real-time nature of the system, this data is immediately active and available once it is entered. There are times, however, when you need to perform data updates either periodically or as a one-off process due to the following reasons:

▶ You may have forgotten to activate a certain functionality when you went live with the system. In this case, the functionality that the activation enables will be missing for all previously posted data. In a situation like this, there are programs you can run to retroactively update all past data with the new activation to ensure consistency of data in the system.

▶ There could be redundant or unnecessary data in the system, which needs to be deleted. In an SAP system, you cannot normally delete data records completely. The common way to delete data is to mark it for deletion so that the system gives a warning message if this data is processed. However, if the records are still visible and can be used, they may lead to potential misuse. Therefore, in some cases (particularly before going live with the system) it may be necessary to run a deletion program that removes the data from the database entirely.

▶ Certain reports may need to be updated with data from another part of the system, but because the data is not automatically linked to the report, you may need to run a program with a batch job to periodically populate the report fields.

This part of the book provides several ideas on how you can run programs to update, delete, and retroactively populate data in the system. These programs are usually required when there is inconsistent data that needs to be corrected or removed to make the system function or be analyzed appropriately.

Tip 81

Enabling Line Item Display for General Ledger Accounts

You can retroactively activate line item management for general ledger accounts that already contain postings.

To display the line items on a general ledger account, select the LINE ITEM DISPLAY checkbox of the general ledger master record, which is located in the CONTROL DATA tab. If you did not originally select this checkbox before postings were made to the account, you can always do so after the fact.

However, this setting will only affect future postings to the account, so all prior postings to the activation will not be displayed. To display these prior postings, you need to run the Line Item Display transaction.

✔ And Here's How...

Before you can run the Line Item Display transaction, you need to perform two steps. The first step is to activate the line item display settings in the general ledger account master record. To do this, go to the General Ledger Master Record transaction (FS00) and enter the relevant account and company code. Then go to the CONTROL DATA tab, click on the CHANGE button (✎), and in the ACCOUNT MANAGEMENT IN COMPANY CODE section, select the LINE ITEM DISPLAY checkbox, as shown in Figure 1.

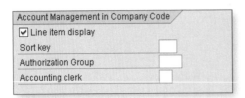

« *Figure 1 Activate Line Item Display*

The second step is to block the account for posting so no one can process the account while the line item change is being made. To do this in the general ledger master, click on the Block icon (🔒). Select the Blocked for Posting checkbox in the Block in Company Code section and save your settings.

Next, go to Transaction FAGL_ACTIVATE_IT and enter the general ledger account and company code. You can choose to display only the lines of certain documents in the account (not shown here) by entering the relevant document numbers in the Document Number field. Click on the Execute button (⊕) to display the screen shown in Figure 2. (Note: The processing time may be a few seconds to several minutes, depending on how many lines exist in the account.)

Doc. no.	Line Items	Year	Remark
300000004	1	1994	Document selected
300000004	1	1994	Document changed
300000004	1	1994	Line items generated in table BSIS
300000005	1	1994	Document selected
300000005	1	1994	Document changed
300000005	2	1994	Line items generated in table BSIS
300000010	1	1994	Document selected
300000010	1	1994	Document changed
300000010	3	1994	Line items generated in table BSIS

« *Figure 2 Documents Generated for Line Item Display*

The system indicates the documents that have been selected and changed, as well as whether line items have been generated in table BSIS (which is the open items index for general ledger accounts). Once the transaction has been executed, you can go to the General Ledger Line Item Display transaction (FAGLL03) to ensure that all of the lines have been transferred. To verify this, you can compare the total balance of this transaction with the one in the General Ledger Balance Display transaction (FAGLB03). If these totals match, then you can unblock the account in Transaction FS00, so postings can be made to the account.

Enabling Open Item Management for General Ledger Accounts

You can enable the clearing of general ledger accounts that were not initially activated for "open item management."

General ledger accounts can only be cleared (that is, matching debit and credit items to total zero) if the OPEN ITEM MANAGEMENT indicator is set in the general ledger master record. However, the system requires that the balance of the account be zero for the OPEN ITEM MANAGEMENT indicator to be changed.

Additionally, changing this indicator manually only applies to future documents, not prior documents. If you want to clear prior documents, there are a few steps you need to take to activate open item management for both the prior and future documents in a general ledger account.

✓ And Here's How...

To activate a general ledger account for clearing, you need to ensure that the LINE ITEM indicator is set in the master record. To do this, go to the General Ledger Master Record transaction (FS00) and enter the relevant account and company code. Then go to the CONTROL DATA tab, click on the CHANGE button (🖉), and select the LINE ITEM DISPLAY checkbox in the ACCOUNT MANAGEMENT IN COMPANY CODE section, as shown in Figure 1.

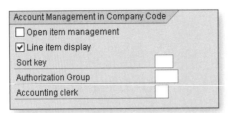

《 Figure 1 *Activate Line Item Display*

If you want to activate line items for historical data, follow the instructions in the first tip in this part of the book.

Once the general ledger is activated for clearing, go to Transaction FAGL_ACTIVATE_ OP and enter the relevant general ledger account, company code, and effective date (which you can either leave as the current date or make a past date) in the ACCOUNT DATA section, as shown in Figure 2.

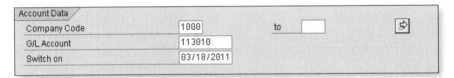

⌃ Figure 2 *Open Item Management Initial Screen*

For open item management to be activated, the account needs to have a zero balance. This means that if, for example, the account has a debit balance of $100, a posting needs to be made to credit this account and debit a "transfer account" with $100, so the original account becomes zero (temporarily). Therefore, you need to enter a DOCUMENT TYPE and ACCOUNT FOR TRANSFER POSTING to make this zero balance posting. This is shown in Figure 3.

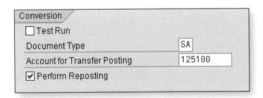

《 Figure 3 *Enter Document Type and Account for Reposting*

Select the PERFORM REPOSTING checkbox so that the posting that is made to bring the balance of the account to zero is reversed after the open item switch has been turned on, which will bring the account back to its original balance. Then click on the EXECUTE button to see the screen shown in Figure 4.

Type	Message Text
☐	Application log FAGL/OPENITEM (transaction SLG1)
☐	Date of the switch is 03/18/2011
☐	Reading data from tables BSIS and BKPF
☐	Reading totals records from table FAGLFLEXT; ledgers involved:
☐	Company code 1000, ledger 0L
☐	--
☐	Company code/ledger 1000/0L: balance 43,641.32 USD Update Currency
☐	Balances from totals record table correspond to amounts of line items
☐	Locking account 0000113010 in company code 1000
☐	--
☐	Company code/ledger group 1000/SPACE: Post 43,641.32 USD (Currency Type:00) to account 0000125100
☐	Document 0100030995 2011 posted with posting date 03/18/2011

⌃ *Figure 4 Log Display for Open Item Activation*

When you click on the EXECUTE button, the system log will show the steps that were carried out to activate open item management. The messages in Figure 4 state that the balance from account 113010 was posted to account 125100 (to make its balance zero), and it specifies the document number that was created. If you scroll further down the screen (not shown in the screenshot), the system will also show how many lines were changed in the general ledger tables and which document number was generated from the reposting.

Once this transaction is complete, all of the line items of the account will be available for clearing, and the OPEN ITEM MANAGEMENT indicator will be activated in the general ledger master record.

Deleting Financial Accounting Master Data

To prepare the system for productive startup, you can delete any redundant finance master data by using a specific program.

During an implementation project, you may have financial master data in your test or productive systems that you want to get rid of. Usually in SAP systems, you cannot totally remove a master data object unless you use an archiving program—you are only able to mark it for deletion. However, there are cases where leaving the data in the system will only cause confusion to the users and may skew reports or transaction processing. You therefore want to remove any master data items that are not going to be used, as long as no transactions have been posted to them. Let's explore how we can accomplish this.

✅ And Here's How...

You can access the deletion program for Financial Accounting master data (customers, vendors, and general ledger accounts) by going to Transaction OBR2. Note that this transaction should only be used either in a test system or in a production system before going live, otherwise you risk deleting productive master data that is to be used for real transactions. When you go to the transaction, you will see a screen like the one shown in Figure 1.

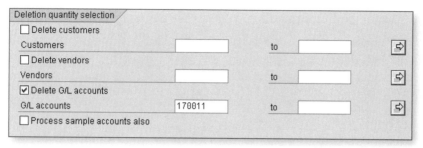

⌃ *Figure 1* *Specify Account to Be Deleted*

In the DELETION QUANTITY SELECTION section, you can choose which type of master data (customers, vendors, or general ledger accounts) you want to delete by selecting the relevant checkboxes. You can also specify the individual account(s) that you want to delete.

In the DELETION DEPTH section, shown in Figure 2, you can choose either to delete master data that has no assignment to a company code, sales, or purchasing area by selecting the ONLY GENERAL MASTER DATA checkbox or to delete a master record that has an assignment to a specific company code.

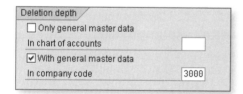

« *Figure 2* *Deletion Indicator for Company Code Data*

In the PROGRAM CONTROL section, you can specify that you want to delete only accounts that have the MARKED FOR DELETION flag activated in their master records. To do this, select the DELETE PER DELETION FLAG ONLY checkbox, shown in Figure 3.

« *Figure 3* *Activate Deletion per Deletion Flag*

When you click on the EXECUTE button, you will see a message asking you if you really want to delete the data. If this is the case, click on the YES button to see the log screen shown in Figure 4.

Table Name	Short descriptn.	Records Read	Records Delete
CDCLS	Change Documents	8	8
SKA1	G/L Account Master (Chart of Accounts)	1	1
SKAS	G/L account master (chart of accounts: key word list)	0	0
SKAT	G/L Account Master Record (Chart of Accounts: Description)	14	14
SKB1	G/L account master (company code)	1	1

☆ *Figure 4 Deletion Log Screen*

The log shows if the deletion has been successful and indicates the tables where the data records have been read and deleted.

Note that when a company code is productive, you need to ensure that this deletion program cannot be run for it, otherwise you may end up deleting live data that is relevant to your business transactions with customers and vendors. To do this, go to Transaction OBR3 and select the PRODUCTIVE checkbox for the relevant company code, as shown in Figure 5.

CoCd	Company Name	City	Productive
3000	IDES US INC	New York	✔

☆ *Figure 5 Select Productive Checkbox in Company Code*

With this activation turned on, if you try to delete the data in that company code, you will see a message saying that the company code is productive, and therefore its data cannot be deleted.

Deleting Financial Accounting Transactional Data

You can use certain deletion programs to reset the balance carryforward of SAP General Ledger or to delete all of the transactional data of a specific company code.

After you have migrated account balances to SAP General Ledger, you might have a situation where the balances that have been brought forward are incorrect and need to be deleted. There can also be cases during an implementation project where test data was accidentally loaded into your production system. In these scenarios, you need to be able to run a program that can delete all of the transactional data from the relevant ledger to prepare the system for production, or in the case of a test system, so the data can be reloaded again.

✅ And Here's How...

To delete the transactional data from a specific ledger for a particular fiscal year, go to Transaction FAGL_DEL, which takes you to the screen shown in Figure 1.

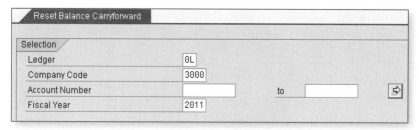

⌃ *Figure 1 Initial Screen for Transactional Data Deletion*

You need to restrict the selection criteria as much as possible so that the deletion is specific to the data in the relevant ledger, company code, and fiscal year. If you only want to delete the transactions of certain general ledger accounts, you can enter these accounts in the ACCOUNT NUMBER field. Note that this selection must be conducted very carefully to ensure the consistency of the data.

In the PROCESSING OPTIONS section, ensure that the OUTPUT LIST checkbox is selected (as displayed in Figure 2) so you can see the statistics of the deletion operations that have been performed.

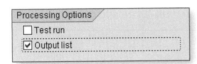

« *Figure 2 Select Output List Checkbox*

Click on the EXECUTE button to see the table the data was deleted from (which will be the SAP General Ledger totals table FAGLFLEXT and all of the other tables involved in the transaction, to ensure data consistency of the database) and the number of records that have been deleted, as shown in Figure 3.

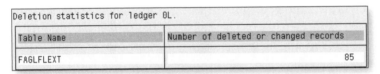

Deletion statistics for ledger 0L.	
Table Name	Number of deleted or changed records
FAGLFLEXT	85

⌃ *Figure 3 Deletion Statistics for Ledger*

If you wanted to delete all of the transactional data in a particular company code to prepare it for productive startup, go to the following configuration menu path to see the screen shown in Figure 4:

FINANCIAL ACCOUNTING (NEW) • GENERAL LEDGER ACCOUNTING (NEW) • PREPARATION FOR PRODUCTIVE START • NEW INSTALLATION • DELETE TEST DATA • DELETE TRANSACTION DATA • DELETE COMPANY CODE DATA

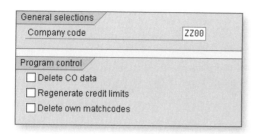

« *Figure 4* *Delete Company Code Data*

Enter the company code whose data you want to reset. You can also delete CO data, regenerate credit limits, and delete custom matchcodes. We recommend that you use a separate program (RKSCUS01) to delete CO data. In program RKSCUS01, you can specify whether you want to delete actual and plan data or actual data only.

Note that this deletion program (and the deletion Transaction FAGL_DEL) does not work if the PRODUCTIVE indicator is set for the company code in Transaction OBR3.

Deleting Fixed Assets Data

You can reset all of the data that has been created and posted in a particular company code by running the fixed assets deletion program.

When you are in the testing phase of your fixed asset conversions, you may need to do several iterations of the data loads until the correct data is in the system. Therefore, it may be necessary to delete all of the fixed assets data in the system before performing a new data load.

In this tip, we will show you the transaction you can use to reset all of the fixed asset data that exists in a particular company code.

 And Here's How...

You can delete all of the fixed asset data in a company code by accessing Transaction OABL or going to the following configuration menu path:

> FINANCIAL ACCOUNTING (NEW) • ASSET ACCOUNTING • PREPARING FOR PRODUCTION STARTUP • TOOLS • RESET COMPANY CODE

This takes you to the screen shown in Figure 1, where you enter the company code you want to be reset. Make sure to take note of the important warning on the screen.

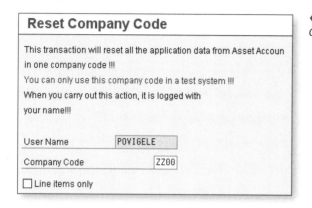

« *Figure 1* *Reset Fixed Assets in Company Code*

If you only want to delete the transactional fixed assets data and not the master data, select the LINE ITEMS ONLY checkbox. Press ⌈Enter⌉, and the system displays the message shown in Figure 2.

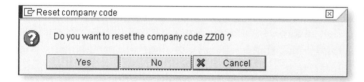

« *Figure 2* *Reset Company Code Message*

Click on the YES button to reset the company code, and a message appears at the bottom of the screen, notifying you that the company code was reset.

Note that when this transaction is executed, it only deletes asset accounting data. If, for example, you deleted asset transactions that are integrated with general ledger transactions, the general ledger transactions will still exist in the system. This would cause an imbalance in the reconciliation between fixed asset accounting and SAP General Ledger. You therefore need to delete all related general ledger transactions by using a separate process (which is demonstrated in Tip 85 of this part of the book). However, as mentioned above, this transaction is only to be used in a test system or during the asset migration from a legacy system, so the emphasis on reconciling SAP General Ledger with fixed asset accounting may not be that stringent.

To make sure that the reset transaction cannot be used in your production system, set up your company code as "Productive." To do this, go to Transaction OBR3 and activate the PRODUCTIVE indicator for the relevant company code.

Deleting Bank Statements that Have Been Posted

If a bank statement needs to be reloaded due to errors, you can use a specific program to delete the original statement.

When you enter a bank statement into the system either electronically or manually, there can be cases where an incorrect statement, or a statement with errors, was loaded. In these cases, you cannot simply reload the same bank statement—the system will not allow you to enter a bank statement in the same house bank and account ID that has an identical statement number. In this situation, it is important to know how to delete the incorrect statement from the system in order to correctly reload it.

✓ And Here's How...

To delete a bank statement from the system, the deletion program requires some specific information, which you need to retrieve from the bank statement transaction. You can find this information by going to Transaction FEBA_BANK_STATEMENT or via the following menu path:

> ACCOUNTING • FINANCIAL ACCOUNTING • BANKS • INCOMING • BANK STATEMENT • REPROCESS

This takes you to the screen shown in Figure 1, where you enter the COMPANY CODE, HOUSE BANK, ACCOUNT ID, and STATEMENT NUMBER information for the statement you want to delete.

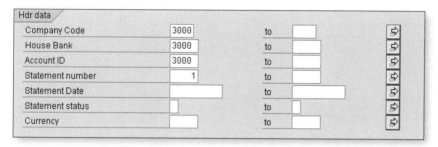

⌃ *Figure 1* *Bank Statement Reprocessing Initial Screen*

When you click on the EXECUTE button, the system takes you to the EDIT BANK STATEMENT screen, which shows the bank statement as a folder and displays all of the statement items within it. You then click on the OTHER DISPLAY button at the top of that screen to see the view shown in Figure 2.

Statement Items

AC	Amount	Posting rule	Value date	MR no
USD	4,000.00	002	12/28/2001	1
USD	2,100.00-	107	12/28/2001	2
USD	2,900.00-	101	12/28/2001	3

« *Figure 2* *Bank Statement Items*

You now need to pull the SHORT KEY column into this view. To do this, click on the PICK button to the right of the CHOOSE LAYOUT icon (⊞▤), select CHANGE LAYOUT, and select the SHORT KEY field from the right part of the screen. Use the ◀ button to pull it to the left part of the screen. When you press Enter, the SHORT KEY column appears in the screen, as shown in Figure 3.

AC	Amount	Posting rule	Value date	MR no	Short key
USD	4,000.00	002	12/28/2001	1	42
USD	2,100.00-	107	12/28/2001	2	42
USD	2,900.00-	101	12/28/2001	3	42

« *Figure 3* *Bank Statement Items Including Short Key*

Make a note of the SHORT KEY number (42 in this example), as you will need it in the deletion program. Now go to Transaction SE38 to delete the bank statement, enter program RFEBKA96 in the PROGRAM field, and click on the EXECUTE button to see the screen shown in Figure 4.

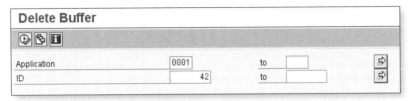

⩔ *Figure 4 Delete Buffer Entry Screen*

Enter the appropriate value in the APPLICATION field (this example refers to the electronic bank statement, so we entered 0001). Press the F4 key in this field to see what the other options are. Now enter the SHORT KEY number (42) that you got from the bank statement view into the ID field. Click the EXECUTE button to see the screen shown in Figure 5.

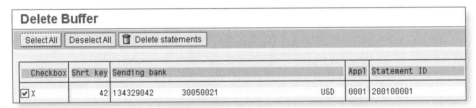

⩔ *Figure 5 Bank Statement to Be Deleted*

The system now shows the bank key and bank account numbers you intend to delete in the SENDING BANK column. Verify these so you know you are dealing with the correct bank.

In the STATEMENT ID column you see the year of the bank statement and the statement number as a continuous string. You should also verify these details. If the selection is correct, click on the DELETE STATEMENTS button and in the message that appears, click on the YES button. The system then gives you a green light signal if everything is correct and specifies from which tables the records were deleted.

Update Withholding Tax Postings Retroactively

After updating the vendor master with the relevant tax code, you can adjust past documents for withholding tax.

When you enable a vendor for withholding tax, all invoices and payments for this vendor are eligible for withholding tax based on the tax code that is entered in the vendor master. However, sometimes you only discover that a vendor is liable for withholding tax after invoices and payments have been made to his account. In this situation, you need to know how to subsequently create withholding tax data after invoices and payments have been processed.

✓ And Here's How...

To create withholding tax data for these documents, first go to Transaction FK02. Enter the appropriate withholding tax code in the ACCOUNTING INFORMATION ACCOUNTING section of the vendor master's COMPANY CODE view (see Figure 1).

Withholding tax		
W. Tax Code	00	Exemption number
WH Tax Country		Valid until
Recipient type		Exmpt.authority

« Figure 1 *Withholding Tax Code in Vendor Master*

The withholding tax code (00) you see in this screen relates to 1099 MISC vendors in the United States. You can press the F4 button in this field to see what the other available options are.

To complete the settings for a withholding tax vendor, go to the CONTROL section of the GENERAL DATA view. Enter the vendor's tax identification or social security numbers in the TAX NUMBER 1 and TAX NUMBER 2 fields, respectively. Once you have saved your settings, run the withholding tax adjustment program. There are two programs you can use to create withholding tax data. They are:

▶ **RFWT0010**

This program is normally used to adjust withholding tax data where extended withholding tax is activated within your company code.

▶ **RFWT0020**

This program is normally used to adjust withholding tax data where the withholding tax rate is 0%.

In our example, we will show you how to make the adjustment using program RFWT0020. Go to Transaction SE38, enter program RFWT0020, and click on the EXECUTE button to see the screen shown in Figure 2. Here, you enter the relevant selection data as we have demonstrated.

Acct Selectn				
Vendor	7777	to		⇨
Tax Number 1		to		⇨
Tax Number 2		to		⇨
Customer		to		⇨
Tax Number 1		to		⇨
Tax Number 2		to		⇨
Company Code	3000	to		⇨
Document Number		to		⇨
Posting Date	01/01/2011	to	03/31/2011	⇨

⌃ *Figure 2 Withholding Tax Adjustment Program Screen*

In the DETAILS ON SELECTED PROCEDURE section (shown in Figure 3), select the ONLY RECREATE DOCUMENTS WITHOUT W/TAX DATA box if you only want to create withholding tax documents where they did not previously exist.

If you want to exchange a previous withholding tax code with the one that is currently in the vendor master, do not select this box. In this situation, you need to specify whether the withholding tax data should be updated on the invoice document or the payment document by selecting the relevant radio button (see Figure 3).

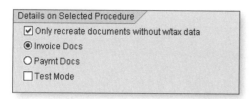

« *Figure 3* *Specify Document for Withholding Tax Update*

Click on the EXECUTE button to see the screen as shown in Figure 4, which shows the documents that have been updated for withholding tax.

	Changed Classic Withholding Tax Data (BSEG)							
CoCd	Vendor	DocumentNo	Clrng doc.	Clearing	Itm	WT	Withhld.tax base	W.tax-exempt amt
3000	7777	1900000002	2000000003	02/08/2011	1	00	0.00	1,000.00
3000	7777	1900000006	2000000004	02/08/2011	1	00	0.00	1,000.00
3000	7777	1900000007	2000000004	02/08/2011	1	00	0.00	1,000.00
3000	7777	1900000008	2000000004	02/08/2011	1	00	0.00	1,000.00

☆ *Figure 4* *Updated Documents for Withholding Tax*

The relevant documents will now be updated with the withholding tax code, and they will be available in the withholding tax reports (for example, with Transaction S_PL0_09000314 for US 1099 Misc) along with any output forms that are produced.

Populating the Check Number in a Payment Document

You can automatically populate the assignment field of a payment document with the check number.

When performing an analysis on the bank account (using Transaction FAGLL03, for example) it is not easy to see what the check number that relates to the payment document is, which you need to see to understand which check made a certain payment. You normally need to drill into the item or select the line and click on the DISPLAY CHECK INFORMATION button (⊠) to see the check number. To bypass this annoyance, you can run a program that will automatically update the PAYMENT DOCUMENT ASSIGNMENT field with the check number so that you can view it in line item reports.

✔ And Here's How...

You can update the check number in a payment document by going to Transaction FCHU and entering the relevant PAYING COMPANY CODE, HOUSE BANK, and ACCOUNT ID, as shown in Figure 1.

Create Reference for Check from Payment Document

⊕ ⟷ ℹ			
Paying company code	3000	to	⇨
House Bank	3000	to	⇨
Account ID	3000	to	⇨

⌃ *Figure 1 Create Check Reference Initial Screen*

In the GENERAL SELECTIONS section, you can further restrict the selection criteria by entering values in fields such as the DATE OF ISSUE and CREATION DATE.

In the TARGET FIELD SELECTION FOR CHECK NUMBER section (displayed in Figure 2), choose in which field in the payment document you want the check number to be populated.

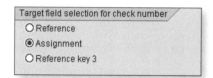

« *Figure 2* Target Field Selection for Check Number

Click on the EXECUTE button to see a list of all of the payment documents that have been updated with their corresponding check numbers (see Figure 3).

CoCd	Payment	Fiscal Yr	House Bank	Acct ID	Pay.Method	Check number
3000	1500000000	2001	3000	3000	C	22671
3000	1500000000	2005	3000	3000	C	00022702
3000	1500000001	2005	3000	3000	C	00022703
3000	1500000002	2005	3000	3000	C	00022704
3000	1500000002	1996	3000	3000	C	10009
3000	1500000003	1996	3000	3000	C	10011
3000	1500000003	2005	3000	3000	C	00022705
3000	1500000004	2005	3000	3000	C	00022706

« *Figure 3*
Documents Updated
with Check Number
Reference

The next time you display the line items in the payment account using Transaction FAGLL03, you will see that the assignment field (if this was the field that was specified) has been populated with the check number. If you have a sort key for this payment account that already populates the assignment field (as described in Tip 32 of Part IV), running Transaction FCHU will override the value populated by the sort key with the check number.

It is best to set up the underlying program (RFCHKU00) that is linked to this transaction as a background job that is run every night. This way, the line item reports are populated every day with the checks that were issued the previous day.

Handling Check Assignment Errors

There are certain transactions you can use to fix the incorrect assignment of manual checks to payment documents.

It is common for errors to be made when manual payments processed with Transaction F-53 are assigned to checks, using Transaction FCH5. A typical example is where you assign check number A with payment document B and check number B with payment document A, which results in a situations where you need to swap the assignments. Also, there are cases where you may have assigned a check number to a payment document that has itself been assigned to a totally different check.

The usual way of fixing these issues is to void the checks, reverse the payment documents, reenter the payment documents, and reassign the checks, which can be quite a quite laborious process. In this tip, we will show you the alternative steps you need to handle these issues expediently.

 And Here's How...

Scenario 1

Below is an example of two payment documents where the check numbers have been incorrectly assigned:

▶ Payment document number 1500000000 has been assigned to check number 00022745 (but should have been assigned to check number 00022746).

▶ Payment document number 1500000003 has been assigned to check number 00022746 (but should have been assigned to check number 00022745).

You can correct these assignments using Transaction FCHT or by going to the following menu path:

ACCOUNTING • FINANCIAL ACCOUNTING • BANKS • ENVIRONMENT • CHECK BALANCE • CHANGE • ASSIGNMENT TO PAYMENT

This takes you to the screen shown in Figure 1, where you can enter the relevant information for both checks.

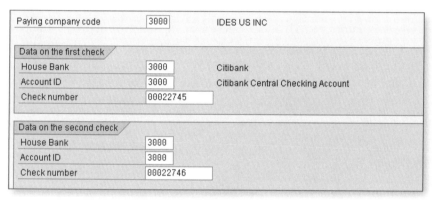

≫ *Figure 1* Check Document Numbers To Be Switched

Click on the CHANGE ASSIGNMENT button, and the system shows you the message shown in Figure 2.

« *Figure 2* Message for Check Number Reallocation

Check that the reallocation has been made correctly by going to Transaction FCH2, entering one of the payment document numbers that you changed (for example, 1500000000 in the above example), and verifying that it has now been assigned to the appropriate check number.

Scenario 2

Payment document number 1500000001 has been assigned to check number 00022744 (but should have been assigned to check number 00022749, which has not been issued).

In this case, you need to delete the assignment of the check number to the payment document. Before you do this, ensure that the check you are deleting is the last number in the check status (that is, no other check has been issued after this one). If the check is not the last number in the check status, go to Transaction FCHI, enter the relevant company code house bank and account ID details, and click on the CHANGE STATUS button to see the screen shown in Figure 3.

Check lots					
Lot number	Short info	Check no. from	Check number to	Next lot	Number status
2	Check Lot 2	00020000	00029999	3	00022748

⌃ *Figure 3 Change Check Number Status*

Here, the current number status is 00022748. You need to change this to the number of the check that you want to delete (00022744). Ensure that you make a note of the current check number (00022748) because you need to reset the status to this number so that the checks are not out of sync. Once you have changed the number (simply by overwriting the current number with the one you want to delete) accordingly, save your changes.

Now go to Transaction FCHF and enter the details of the incorrectly assigned check number, as shown in Figure 4.

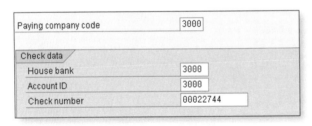

Paying company code	3000

Check data	
House bank	3000
Account ID	3000
Check number	00022744

≪ *Figure 4 Delete Check Number Entry Screen*

Once you have entered the details, click on the EXECUTE button and press the ⌈Enter⌉ key to delete the check number. Ensure that this deleted check number (00022744) is accounted for in the system. It should either be voided (by using Transaction FCH3) or assigned to its appropriate payment document (by using Transaction FCH5).

Now go back to the Check Lot Maintenance transaction (FCHI) and change the number status back to what it was originally (in this case 00022748). The payment document (1500000001) is now freed up to be assigned to its correct check number 00022749. Assign the correct check number by going to Transaction FCH5.

Once you have entered the relevant information, press the ⌈Enter⌉ key to verify the check information and save your settings.

Transfering CO Planning Documents to SAP General Ledger

You can copy data from Overhead Cost Controlling (CO-OM) to SAP General Ledger by running a transfer program.

Planning in FI was not generally used until New General Ledger (now called SAP General Ledger) was introduced. So therefore, if you want to transfer plan data from the Controlling component to SAP General Ledger (on a "plan" to "plan" basis), you need to know what steps to take before the transfer and which program should be run to execute the transfer. This will save the time you need to recreate plan data (which already exists in the Controlling component) in SAP General Ledger.

✔ And Here's How...

To copy planning data from Overhead Cost Controlling to General Ledger Accounting, first activate integrated planning in SAP General Ledger. You can do this by following the configuration menu path:

> FINANCIAL ACCOUNTING (NEW) • GENERAL LEDGER ACCOUNTING (NEW) • PLANNING • PLAN VERSIONS • DEFINE PLAN VERSIONS

Click on the NEW ENTRIES button and enter the details, as shown in Figure 1.

Ld	Ver	Man. plan	Integ.plan	Version Description
0L	0	☐	☑	Standard Plan Version

≪ Figure 1 *Activate Integrated Planning*

You now need to assign the plan version to a fiscal year and activate line item planning for the version. You do this by going to the following configuration menu path:

> FINANCIAL ACCOUNTING (NEW) • GENERAL LEDGER ACCOUNTING (NEW) • PLANNING • PLAN VERSIONS • FISCAL-YEAR-DEPENDENT VERSION PARAMETERS • ASSIGN PLAN VERSION TO FISCAL YEAR AND ACTIVATE

Click on the NEW ENTRIES button and enter the details, as shown in Figure 2.

Ld	Ver	CoCd	Year	Locked	LItem	OpBal
0L	0	3000	2011	☐	☐	☐

« *Figure 2 Assign Fiscal Year to Plan Version*

Press Enter to activate the LITEM indicator. You also need to activate integrated planning in the Controlling component. You can do this by accessing Transaction KP96 and entering the relevant version and fiscal year, as shown in Figure 3.

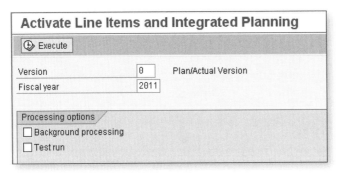

« *Figure 3 Activate Integrated Planning in Controlling*

When you click on the EXECUTE button, the system will issue a message saying "Integrated planning activated successfully." This means you can now run the transfer program. You can do this with Transaction FAGL_CO_PLAN or by going to the configuration menu path:

> FINANCIAL ACCOUNTING (NEW) • GENERAL LEDGER ACCOUNTING (NEW) • PLANNING • TRANSFER PLANNING DATA FROM CO-OM

You now see the screen shown in Figure 4, where you enter the relevant selection data as shown.

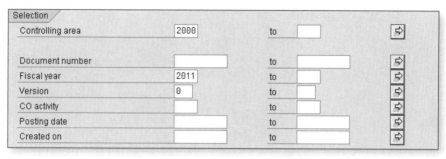

⌃ *Figure 4* Transfer Planning Data Initial Screen

In the Processing Options section (displayed in Figure 5) select the List posted records checkbox to see all of the records that were posted, as well as the Check for existing records checkbox so that the system checks whether the data record already exists before posting it.

« *Figure 5* Select Processing Options

Click on the Execute button to see a log of the documents that were processed and a list of the ones that were posted correctly, as shown in Figure 6.

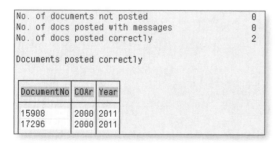

« *Figure 6* List of Documents Posted Correctly

If you double-click on any of the lines displayed, the system takes you to the original plan cost document that was transferred to SAP General Ledger.

Part 10

Technical

Things You'll Learn in this Section

You use the technical processes in the Financial Accounting component in cases where the master data and configuration settings are not sufficient. The degree of technical activities can vary from creating a background job to modifying a program. Depending on how technical the activity is, it could be performed by the SAP technical team (that is, a Basis person or an ABAP programmer) as opposed to someone in the finance department. For example, tasks such as creating transaction codes and scheduling background jobs may be performed by the Basis team, while tasks such as changing screen variants and creating validation rules may be carried out by an ABAP programmer.

However, it is important for people who use the Financial Accounting component to be aware of the technical tasks that can be carried out to improve their periodic processes. This is even more relevant where finance users are responsible for carrying out these tasks themselves, as it saves them from having to solicit outside help (either from another team or an external consultant) to perform these functions.

This section of the book will provide some technical tips you can use to enhance and streamline finance processes such as how to create transaction and screen variants for certain financial accounting transactions, how to dynamically schedule background jobs for processes that are carried out repeatedly with the same input data, and how to control the posting of general ledger accounts to specific cost centers by using validation rules. We recommend keeping technical enhancements and changes to a minimum as much as possible to keep the system stabilized. Also, there is a concern that any technical changes that are not part of the standard system could be impacted when there is a system upgrade or an enhancement package is applied.

Configuring Transaction Variant for FI Enjoy Transactions

You can customize the field layout of FI enjoy transactions by using screen and transaction variants.

When you process any of the enjoy transactions in Financial Accounting such as Transactions FB50, FB60, and FB70, there may be certain field and column settings that you want to reconfigure to make the screen more relevant to your processing needs. You may also want to hide certain buttons to prevent users from accessing them. To do this, you need to create a transaction variant and configure the screen settings within this variant.

✓ And Here's How...

We will use an example where you want to hide the Tax tab in the transaction for parking vendor invoices (FV60). To create a transaction variant, go to Transaction SHD0 and enter the relevant transaction code and a transaction variant, as shown in Figure 1.

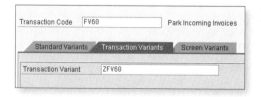

« Figure 1 *Create Transaction Variant*

Now click on the CREATE button (🗋) to go to the processing screen for that transaction, which in this example is the BASIC DATA screen of the Park Vendor Invoice transaction (FV60), as shown in Figure 2.

Figure 2 Park Vendor Invoice: Basic Data Screen

When you have entered the relevant information, as shown in Figure 2, press Enter, which takes you to the Confirm Screen Entries screen. To make the TAX tab invisible, select the INVISIBLE checkbox in the TAX row, as shown in Figure 3.

⌃ *Figure 3* Make Tax Tab Invisible

Now click on the EXIT AND SAVE button to go to the Change Transaction Variant screen, where you can give the screen variant a short text and click on the SAVE button. This takes you back to the original screen, where you can see that a screen variant has been assigned to the transaction variant you created. This screen variant is a combination of the transaction variant name (ZFV60 in this example) and the screen number (in this example 1100).

The next time you go to the Park Vendor Invoice transaction (FV60) you will see that the TAX tab does not appear (see Figure 4).

⌃ *Figure 4* Park Vendor Invoice Screen without Tax Tab

You can also use the transaction variant functionality to assign default values to fields, suppress fields for entry, hide or change the order of columns in the line items section, or hide icons and buttons on the screen.

Designing Screen Layout for Transaction MIRO

You can customize the field layout of logistics invoice verification transactions by using screen and transaction variants.

In the Logistics Invoice Verification transaction (MIRO), you may want to set up the screen so that the fields displayed are only the ones you need to process an invoice. Instead of having to scroll to the right part of the screen to access fields that are used all the time, you may want them available as soon as the transaction is accessed. Also, you may want to suppress certain fields and buttons that you do not need, make certain key fields required for entry, and default the values in selected fields. This will reduce the time it takes to process logistics invoices and reduce possible user entry errors.

To accomplish this, you need to create a screen variant for Transaction MIRO where you can sort or hide the columns or define their sequence and width.

✔ And Here's How...

For this tip, we will configure the general ledger account and cost center to show in the initial screen of the logistics invoice verification transaction without having to scroll to the right part of the screen (as you do with the standard layout). You can change the screen variant for the MIRO transaction by going to Transaction OLMRL-IST or via the following configuration menu path:

> MATERIALS MANAGEMENT • LOGISTICS INVOICE VERIFICATION • INCOMING INVOICE • MAINTAIN ITEM LISTS VARIANTS

Enter "MIRO" in the TRANSACTION field and "ZMIRO" (for example) in the SCREEN VARIANT field, as shown in Figure 1.

Transaction	MIRO
Screen variant	ZMIRO
Program	SAPLMR1M
Screen	6310

✯ *Figure 1 Create Screen Variant for MIRO Transaction*

Click on the CREATE button, which takes you to the Enter Incoming Invoice screen. You can enter any relevant data to validate the screen and then proceed to move the columns as necessary. In our example, we will move the G/L ACCOUNT and COST CENTER columns from the right part of the screen to the part of the screen that makes them visible when you initially access the transaction (shown in Figure 2). To move a column, you can simply left-click on and hold down on the title of the column and drag it to where you want it to be positioned.

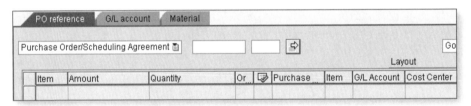

✯ *Figure 2 G/L Account and Cost Center Columns in Initial Screen*

Press the ⌐Enter¬ key, which brings up the Confirm Screen Entries screen. Here you can give the screen variant a short text and select the ADOPT COLUMN SEQUENCE checkbox, as shown in Figure 3.

Click on the EXIT AND SAVE button, which takes you to the Change Screen Variant screen. Save your work.

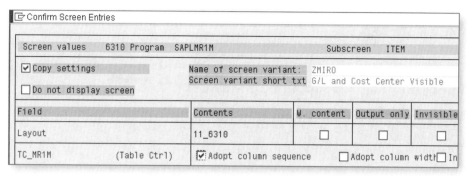

⚞ *Figure 3* *Adopt Column Sequence*

To test the transaction, click on the BACK button (⬅) to go back to the original Screen Variants screen and then click the TEST button (🖳). This takes you into the MIRO transaction screen and shows the columns (shown in Figure 4) that you moved into the initial view.

	Item	Amount	Quantity		Or	🗒	Purchase	Item	G/L Account	Cost Center

⚞ *Figure 4* *Test MIRO Transaction Screen*

Go back to Transaction MIRO and drop down in the LAYOUT field on the right part of the screen. Here you can see the screen variant that you created in the list, as shown in Figure 5.

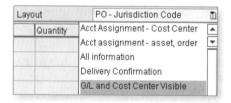

≪ *Figure 5* *New Screen Variant Included in Layout Options*

When you select this screen layout it will remain defaulted in this transaction even after you have logged out of the system, unless you decide to change it again.

Making Financial Statement Version Modifiable in Production Client

You can directly modify the financial statement version in your productive system by changing the application area message.

The financial statement version represents the chart of accounts reporting structure and can be freely defined according to the needs of a country, industry, or business. It is usually set up in the configuration client and then transported to the production client. This is because the development client is open for configuration changes, while the production client is not, and the financial statement version is based on a configuration object.

However, in reality, because general ledger accounts are usually modified directly in the production client, the financial statement version should also be enabled for direct modification in this client. If you do not allow direct modification of the financial statement version, you will have to open up the production client every time you want to make a change, and this presents the risk of other users accidentally modifying configuration tables directly in the productive system.

✔ And Here's How...

To make the financial statement version modifiable in production, there are a few steps you need to take. First, find out what application area and message number are issued when you try to modify the financial statement version. To do this, go to Transaction FSE2 in your production system, and you will usually receive an error message such as the one shown in Figure 1.

« *Figure 1* Error Message
from Modifying Financial
Statement Version

Click on the HELP button (⊚) to display the long text of the message (see Figure 2).

« *Figure 2* Error Message Long Text

The message number is FE146, which means the application area is FE and the message number is 146.

Next, switch off this error message by changing the message control settings. To change the settings on this message, go to Transaction OBA5 (in your development system), enter APPLICATION AREA "FE," and press the ⎡Enter⎤ key. Now click on the NEW ENTRIES button, enter the relevant settings as shown in Figure 3, press the ⎡Enter⎤ key again, and click on the SAVE button (🖫) to save your changes.

Area	FE	CO-PA module pool messages				

Message Control by User						
	Msg.	Message Text	User Name	Online	Batch	Standard
	146	Client &1 has status 'not modifiable'		-	-	E

⌃ *Figure 3* Change Message Settings

You can now go to the production client and attempt to modify the financial statement version by going to Transaction FSE2. Enter the relevant financial statement version and click on the EXECUTE button (⊕). When you make your changes and click on SAVE, you will see a message, as shown in Figure 4.

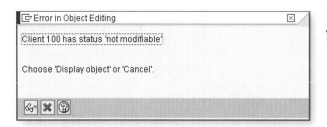

« *Figure 4* *Message from Modifying Financial Statement Version*

If you press the [Enter] key, the system will display a message saying that the financial statement version has been changed and your changes will have taken effect.

Maintaining Selection Variables in Variants

You can dynamically maintain the variants of several reports by using selection variables.

There are several reports that are run during period end that are used to analyze the transactions that occurred during that period or cumulatively. Usually you set these reports up as background jobs to ease the system processing time and the effort involved in the online execution of the programs. As is the case with background jobs, you need to maintain variants that specify the entry fields to be populated when the report is run.

However, if certain values (such as period, year, posting date, and so on) need to be changed each month, it could become rather painstaking to update the variants of all of the reports that need to be run in the background. In this tip we will show you how to set up a dynamic way of changing the fields of these variants.

✔ And Here's How...

As an example, we will set up a selection variable for the POSTING DATE field for multiple reports. First, go to one of the reports (in our example we will use the Use and Sales Tax report in Transaction S_ALR_87012394) and enter the necessary fixed values that you want to save in your variant. In the top menu select:

> GOTO • VARIANTS • SAVE AS VARIANT

This takes you to the VARIANT ATTRIBUTES screen, where you can scroll down to the POSTING DATE line in the OBJECTS FOR THE SELECTION SCREEN section and check which selection type this field is assigned to. In Figure 1 you can see that the posting date is assigned to SELECTION TYPE S (which stands for "selection" as opposed to P for "parameter").

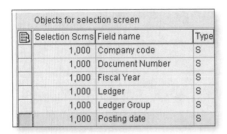

« Figure 1 *Selection Type for Posting Date*

You can then go to the top menu ENVIRONMENT • MAINT. SEL. VARIABLES, and in the screen that appears, go to the SELECTION OPTIONS tab (because the selection type for the posting date field was S). Click on the CHANGE button (🖉) and the CREATE button (📄), and enter the values as displayed in Figure 2.

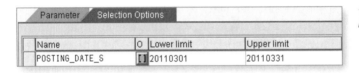

« Figure 2 *Values for Posting Date Variable*

You can give the variable any name you want. In this example we use POSTING_DATE_S. This indicates that it relates to the POSTING DATE field in programs where the selection type is S. It is possible for there to be some programs where the posting date has a selection type of P, and you can therefore distinguish the fields by using this designation.

Next, click on the button in the O (for "option") column. Click on the ⬛ symbol to indicate that you want to choose a range of dates. Now enter the start and end dates of the month (in numerical format) in the LOWER LIMIT and UPPER LIMIT columns, and then save your settings.

Click on the BACK (⬅) button to go back to the Variant Attributes screen. On the POSTING DATE line, drop down in the SELECTION VARIABLE field and select T (table variable from TVARC). Also, drop down in the NAME OF VARIABLE INPUT ONLY USING F4 field and select the variable you created (in our example POSTING_DATE_S), as shown in Figure 3.

	Selectio	Field name	Ty	Protect field	Hide field	Hide field 'BIS'	Save	Switch	Required	Selection variable	Option	Name of Variable (Input Only Using F4)
		Objects for selection screen										
	1,000	Company code	S	☐	☐	☐	☐	☐	☐			
	1,000	Document Number	S	☐	☐	☐	☐	☐	☐			
	1,000	Fiscal Year	S	☐	☐	☐	☐	☐	☐			
	1,000	Ledger	S	☐	☐	☐	☐	☐	☐			
	1,000	Ledger Group	S	☐	☐	☐	☐	☐	☐			
	1,000	Posting date	S	☐	☐	☐	☐	☐	☐	T		POSTING_DATE_S

⌃ **Figure 3** *Assign Selection Variable to Posting Date Field*

Now give the variant a name and description as normal, and then click on the SAVE button. You can repeat the setting shown in Figure 3 for all other reports where the posting date has an S selection type. This way, instead of changing the variants of each report (and there could be hundreds of them) every month, you simply need to follow these steps: Go to Transaction STVARV and click on the SELECTION OPTIONS tab, scroll down to the POSTING_DATE_S line, and change the date range to the relevant month. This updates all of the reports that contain this selection variable in their variants.

Creating Transaction Codes for Report Painter Reports

You need to know which screen fields and values to use if you want to assign transaction codes to Report Painter reports.

Report Painter (or Report Writer) reports are normally created when the layout or data that exists in standard reports is not suitable for your reporting needs. The advantage of Report Painter reports is that you do not need to use ABAP programming to create them and you can make them more customized to your requirements than the standard reports.

You can run Report Painter reports by executing the relevant report group in Transaction GR55. However, if you do not want all users to have access to all of the Report Painter reports, then you need to assign them to transaction codes. To do this you need to know which default values to use in the transaction code.

✓ And Here's How...

To assign a Report Painter report to a transaction code, you first need to establish in which report group the report exists. This is because it is the report group that you assign to the transaction code. Therefore, if you have several reports in a report group, they will all be executed simultaneously with the transaction.

To do this, go to the relevant report (using Transaction GR55 or GRR3) and select Environment • Technical Information from the initial screen to see the screen shown in Figure 1.

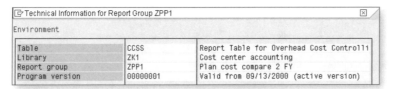

Figure 1 shows:

Table	CCSS	Report Table for Overhead Cost Controlli
Library	ZK1	Cost center accounting
Report group	ZPP1	Plan cost compare 2 FY
Program version	00000001	Valid from 09/13/2000 (active version)

⨠ *Figure 1 Technical Information for Report Group*

You can see that the report group in this example is ZPP1. Now go to the transaction for maintaining transaction codes (SE93), enter a transaction code beginning with Z, and click on the CREATE button. In the CREATE TRANSACTION dialog box that appears, give the transaction code a short text, select the TRANSACTION WITH PARAMETERS (PARAMETER TRANSACTION) radio button (as shown in Figure 2), and press ⌑Enter⌑.

⨠ *Figure 2 Create Custom Transaction Code*

In the CREATE PARAMETER TRANSACTION screen that appears, go to the DEFAULT VALUES FOR section, select the SKIP INITIAL SCREEN checkbox, and enter "START_ REPORT" in the TRANSACTION field, as shown in Figure 3.

《 *Figure 3 Default Values for Section*

Scroll down to the DEFAULT VALUES section and enter the values, as shown in Figure 4.

Default Values	
Name of screen field	Value
D_SREPOVARI-REPORTTYPE	RW
D_SREPOVARI-REPORT	ZPP1

« *Figure 4* *Enter Screen Field Values*

The values that appear in this screen can be explained as follows:

▶ **D_SREPOVARI-REPORTTYPE**
This refers to the type of report. Enter the value "RW" (for Report Writer).

▶ **D_SREPOVARI-REPORT**
This refers to the report group. Enter the report group that is linked to the report (ZPP1 in this example).

Once you save the new transaction code, you will be able to directly access the report by executing the transaction. You can then ask your Basis team to assign the transaction codes for different Report Painter reports to different user roles so that only the authorized users can access the reports.

Creating Transaction Codes for SAP Query Reports

You need to know which screen fields and values to use if you want to assign transaction codes to SAP Query reports.

When you use Transaction SQ01 to create an SAP Query report, you can assign the reports to transaction codes. In turn, you can assign the transactions to user roles so that only certain users can access the reports. However, it is important to know that you cannot simply assign the query program (which normally begins with "AQ....") to the transaction codes, as these programs can be different for the same query in each client.

You should also note that any modifications to the Infoset will lead to a change in the program name. If the query is not regenerated in your production system, the transaction code will read the incorrect program. To avoid this situation, you need to create a transaction code for the query that can be executed correctly in all clients.

✔ And Here's How...

To assign a standard SAP Query report to a transaction code, go to the transaction for maintaining transaction codes (SE93), enter a transaction code beginning with Z, and click on the CREATE button. In the CREATE TRANSACTION dialog box that appears, give the transaction code a short text, select the TRANSACTION WITH PARAMETERS (PARAMETER TRANSACTION) radio button (as shown in Figure 1) and press Enter.

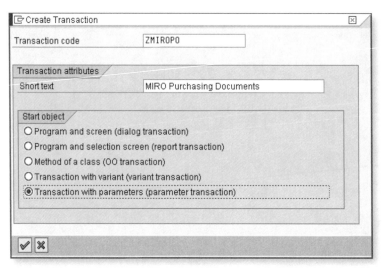

⌃ **Figure 1** *Create Custom Transaction Code*

In the Create Parameter Transaction screen that appears, go to the DEFAULT VALUES FOR section, select the SKIP INITIAL SCREEN checkbox, and enter "START_REPORT" in the TRANSACTION field, as shown in Figure 2.

« **Figure 2** *Default Values for Section*

Scroll down to the DEFAULT VALUES section and enter the values, as shown in Figure 3.

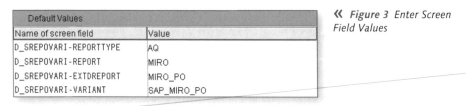

« **Figure 3** *Enter Screen Field Values*

The values that appear in this screen can be explained as follows:

- **D_SREPOVARI-REPORTTYPE**

  This refers to the type of report on which the transaction code is based. Enter the value "AQ" (for SAP Query).

- **D_SREPOVARI-REPORT**

  This refers to the user group to which the query is assigned. Enter the relevant user group name (which is MIRO in this example).

- **D_SREPOVARI-EXTDREPORT**

  This refers to the name of the query. In this example, the name of the query is MIRO_PO.

- **D_SREPOVARI-VARIANT**

  If you want the transaction to be executed with a variant, you can enter the variant name in this field. In this example we have entered the variant SAP_MIRO_PO.

When you save the new transaction code, you will be able to directly access the report by executing the transaction.

You can ask your Basis team to assign the transaction codes for different SAP Query reports to different user roles so that only the authorized users can access the reports.

Tip 97

Scheduling Materials Management Period Close

By using a dynamic selection variable on the posting date, you can schedule the Materials Management period close indefinitely.

The Material Master Period Close program is run at the beginning of every month so that inventory postings can be made in the new month. You can run this program manually by using Transaction MMPV; however, it would need to be run as early as possible on the first day of the new month (there could be other inventory-related jobs that are run in the early hours of the morning that rely on this program in order to be posted in that month).

Therefore, it is beneficial to set up this program as a background job. Because the period in the program needs be changed every month, you could create a variant for every period and schedule each variant as a different step to be run in its relevant period. However, this means you would need to change the batch job every year, and it is possible to forget to do this. You therefore need a more dynamic way of creating this batch job to run for every period, which we will go over in this tip.

✅ And Here's How...

To create a dynamic variant for the Material Master Period Close program, go to Transaction MMPV and enter the relevant company codes in the FROM and To company code fields. Click on the SAVE AS VARIANT button (🖫) and give the variant an appropriate name and description (such as PERIOD_CLOSE, which we use in this example).

In the Objects for Selection Screen section, scroll to the Date field, drop down in the Selection Variable field, and select D (dynamic date calculation). Now drop down in the Name of Variable Input Only Using F4 field and select First Day of the Current Month. The screen should now look like the one shown in Figure 1.

	Selection	Field name	Ty	Protect	Hide	Hide	Save	Switch	Required	Selection variable	Option	Name of Variable (Input Only Using F4)
	1,000	From company code	P	☐	☐	☐	☐	☐	☐			
	1,000	To company code	P	☐	☐	☐	☐	☐	☐			
	1,000	Period	P	☐	☐	☐	☐	☐	☐			
	1,000	Fiscal year	P	☐	☐	☐	☐	☐	☐			
	1,000	Date	P	☐	☐	☐	☐	☐	☐	D		First day of current month

(Objects for selection screen)

≫ *Figure 1* Selection Variable for Posting Date

Click on the Save button to save the variant.

Next, you need to schedule the background job by going to Transaction SM36. Enter a name for the job in the Job Name field and click on the Start Condition button, which displays the Start Time dialog box. Here you can click on the Date/Time button and enter the first day of the next month (note that you only need to this once, as the system will subsequently always use the first day of the current month), and the time you want the program to run. In our example, we choose 12:30 a.m. (see Figure 2). We provide the time cushion of 30 minutes in our example in case there is an issue with the system time, where there is a lapse between system date/time being updated with the actual date/time.

Date/Time					
Scheduled start	Date	04/01/2011	Time	00:30:00	
No Start After	Date		Time		

≫ *Figure 2* Schedule Start Date and Time

Now, select the Periodic Job checkbox, which is located at the bottom of the screen. Click on the Period Values button, which displays a Period Values pop-up box. Click on Monthly, the Check button, and Save to be taken back to the Start Time dialog box. Click on Check and Save again to go back to the Define Background Job screen.

Now click on the STEP button, enter the period closing program name (RMMMPERI) in the NAME field, and enter your variant in the VARIANT field, as shown in Figure 3.

« *Figure 3 Enter Period Closing Program and Variant*

Next, click on the CHECK and SAVE buttons, and the STEP LIST OVERVIEW screen shown in Figure 4 is displayed.

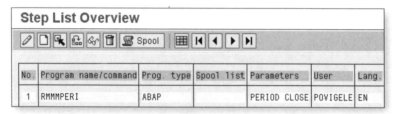

≪ *Figure 4 Step List Overview Screen*

Click on BACK and then SAVE to save the background job. As the variant was set up using a dynamic variable of the start of the month and the background job was set up monthly on the first day of the month, the system will use the first day of each month as the posting date for the period closing program.

Maintaining Custom Reports in an Area Menu

You can use area menus to create and maintain custom transaction codes for reports in a default reporting tree.

If you have many custom reports in your system (created using various tools such SAP Query, Report Painter/Writer, ABAP programs, and so on), you may want to streamline the access to these reports by assigning them to transaction codes and an area menu; otherwise, it can be hard to find the reports you need. You can then copy the area menu into a role menu so that users can access all their authorized custom transactions in their default SAP menu tree.

✅ And Here's How...

To create an area menu, go to Transaction SE43. In the AREA MENU field, enter "S000" and click on the COPY (📋) button. In the resulting pop-up box, enter a name and description for your area menu, as shown in Figure 1.

Figure 1 Copy Area Menu Screen

Next, click on the COPY button and choose the language in which the copy is to be created. The system prompts you to assign the area menu to a development package (you can check with your Basis team about which package you should use).

Now, click on the CHANGE button (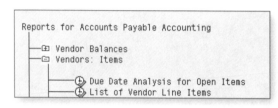) to see the standard SAP menu tree. (You have the option to navigate this tree to where you want to insert your custom report. We are going to use the accounts payable menu path to illustrate our example, although this process can be applied to any area of the SAP menu.) We have navigated the menu tree as follows:

> ACCOUNTING • FINANCIAL ACCOUNTING • ACCOUNTS PAYABLE • INFORMATION SYSTEM • REPORTS FOR ACCOUNTS PAYABLE ACCOUNTING • VENDORS: ITEMS

This takes you to the screen shown in Figure 2.

Reports for Accounts Payable Accounting

— ⊞ Vendor Balances
— ⊟ Vendors: Items

       ⊕ Due Date Analysis for Open Items
       ⊕ List of Vendor Line Items

« Figure 2 *Reports for Accounts Payable Accounting Menu Tree*

Click on the VENDORS: ITEMS node and click on the ADD ENTRY AS SUBNODE button (⬛). In the resulting screen, click on the REPORT button. This takes you to the Transaction Code for Reports screen, where you choose the type of report for which you want to create a transaction code.

In Figure 3, we have chosen SAP QUERY for REPORT TYPE, specified that it is a GLOBAL AREA query, and entered the relevant USER GROUP and QUERY.

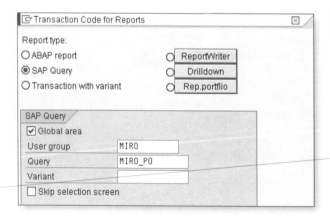

« Figure 3 *Choose Report Type for Transaction Code*

If you click on the DISPLAY OTHER OPTIONS (▣) button at the bottom of the screen, you can see that GENERATE AUTOMATICALLY and ADOPT REPORT DESCRIPTIONS are automatically activated. This means the system will generate the transaction code internally and will adopt the transaction description from the report description. If you want to give the transaction your own code and description, then you need to unselect these boxes and manually enter a Z transaction code and description.

In our example, we will leave these boxes selected. Press the ⌈Enter⌋ key to accept and move on, and the system again prompts you to assign a package to the development object. If it defaults the last package that you entered, simply click on the SAVE button; otherwise, enter the package your Basis team provided. The system then displays the new transaction code and description that was generated for the report, as shown in Figure 4.

≫ **Figure 4** *Transaction Code Generated for Report*

Click on the COPY button to add the transaction to the area of the menu tree that you highlighted. The area menu now looks like the screen shown in Figure 5 (that is, with the Purchasing Documents transaction included in the VENDORS: ITEMS node).

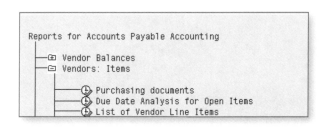

« **Figure 5** *Area Menu Including New Report Transaction*

Save your changes. If you want to default this area menu for a user (in reality, the Basis team will assign the area menu to all of the relevant users on a mass basis), go to Transaction SU01, enter the person's user name, and click on the CHANGE button. Then go to the DEFAULTS tab and in the START MENU field enter the area menu you created, as shown in Figure 6.

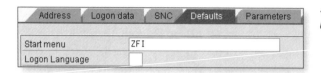

« *Figure 6* *Enter Area Menu in User Profile*

By doing this, the next time the user logs into the system they will be able to access the new transaction (and all other custom report transactions that were created) by going to the relevant node in the SAP menu. An example of this is shown in Figure 7.

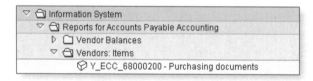

« *Figure 7* *SAP Menu Including New Transaction Code*

The custom report Transaction Y_ECC_68000200 has been added to the VENDORS: ITEMS node of the SAP menu. You can add the other custom reports to their relevant nodes in that area menu by going through the same process.

Validating Account and Cost Center Combinations

If you want to validate postings to general ledger accounts against a certain cost center, you can create validation rules.

When most profit and loss accounts (with a cost element category of "1") are posted to manually, a cost object (usually a cost center) needs to be entered in the posting. Because you are allowed to pick any cost center in the dropdown list to assign to the posting, there are times when the incorrect general ledger account/cost center combination is selected. This may lead to several adjustments at month end and is complicated even further if you run assessments and the values in the incorrect cost center have already been reallocated somewhere else.

It is important for the system to be able to issue an error message when certain general ledger accounts have not been given the correct cost center assignments. You can set up validation rules in the system to accomplish this, which we will describe in this tip.

✔ And Here's How...

Before you create the validation rule, you need to gather a list of general ledger accounts that are to have cost center restrictions and include them in a set. In our example, we want all general expense accounts (in the range of 476100 to 476999) to be assigned only to the operations cost center (403). To do this, go to Transaction GS01, give the set a description, specify the relevant source table, and select the BASIC SET radio button, as shown in Figure 1.

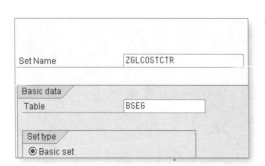

« Figure 1 Create Set

Press the Enter key, which displays a pop-up box where you enter the field name for general ledger accounts (HKONT), as shown in Figure 2.

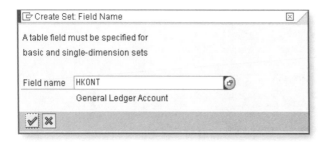

« Figure 2 Enter Field Name for Set

Press the Enter button again and give the set name a description. Next, enter the range of accounts that you want to be included in the set. If the accounts are not in chronological order, you can also enter the individual accounts in separate lines. In our example (shown in Figure 3) we have entered the range of 476100 to 476999.

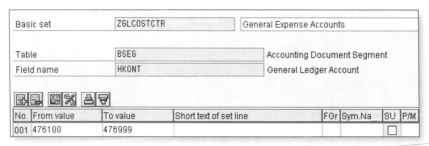

⋀ Figure 3 Enter General Ledger Account Set Range

Validation Rules

Now save the set and proceed to create the validation rule. To do this, go to Transaction OB28, click on the NEW ENTRIES button, and enter the relevant values, as shown in Figure 4.

CoCd	CallPnt	Validation	Description	Activtn leve
3000	2	ZGLCTR		

⌃ *Figure 4 Create Validation*

Enter the company code, call point 2 (which is on a line item level), and give the validation a name.

Now access ENVIRONMENT • VALIDATION from the top menu and click on the YES button in the message that appears. In the Create Validation: (Header Data) screen click on the STEP button, give the validation step a description in the right part of the screen, and double-click on the PREREQUISITE button in the left part of the screen. Then go to the top menu and elect SETTINGS • EXPERT MODE and type the following formula in the Prerequisite screen:

```
BSEG-HKONT IN ZGLCOSTCTR
```

This formula means you are selecting all general ledger accounts in the set ZGL-COSTCTR. Next, go to the left part of the screen, double-click on the CHECK button, and type in the formula shown here:

```
BSEG-KOSTL = '403'
```

Go to the left part of the screen, double-click on the MESSAGE button, and click on the MAINTAIN MESSAGE button (🖉) in the right part of the screen.

Next, click on a message number that does not have any text and click on the INDIVIDUAL MAINT. button. This creates an entry text field in front of your message number, where you can type in the message you want to be displayed if the conditions of your validation are not met (shown in Figure 5).

Message number	
026 G/L Account & is not valid with cost center &	

» *Figure 5 Enter Validation Message*

We used the ampersand sign (&) because the cost center and general ledger account we want to display in the message will vary depending on the posting. Therefore, we have set up this variable key and will specify its values that should be populated later. Click on the SAVE and BACK buttons to go back to the initial screen.

Variables

Enter "E" (for error message) in the MESSAGE TYPE field, the message number you maintained in the MESSAGE NUMBER field, and the values for the variables, as shown in Figure 6.

Message variables

1	BSEG	-	HKONT	2	BSEG	-	KOSTL
3		-		4		-	

« *Figure 6 Enter Message Variables*

These message variables (which are the technical table and field names, which you can select by clicking in the field and pressing the F4 button to see the options) indicate that the first variable specifies the general ledger account and the second variable specifies the cost center specific to the posting.

Save the validation and go back (using the BACK button) to the original screen to activate it. To activate, enter "1" in the ACTIVTN LEVEL column, as shown in Figure 7.

CoCd	CallPnt	Validation	Description	Activtn leve
3000	2	ZGLCTR	New validation	1

⌃ *Figure 7 Activate Validation*

Result of Validation

Now when a user tries to assign any other cost center to a general ledger account that is in the 476100 to 476999 range, they will see the error message you created in the validation rule, as shown in Figure 8.

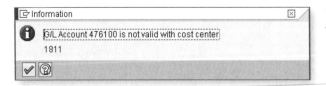

Information   ⊠

ⓘ G/L Account 476100 is not valid with cost center
   1811

✔ ⓘ

« *Figure 8 Validation Message During Posting*

You cannot post the document until the cost center is changed appropriately. You can extend the settings explained in this tip to different combinations of general ledger accounts and cost centers by creating each combination as a different set in your validation.

Scheduling Payment Program Automatically

You can ease the burden of periodically creating several payment runs by automatically scheduling the payment program.

If you use SAP software, then you are probably using the automatic payment program to process some of your payments. The automatic payment program (also known as the payment run) is usually run every week or every two weeks in most companies.

Additionally, several versions of the payment program are usually run in a period to represent local and foreign payments or payments based on different methods such as checks, wires, ACH, or bank transfers. This can result in a considerable amount of time spent entering payment run parameters every week, even though most of the values are the same and the only item that changes is the date.

To eliminate the time spent creating payment runs, there is a transaction that you can use to save all of the values you enter in the payment program as a variant, set the date fields as dynamic variables, and schedule the program as a background job.

And Here's How...

You can schedule the payment run automatically by going to Transaction F110S or following the menu path:

> ACCOUNTING • FINANCIAL ACCOUNTING • ACCOUNTS PAYABLE • PERIODIC PROCESS-ING • SCHEDULE PAYMENT PROGRAM PERIODICALLY

All of the information that was available in different tabs in the Payment Run transaction (F110) is available on just one screen in Transaction F110S. Enter the RUN DATE and IDENTIFICATION as in the PAYMENT RUN section, as shown in Figure 1.

≫ *Figure 1 Payment Run Section*

Do not select the PROPOSAL RUN checkbox unless you want to issue only a payment proposal and not an actual payment run.

In the PARAMETERS section, enter the DATE SPECIFICATIONS, PAYMENTS CONTROL, and relevant ACCOUNTS to be selected for payment, as shown in Figure 2.

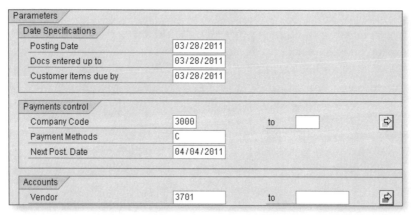

≫ *Figure 2 Parameters Section*

In the ADDITIONAL LOG section (near the bottom of the screen) select the necessary REQUIRED LOGGING TYPE checkboxes and enter the accounts that are to be made available for a detailed log (which should include at least the same accounts selected for payment). These settings are displayed in Figure 3.

⌄ *Figure 3* *Additional Log Section*

In the PRINT AND DME section, select both of the PRINT CONTROL checkboxes, enter the output program name and variant to be used for form printing or data medium exchange (DME), and enter the program name for proposal and payment lists, as shown in Figure 4.

⌄ *Figure 4* *Print and DME Section*

Create a Variant

Once you have made all of the necessary entries (which should be no different than the entries that you make in a typical payment run), click on the SAVE button to create a variant. This takes you to the VARIANT ATTRIBUTES screen, where you go to the OBJECTS FOR SELECTION screen and enter the relevant dynamic variables for the DATES fields, as shown in Figure 5.

	Objects for selection screen										
	Selectio	Field name	Type	Protect	Hide	Hide	Save fie	Switch GPA off	Required field	Selection variable	Option	Name of Variable (Input Only Using F4)
	1,000	Run Date	P	☐	☐	☐	☐	☐	☐	D		Current Date
	1,000	Identification	P	☐	☐	☐	☐	☐	☑			
	1,000	Proposal run	P	☐	☐	☐	☐	☐				
	1,000	Target computer	P	☐	☐	☐	☐	☐	☐			
	1,000	Posting Date	P	☐	☐	☐	☐	☐	☑	D		Current Date
	1,000	Docs entered up to	P	☐	☐	☐	☐	☐	☑	D		Current Date
	1,000	Customer items due by	P	☐	☐	☐	☐	☐	☐	D		Current Date
	1,000	Company Code	S	☐	☐	☐	☐	☐	☑			
	1,000	Payment Methods	P	☐	☐	☐	☐	☐	☑			
	1,000	Next Post. Date	P	☐	☐	☐	☐	☐	☑	D		Current date + 7 days

⌃ *Figure 5 Objects for Selection Screen*

All of the date fields in the program variant should be set to be "Dynamic" so that they can be changed accordingly, depending on when the background job is run. The date settings are specific to each individual business; however, it is normal for all of the date fields to be set to the current date, while the NEXT POST. DATE field is set to the next day, the next week, or some other point in the future (we used the next week in our example).

To have your VARIANT ATTRIBUTES screen look like the one in Figure 5, simply drop down in the SELECTION VARIABLE field and select D (for dynamic date calculation), drop down in the NAME OF VARIABLE (INPUT ONLY USING F4) field, and select CURRENT DATE.

For the NEXT POST. DATE field, instead of selecting CURRENT DATE, select CURRENT DATE +/- ??? DAYS. In the resulting pop-up box, enter the number of days from the current date that you want to be displayed, as shown in Figure 6.

« *Figure 6 Date Calculation Parameters Screen*

For positive days, enter just the number, and for negative days enter the number and a dash sign (-) after it.

Once you have saved the variant, you will be taken back to the original screen, where you can select PROGRAM • EXECUTE IN BACKGROUND from the top menu and proceed to set up the job as a weekly (or whatever frequency is required for your business) scheduled job.

Glossary

Access sequence The order in which the system works through the condition tables when searching for particular condition records. It starts with the more specific condition records and proceeds to more general condition records.

Account assignment category Determines which account assignment details are required for the line item of a purchase order, such as the general ledger account or cost center.

Account assignment template A model document that can be used for recurring financial transactions.

Account category reference A group of valuation classes the system uses to validate whether the valuation class you have entered in the material master accounting is allowed.

Account detective A report that shows the general ledger accounts that are automatically assigned in the system and the source tables where they are assigned.

Account determination An automatic function that determines the accounts for amounts that are posted in Financial Accounting.

Account groups An object that determines the data that is relevant in the creation of master records and the number range from which numbers are selected for these master records.

Account ID Together with the house bank, the account ID represents a specific bank account that belongs to a company code.

Account key The account key enables the system to post amounts to different types of accounts such as revenue, freight, discount, or tax. It is used to distinguish general ledger accounts that are posted automatically through the use of condition types

Account type A key that specifies the area to which an account belongs. Because the same account number can be used for (for example) an asset, customer, vendor, or general ledger, the account type is used in addition to the account number to identify an account.

Accounting principle A set of rules and principles for financial statements preparation and legal accounting reporting such as the International Accounting Standards (IAS) and General Accepted Accounting Practices (GAAP).

Accrual key A key that identifies different types of general ledger accounts for accruals or provisions, such as freight and rebate accruals.

Activation level Specifies the activation level of validation or substitution for a company. The activation level can be set to active or inactive.

Active splitting A type of document splitting you can control in customizing to split the line items according to the classification of the document for a business transaction and the assigned splitting rule.

Alternative reconciliation account A different reconciliation account from the one entered in the master record, which you can select when making a posting to a vendor or customer.

ALV report   A user-friendly report that is displayed in a tabular format and allows the user to sort, filter, and sum the data in tables.

Application area   A set of commonly related work processes made up of the transaction, programs, and screens that relate to these processes.

Area menu   An area menu enables you to group menus that contain a set of functions that are used to perform particular tasks in an organization.

Attachment list   A list of the external documents that have been attached to an SAP object by using the "Services for objects" function. (See *services for objects*.)

Background job   A scheduled set of tasks that contains one or more ABAP programs and is executed in background processing.

Bank key   A key that uniquely identifies a particular bank in the system. It can refer to the routing number or the sort code, depending on the country where it is located.

Base item categories   Item category whose document line items are used to determine the account assignments into which the document line item to be processed is split.

Batch input session   Contains all of the information and data required for a data transfer with a batch input. It is made up of a sequence of transaction calls, including input data and user actions.

Billing document   A generic term for a document that is issued for a customer account such as invoices, credit memos, debit memos, pro forma invoices, and cancellation documents.

Billing type   Controls certain functions used in the processing of invoices, credit memos, debit memos, and cancellation documents.

Business transaction variant   Further restricts the item categories specified in the business transaction.

Calculation schema   Used in the Materials Management component to determine the costs, prices, rebates, and taxes that are calculated when the relevant condition types are selected in a purchasing document.

Chart of accounts   Consists of a list of general ledger accounts in accordance with an ordered numbering structure. The chart of accounts contains the account number, the account name, and technical information for each general ledger account.

Check number status   Represents the last check number assigned in a check lot.

Cleared items   Items that have been matched off with a corresponding contra item, such as a payment with an invoice or a reversal document with its original document.

Company   A company can consist of one or more company codes that use the same transaction chart of accounts and the same fiscal year breakdown. Companies are usually used for consolidation purposes.

Company code   The smallest organizational unit of Financial Accounting for which a complete self-contained set of accounts can be drawn up for purposes of external reporting.

Company code currency   Currency into which all transacted currencies in the company code are translated. It usually represents the currency of the country in which the company code resides.

Complex posting A multi-screen transaction that allows you to enter more data than you would in an enjoy transaction, such as manually entering tax amounts in general ledger postings and accessing reference 1, 2, and 3 fields.

Condition record Contain master data tables that use variable factors such as the customer, the product, order quantity, or date to determine the final price the customer gets.

Condition table Determines the field combinations that an individual condition record should consist of.

Constant profit center The default profit center for specific line items in processes for which it is not possible to derive the correct profit center through document splitting when the document is posted. This is the case if the required profit center is not yet available when the posting occurs.

Controlling area An organizational unit within a company that is used to represent a closed system for cost accounting purposes.

Copying control Allows you to define control data for the document flow of delivery and billing documents. You can specify which document type is to be assigned to copied reference documents and which item categories are to be copied for a particular delivery or billing type.

Cost center An organizational unit within a controlling area that represents a defined location of cost incurrence and can be based on functional requirements, allocation criteria, physical location, or responsibility for costs.

Cost element The classification of the organization's valuated consumption of production factors within a controlling area.

Cost element category The classification of cost elements according to their usage or origin.

Cost of sales accounting Type of profit and loss statement that matches the sales revenues to the costs or expenses involved in making the revenue.

Currency type Key that identifies the role of a currency in the system such as group currency, hard currency, index currency, or global company currency.

Data medium exchange Enables you to define file formats that meet the requirements of your banks. By doing so, you can model an externally defined bank format in SAP ERP, which allows you to send or receive data in the form of DME files in this format.

Debit/credit shift This functionality in the financial statement version allows you to assign one financial statement item to another as a contra item. This means the display for the group of accounts that is summarized in these financial statement items is dependent on whether the total balance of the accounts is in credit or in debit.

Default profit center Profit centers that are used to collect costs, revenues, or postings made to balance sheet accounts within a posting period.

Deferred revenue account The general ledger account number that is used to track deferred revenue (the amount of revenue that has been invoiced and not recognized).

Direct quotation A currency value expressed in units of the local currency (or "To" currency in the exchange rate table) per unit of the foreign currency (or "From" currency in the exchange rate table).

Distribution channel Channel through which saleable materials or services reach customers, such as by wholesale, retail, and direct sales.

Division   An organizational unit based on responsibility for sales or profits from saleable materials or services.

Document class   Defines the technical format of a document and is assigned to a global document type for bar code activation.

Document number range   Used to specify a number interval from which document numbers are selected and the type of number assignment (internal or external). You can assign one or more document types to each number range so that the number range becomes effective through the document type specified in document entry and posting.

Document overview   The display of the line items of a document that has been posted or is about to be posted, including any automatically calculated lines such as for tax and exchange rate differences.

Document splitting   An automatic procedure for organizing line items in the document according to selected dimensions, such as organizing receivable lines by profit center or segment.

Document splitting characteristics   An account assignment object for which document splitting can be performed. It generally corresponds to a field in the data structure of the general ledger such as PROFIT CENTER, SEGMENT, BUSINESS AREA, and CUSTOMER.

Document type   A key that distinguishes the business transactions to be posted. It determines the number range that will be used in posting the document and the account types to be posted.

Down payments   Part of the full price paid at the time of purchase or delivery with the balance to be paid later. They are shown separately from other receivables and payables on the balance sheet.

Drill-down report   A means of evaluating the data of an application according to its characteristics and key figures. Drill-down reporting enables users to generate simple ad hoc reports and complex formatted reports based on forms.

Dummy profit center   The profit center to which all Profit Center Accounting data is transferred from objects that are not assigned to a profit center.

Editing options   Can be used to make user-specific settings for document entry and to default the document currency for both standard and enjoy financial transactions.

Enjoy transaction   Used to perform financial accounting postings such as entering, holding, parking, and posting documents in a single-screen transaction with a minimum amount of entries.

Exchange rate type   A key representing a type of exchange rate in the SAP system, such as buying rate, bank selling rate, or average rate. It is used when translating currency amounts in the system.

Entry view   This document display view is based on the classic General Ledger. It does not include the effects of SAP General Ledger such as document splitting and individual ledger display.

External number range   Contains document numbers that are specified by the user when they post a transaction, as opposed to letting the system internally generate the document numbers.

Field catalog   Defines fields that can be used as search fields for condition records.

Field status group   Determines which fields are ready for input, which are required entry fields, and which are hidden during document entry.

Field status variant   A field status variant groups several field status groups together and is assigned to a company code. This allows you to work with the same field status groups in any number of company codes.

Financial statement items   Used for accounting purposes within the balance sheet, income statement, and for statistical purposes to produce the group reports.

Financial statement version   Represents a hierarchical positioning of general ledger accounts. It can be based on specific legal requirements or for specific organizational purposes.

Fiscal year dependent   An indicator that the allocation of posting periods to calendar days must be made individually for each year. It is used if the end of the period is not linked to a fixed calendar day.

Fiscal year independent   Indicates that the allocation of posting periods to calendar days is based on the period end days of the calendar year.

Fiscal year variant   A variant that defines the relationship between the calendar and fiscal year. It specifies the number of periods and special periods in a fiscal year and how the SAP system is to determine the assigned posting periods.

Functional areas   An organizational unit in accounting that classifies the expenses of an organization by functions such as Administration, Sales and Distribution, Marketing, Production, and Research and Development. This classification is used to meet the needs of cost-of-sales accounting.

General ledger account   A structure that records value movements in a company code and represents the general ledger account items in a chart of accounts.

General ledger view   A document display view that includes the effects of SAP General Ledger such as document splitting and individual ledger display.

General modifier   A three-digit key that is used to differentiate the account determination, depending on the business transaction. Also known as the account grouping code or the account modifier.

Global query   Queries that exist in the global query area and are available throughout the system and in all clients. Query objects in the global area are connected to the Workbench Organizer, and their transports are created automatically without any manual preparation.

Goods receipt   A term from inventory management that denotes a physical inward movement of goods or materials.

Goods receipt/invoice receipt (GR/IR) account   An accrual account that is posted to when a goods receipt (as a credit) or invoice receipt (as a debit) transaction is posted. It is meant to be cleared regularly so that the open items that match up against each other do not show up when analyzing the items in the account.

Group currency   The currency that is defined at the client level in table T000. It is also used for cross-company postings in controlling and for consolidation purposes.

Grouping key   You use this key to specify a maximum of three fields from the database tables BSIK (vendors) or BSID (customers) to enter in the customer/vendor master record so that open items containing the same entries in the specified fields are settled together.

Hard currency A country-specific second currency used in countries with high rates of inflation.

Held documents An incomplete document that is temporarily saved by a user and can only be completed and posted by that user.

House bank A unique bank ID of the company code in the system.

IBAN A standardized, uniform representation of complete bank details in accordance with the European Committee for Banking Standards (ECBS).

Indirect quotation A currency value expressed in units of the foreign currency (or "From" currency in the exchange rate table) per unit of local currency (or "To" currency in the exchange rate table).

Integrated planning Used to determine whether to transfer plan data from the cost center accounting component (CO-OM-CCA) to other components (such as the Special Purpose Ledger or the Profit Center Accounting component), and whether to write line items for each change in the plan data.

Internal number range Contains document numbers that are internally generated by the system.

Internal order An instrument used to monitor costs and revenues of an organization such as with short-term jobs or services.

Investment order An internal order that is assigned to an asset and is used for budget control purposes.

Invoice receipt Describes the receipt of an invoice issued by a vendor such as invoice receipt referencing a purchase order, invoice receipt referencing a goods receipt, or invoice receipt without reference.

Item categories The item category characterizes the items of an accounting document such as customer, vendor, asset, cash discount clearing, and exchange rate difference accounts. It is derived from the account type and is required for document splitting.

Layout variant A variant you can use to create different views of a standard SAP report by adding, hiding, subtotaling, filtering, and sorting the data and saving it as a variant to be accessed in that format in the future.

Leading ledger A ledger that applies the same accounting principle as that used for drawing up the consolidated financial statement. It is integrated with all subsidiary ledgers and is updated in all company codes. You can only specify one ledger as the leading ledger in General Ledger Accounting.

Ledger group A combination of ledgers for the purpose of applying the functions and processes of General Ledger Accounting to the group as a whole. By specifying a ledger group, you can post data only to the ledgers in that group. A ledger group is automatically created for each ledger and carries the same name as that ledger.

Line item display A display of line items from one or more accounts. This is mandatory for customer and vendor accounts. For general ledger accounts, this setting must be defined in the master record of the account.

Local currency The currency of a company code in which the local ledgers are managed.

Logistics invoice verification A process that is situated at the end of the logistics supply chain that includes purchasing, inventory management, and invoice verification. It updates the data saved in the invoice documents in Materials Management and Financial Accounting.

Legacy System Migration Workbench (LSMW)   An SAP system tool that supports one-time and periodic data transfers from external systems to SAP ERP systems. It facilitates the conversion of data to the necessary format and can be processed using batch input, call transaction, direct input, BAPIs, and EDI.

Manual clearing   The process of using one of the manual clearing transactions to match a debit and credit item that balances to zero or within a clearing tolerance.

Mass reset   The mass process of changing the status of line items from "cleared" to "open" and breaking the link between the cleared document and its original open item.

Master data   Nontransient data that is used in transactional processing and displaying reports. It is key business information that may include data about general ledger accounts, cost centers, customers, vendors, materials, and employees, to name a few.

Material group   Grouping of materials that can be used for reporting purposes or account assignment.

Material ledger   Enables material inventories to be valuated in multiple currencies and valuation approaches and is the basis of actual costing. It collects transaction data for materials whose master data is stored in the material master and uses this data to calculate prices to valuate these materials.

Message control   The process of changing the severity of a message from (say) an error to a warning.

Message number   The numerical identification of a message in a message class.

Movement type   A classification key indicating the type of material movement such as goods receipt, goods issue, or physical stock transfer. It enables the system to find predefined posting rules determining how the general ledger accounts are to be posted and how the inventory fields in the material master record are to be updated.

Multi-level price determination   Takes into account the use of one material in another material, where single-level price differences exist for the input material, and it results in multilevel price differences. In this way, differences are rolled up from raw materials through semifinished products to finished products.

Non-leading ledger   When parallel ledgers are used, one of them must be specified as the leading ledger and the other parallel ledgers then become non-leading ledgers.

Noted items   A special item that does not affect any account balance. When you post a noted item, a single-entry document is generated that can be displayed using the line item display if you select the NOTED ITEMS checkbox.

Number range interval   An interval of consecutive numbers and/or other alphanumeric characters within a number range.

Number range status   Represents the last number that was assigned in a number range.

Open item management   A stipulation in the general ledger master record that the items in an account must be used to clear other line items in the same account. These items must balance out to zero before they can be cleared.

Open items   Items in general ledger accounts that have not been matched with their corresponding contra items.

Parameter ID Allows a field to be filled with proposed values from SAP system memory.

Parameter A component of a selection screen, which is displayed as a single input field and internally as an elementary data object.

Parameter value The value entered in a parameter ID that defaults into the field that carries that parameter ID.

Parked documents Documents that are stored temporarily with incomplete information (such as where the balance is not zero). You can go back to the document to complete it so it can be posted.

Partner bank types A key you enter in the customer vendor master or line item to specify which business partner's bank the system should use when several bank accounts exist.

Passive splitting Document splitting processes you cannot influence by settings in Customizing. It is used mainly when a document line inherits its account assignment from another line that had previously been actively split.

Payment document The accounting document that is generated when a payment is made to a customer or vendor.

Payment groupings Used to define the grouping keys that are used to settle a customer or vendor's open items together.

Payment method A method that specifies how payment is to be made, such as by check, bill of exchange, or bank transfer.

Payment program The program for making the payments specified in payment requests. The payment program generates documents

in Financial Accounting and payment media to create payment forms and lists.

Payment proposal A selection of open items that are due for payment according to the parameters specified in the payment program.

Payment term The conditions of payment agreed to between business partners with respect to goods supplied or services provided.

Period texts The descriptions of periods that can be shown in balance display reports.

Periodic unit price (PUP) A price that changes periodically as a result of goods movements and invoice entries. It is calculated by dividing the value of the material by the quantity of that material in inventory and references the base unit of measure and price unit in the material master record.

Planned delivery costs Delivery costs that are planned in a purchase order and are posted to an accrual account when a goods receipt of that purchase order is made.

Plant An organizational unit for dividing an enterprise according to production, procurement, maintenance, and materials planning. It is a place where materials are produced or goods and services are provided.

Post goods issue The process made on outbound deliveries that relieves the material from inventory and records a cost of goods sold in accounting.

Post with reference The process of using one document as a template for posting another document.

Posting key A two-digit numerical key that determines the way line items are posted. It determines several factors including the account type, type of posting (debit or credit), and field status of the entry screens.

Posting period variant Describes the specifications for a posting period and hence determines the accounting periods that are open for transaction processing.

Prerequisites A Boolean statement that is used for selecting data for validation and substitutions. If the prerequisite statement is false, the entered value is not selected for validation or substitution. If the prerequisite statement is true, the entered value is checked against the check statement entered in the CHECK field for a validation and is replaced with the specified field in a substitution.

Pricing procedure Defines the conditions that are permitted for a document and the sequence in which the system takes these conditions into account during pricing.

Primary cost element A cost element whose costs originate outside of the Controlling component and accrual costs that are used only for controlling purposes. Primary cost elements usually have a corresponding general ledger profit and loss account of the same number.

Profit center An organizational unit in accounting that reflects a management-oriented structure of the organization for the purpose of internal control. Operating results for a profit center can be analyzed using either the cost of sales approach or the period accounting approach.

Program variant A variant that can be used to store the attributes of the screen in a program and is saved so that it can be called during online or background processing of the program.

Provision account Used when there are conditions that are relevant for accrual; for

example, rebate conditions. If this is the case, account determination takes place in the billing document with the field account key—Accrual (KVSL2). This field is assigned to the condition type in the pricing procedure. Normally account determination for general ledger accounts takes place in the billing document with the field account key (KVSL1). The account key field is also assigned to the condition type in the pricing procedure.

Purchasing organization An organizational unit in logistics that subdivides an enterprise according to the requirements of purchasing.

Reconciliation accounts General ledger accounts that are assigned either directly or indirectly to the subsidiary ledgers (such as in the customer, vendor, or assets areas) so that any postings to these subledgers will update SAP General Ledger automatically.

Report Painter Report Painter uses a graphical report structure that forms the basis for the report definition and enables you to report on data from various applications. When defining the report, you work with a structure that corresponds to the final structure of the report when the report data is output.

Report Writer Report Writer enables you to report on data from multiple applications using functions such as sets, variables, formulas, cells, and key figures. You can create complex reports that meet more specific reporting requirements than when you use the Report Painter tool.

Representative ledger The ledger of a ledger group used by the system to determine the posting period during posting and to check whether this posting period is open. Each ledger group must contain only one representative ledger.

Revenue recognition   The point at which revenue is credited to a revenue account in SAP General Ledger. It can either be standard (as in when the customer is billed), time-based (at specified dates in a project), or performance-based (at certain performance milestones in a project).

Sales document item category   A classification that distinguishes between different types of sales item (for example, free of charge items and text items) and determines how the system processes the item.

Sales document type   An indicator for controlling the sales documents defined in the system that allows the system to process different business transactions in different ways. You can either use the standard sale document types or define your own.

Sales organization   An organizational unit in logistics that structures the company according to its sales requirements. A sales organization is responsible for selling materials and services.

SAP Query   A tool that allows users to define and execute their own reports without needing knowledge of ABAP programming.

Scenario   Business views that are assigned to ledgers and specify which posting data is transferred from different application components to General Ledger Accounting. Scenarios specify which fields of the ledger are filled with posting data from other application components.

Schedule line category   An indicator that allows each schedule line to be controlled differently and influences how functions such as inventory management, material requirements planning, and availability check are performed for each schedule line.

Screen variant   An object that determines the input fields, buttons, and checkboxes that are displayed on a data entry screen.

Secondary cost element   A cost element that is used to allocate costs for internal activities. They are used only in Controlling and do not correspond to any general ledger account in Financial Accounting.

Segment   A division of a company that can create its own financial statements for external reporting. A segment can be entered in the master record of a profit center. The segment is then derived from the assigned profit center during posting. It can also be derived by using a substitution rule, a BAdI, or through direct entry.

Selection type   Specifies whether a field in a program variant has a "parameter" option (where only a single value is permitted) or a "selection" option (where intervals and free selection options such as >, <, <> ...) can be entered.

Selection variable   Used to supply the relevant selection criterion with values by a table variable or a function module.

Sensitive fields   Fields that require separate authorization when changes are made to them before further processing can be carried on the master data in which they are contained.

Services for objects   A button that exists in applications that contain objects in SAP BusinessObjects Repository. It allows you to store external documents, Internet addresses, and notes on objects; start workflow tasks; and enter bar codes, among other things.

Set   An object that groups specific values or ranges of values under a set name. The set values reside within one or more dimensions of a database table.

Short key   A unique ID that is given to every bank statement that is posted in the system.

Single-level price determination   Takes into account the price and exchange rate differences that arise directly when a material is procured to calculate the periodic unit price of the material.

Sort key   Indicates the layout rule for the Assignment field in the document line item.

Sort version   Determines the sort levels and the summation levels of the displayed fixed asset reports to which it is assigned.

Sort variant   You can use this to define the fields for up to three levels by which the line items are to be sorted.

Special general ledger transactions   Special transactions in accounts receivable and accounts payable that are shown separately in the general ledger and subledger. They include bills of exchange, down payments, and guarantees.

Special periods   A posting period that is used to divide the last regular posting period for closing operations. A maximum of twelve posting periods and four special periods make up a fiscal year.

Splitting method   Contains the rules governing how the individual item categories are dealt with.

Splitting rule   Defines rules for document splitting according to the splitting method, business transaction variant, and item categories.

Standard query   This is where all query objects (queries, InfoSets, user groups) are created and managed specifically for each client. Query objects are not attached to the Workbench Organizer, which means they

cannot be created and transported according to standard correction and transport procedures, but instead require manual preparation of a transport.

Statistical cost element   A cost element that is linked to a balance sheet account such as a fixed asset reconciliation account that is used with an investment order for budget controlling.

Subcontracting accounts   The accounts that are used in the subcontracting process to record the offsetting entries of the inventory accounts that are issued and produced, as well as the service fee that is charged by the subcontracting vendor.

Substitution rule   An automatic process for replacing values as they are entered into the SAP system. Entered values are checked against a user-defined Boolean statement, which is called a prerequisite. If the statement is true, the system replaces the values concerned.

Symbolic account   A customizing object used for posting payroll results and travel management data from the Human Resources component to accounting.

Text determination   A group of text types that you want to display or maintain in a business context.

Third-party order   A sales order outsourced to a third-party company that delivers the ordered products to the customer.

Tolerance group   The tolerance groups represent amounts or percentages by which receivables may be underpaid or overpaid.

Tolerance limit   The percentage or absolute tolerated differences between the transacted values and the open value.

Totals table A database table containing totals records. The total of all line items posted under a reconciliation key that could be grouped according to criteria in General Ledger Accounting and other downstream accounting systems.

Trading partner A legally independent company belonging to the group.

Transaction key Used to determine accounts or posting keys for line items, which the system creates automatically.

Transaction variant Allows you to create different variants for the same transaction so you can assign default values to fields, suppress and change the readiness for input of fields, or suppress whole screens.

Transactional data Refers to data that is short-lived and assigned to certain master data such as individual posting documents. For example, the total sales to a customer consist of the data of the individual business transactions that is the transaction data.

Translation date type Determines which date should be used for the translation of the amounts according to the exchange rate table.

Travel expense type Used to record expenses that are incurred on business trips and are recorded in Travel Management. They are used to distinguish individual receipts such as hotel bills and trip expenses that are accounted by per diem or flat rates such as advances.

Tree options An option available in enjoy transactions that allows you to access account assignment templates and parked and held documents.

Unbilled receivables account The account that is posted to when the revenue reco-

gnition program has been run before the customer has been billed.

Unplanned delivery costs Delivery costs that are not planned in a purchase order and are not entered in the system until the invoice is received.

User profile An element in the authorization system that enables the system to check all of the profiles in a user master record for the appropriate authorization when a user accesses an area of the system.

User role Collection of activities that an employee performs within an organization.

Validation rule The process of checking values and combinations of values as they are entered into the SAP system. Entered values are checked against a user-defined Boolean statement known as a prerequisite. If the statement is true, the system validates the data using a second Boolean statement known as a *check*. If the check statement is true, the system posts the data. If the check statement is false, it issues a user-defined message, which depending on the message type could be an error or warning.

Valuation area An organizational unit in logistics that subdivides an enterprise for the purpose of uniform and complete valuation of material stocks. It can be based at either the plant or company code level.

Valuation area (foreign currency) Valuation areas enable you to use different valuation approaches and post to different accounts. You can therefore use different valuation areas to store exchange rate differences according to the different currency types of your company code.

Valuation method A method that can be used for multiple charts of accounts to determine the method with which a foreign currency valuation is to be performed as part of the closing procedures.

Valuation modifier   Indicates a grouping of valuation areas and is used with a general modifier to determine the general ledger accounts to which a goods movement is posted in the automatic account determination tables.

Valuation view   A method of valuing the business transactions of company code, the group as a whole, or profit center within the organization.

Variant attributes   Used to select the attributes of a program variant such as whether the variant should be protected, whether it is a system variant, or if it is only for background processing. You can also use it to specify whether the fields in the program are to be made hidden, required, or for display purposes only.

Wage type   An object in Payroll and Personnel Administration in which the user or the system stores amounts and time units that are used, for example, for calculating pay or

for determining statistics. They are also used in the travel expense module to classify the expense type and to assign the expense to a general ledger account.

WBS element   A structural element in a work breakdown structure representing the hierarchical organization of a project. A WBS element describes a task or a partial task that can be divided.

Workbench Organizer   Allows you to organize development objects in the system according to change requests.

Worklists   Used to store object values so you can quickly display a report or process a transaction by entering the worklist name as opposed to the individual values of the object. In Financial Accounting, they can be used for general ledger, customer, vendor, and asset accounts, as well as exchange rates.

Zero balancing   The setting that ensures that a document splitting characteristic (such as profit center or segment) balances to zero in every financial document.

Additional Resources

You can access other useful information about the Financial Accounting module in SAP ERP by accessing the following sources:

- **SAP Help Portal:** *http://help.sap.com/*
  You can navigate to the Financials section, which is located under the ERP Central Component section.

- **SAP Service Marketplace:** *http://service.sap.com/*
  If you are a member, you can access SAP's Online Service System (OSS) notes for support and consulting messages in the Financial Accounting area. You can also access the SAP Community Network from here, where you can find various discussion threads on a variety of Financial Accounting issues.

- **Financial Experts Online:** *http://www.financialsexpertonline.com/*
  Here, you can access various articles written by SAP experts on various Financial Accounting topics.

- **WIS Financials Conferences:** *http://www.wispubs.com/sap/conferences.html*
  These conferences are held in various parts of the world for SAP Financial Accounting users. They provide detailed sessions on all areas of the Financial Accounting modules and offer opportunities to have one-on-one discussions with experts and peers.

- **Paul Ovigele's website:** *http://www.ovigele.com/*
  I offer assistance with implementations, upgrades and support, spot consulting, quality assurance, system optimization, and strategy mapping of the finance and controlling landscape.

The Author

Paul Ovigele is an independent SAP ERP financials consultant. He is a certified chartered accountant (ACCA, United Kingdom) and holds an MBA from Imperial College Business School, London. He has worked as an ERP financials consultant for over 13 years in both North America and Europe, specializing in implementing the Financial Accounting and Controlling components along with their integrated areas for companies in the chemical, logistics, pharmaceuticals, apparel, and entertainment industries, among others.

Paul has delivered numerous training sessions to finance professionals at both the functional and managerial levels, has had several articles published in *FinancialsExpert*, where he also serves as a technical adviser, and has presented at various SAP financials conferences in both Europe and the United States.

You can reach Paul at *paul@ovigele.com*.

Index